# Trembling Earth

MEGAN KATE NELSON

# Trembling Earth

## *A Cultural History of the Okefenokee Swamp*

The University of Georgia Press *Athens and London*

Paperback edition published in 2009 by
The University of Georgia Press
Athens, Georgia 30602
www.ugapress.org
© 2005 by Megan Kate Nelson
All rights reserved
Set in Bethold Baskerville by
Graphic Composition, Inc., Bogart, Georgia

Most University of Georgia Press titles are
available from popular e-book vendors.

Printed digitally

The Library of Congress has cataloged the hardcover
edition of this book as follows:
Nelson, Megan Kate, 1972–
    Trembling earth : a cultural history of the
  Okefenokee Swamp / Megan Kate Nelson.
    xiii, 262 p. : ill., map ; 24 cm.
    Includes bibliographical references (p. [227]–248) and index.
    ISBN 0-8203-2677-1
    1. Okefenokee Swamp (Ga. and Fla.)–History. I. Title.
    F292.O5 N45 2005
    975.8'752–dc22        2004018185

Paperback ISBN-13: 978-0-8203-3419-6

British Library Cataloging-in-Publication Data available

A version of chapter 1 appears as "'Hidden Away in the Woods
and Swamps': Slavery, Fugitive Slaves, and Swamplands in the
Southeastern Borderlands, 1739–1845" in *"We Shall Independent Be":
African American Place-Making and the Struggle to Claim Space in the
United States* (Boulder: University Press of Colorado, 2005).

FOR MY PARENTS

CONTENTS

# ILLUSTRATIONS

## ACKNOWLEDGMENTS

One of the many benefits of finishing a book manuscript is the chance to acknowledge the people whose support was vital to its completion. Laura Rigal was an exemplary graduate and dissertation adviser whose questions and comments on countless drafts were invaluable. Leslie Schwalm, Joni Kinsey, and Ed Folsom taught excellent courses that led me to environmental and southern studies; they shaped *Trembling Earth* as a dissertation and book project in the years since. The faculty and staff of the American Studies Department at the University of Iowa were my guides in all manner of ways. John Raeburn was always a voice of reason and humor during my years of coursework, research, and writing. Rich Horowitz, Carrie Louvar, and Laura Kastens kept me in contact with the program after I left Iowa to work on my dissertation from Boston. I also benefited from contact with excellent teachers at the secondary and collegiate level: Lawrence Buell, Marlys Ferrill, William Gienapp, Anne Moore, Judy Vlasin, and Ted Widmer, in particular, encouraged my interest in interdisciplinary methodology and my desire to earn a PhD in American studies.

For their vivacity, support, and general good natures that made graduate school what is rather rare in academe – a good time – I have to thank my fellow students in American studies at the University of Iowa: Leslie Abadie, Michael Augspurger, Mary Crippen, Jennifer Denniston, Sarah Fields, Russell Peterson, Jen Pustz, Kevin Quirk, and Barb Shubinski. Jane Simonsen read several drafts of the introduction, and her suggestions improved it tremendously. Many other friends and colleagues have supported the project from its inception. Jen Medearis Costello offered insights into epidemiological theories and their connection with swamplands and public health. Nora Titone helped me to refine ecolocalism as a concept and was unceasingly supportive throughout the writing process. Amy Blair, Chris Capozzola, Paul Erickson, Michael Keogh, Timothy McCarthy, Debbie Palliser, and Beth Johnston were always ready with smiles, laughter, and martinis during months of revisions. The members of the Nineteenth-Century Writing Workshop at Harvard University consistently asked challenging and insightful questions: Dara Baker, Christine Dee, Paul Erickson, Jennie Goloboy, and Dan Hamilton, in particular, brought their expertise in early American history to bear on the project. Also, audience response at American Studies Association conferences, Association for the Study of Environmental History meetings, the McNeil Center Spaces and Places graduate student conference (2001), and the Symposium on Georgia History (2002) helped me to see the project in new ways and encouraged me to convert the dissertation into a book manuscript.

At Texas Tech University I have outstanding colleagues and friends: Christina Ashby-Martin, Gary Bell, Kambra Bolch, Jim Brink, Tita Chico, Stefano D'Amico, Ken Davis, Gary Elbow, Don Haragan, Michael Kimball, Randy McBee, Ron Wilhelm, Julie Willett, and Aliza Wong. Susan Tomlinson was an ideal reader and narrative writing consultant—I am grateful for her comments and encouragement.

I could not have completed research for the dissertation or the manuscript without funding from the Woodrow Wilson Foundation, the University of Iowa Graduate College, the University of Iowa American Studies Department, and Harvard University Departments of History and History and Literature.

During my years of research, I benefited from the knowledge and generosity of scholars, archivists, and librarians. Brice McAdoo Clagett sent me typed transcripts of Charles Rinaldo Floyd's diary, a text that is invaluable to my conception of the role of the Okefenokee in the Second Seminole War. Chris Trowell's numerous compilations of Okefenokee primary documents gave me a rich archive to absorb and analyze. I am indebted to the staff at the Hargrett Rare Book and Manuscript Library at the University of Georgia for locating eighteenth- and nineteenth-century Okefenokee hinterland documents. Susan Dick and her staff at the Georgia Historical Society made it possible for me to see uncataloged items and to photocopy thousands of pages of manuscripts and pamphlets. Karen Cook, a Special Collections librarian at the University of Kansas Kenneth Spencer Research Library, and Marvin Goss of Georgia Southern University tracked down several of Francis Harper's photographs that illustrate the complex relationship between Harper and Okefenokee Swampers. Lois Barefoot Mays opened the doors to the Charlton County Historical Society in Folkston, Georgia, and shared her transcripts of late-nineteenth-century Charlton County newspapers with me. Her generosity is typical of those devoted to the study of local history in the

Okefenokee hinterlands. Roger and Genna Wangsness provided me with luxurious room and board during my visit to Folkston and southern Georgia's public libraries in the spring of 2001. The librarians at the Charlton County Public Library in Folkston and the Okefenokee Regional Library in Waycross located books and newspaper articles that shaped my arguments regarding Swampers and preservation in particular – for these contributions to the manuscript I thank them. Chip Campbell provided a gator's view of the Okefenokee on our morning canoe trip in the swamp in April 2001; his enthusiasm for the project convinced me that I was at least heading in the right direction.

At the University of Georgia Press, Nancy Grayson has been a champion of the manuscript since we met at the Georgia Symposium more than two years ago. Jon Davies has been an exemplary project editor, answering all of my questions and fielding numerous anxious e-mails. He and my copyeditor, Jeanée Ledoux, improved the writing of the entire manuscript and encouraged clarity and conciseness in the notes and bibliography. The comments of two anonymous readers challenged me to tighten the focus of the project from the southeastern borderlands to the Okefenokee hinterlands, a change that has improved the manuscript tremendously. My thanks also to the members of the design staff at the press who saw the book through to completion.

Although my husband, Dan, has not ever been with me in an Okefenokee canoe, he has been with me throughout the research and writing of *Trembling Earth*. He was there when the idea for a cultural study of swamps came to me one summer day in Harvard's Lamont Library; he was on the phone with me, listening to the printer churn out the final draft of the dissertation on a rainy day three and a half years later; and he was with me in Texas when I finished the book manuscript and mailed it off to the University of Georgia Press. His support – emotional and intellectual – has been unwavering. He has been my refuge.

*Trembling Earth* officially originated that day in Lamont, but it has a longer back story that is rooted in a childhood filled with reading and writing. My parents took me to bookstores and libraries as if they were candy shops, urged me to hone my writing skills, and made great sacrifices to send me to Harvard for my undergraduate education. It is in recognition of these sacrifices and a lifetime of encouragement that I dedicate this – my first book – to them.

Alexander Key, "The Birthplace of the Suwannee Okefenokee Wildlife Refuge, Georgia."
From Cecile Hulse Matschat, *Suwannee River: Strange Green Land* (New York: Literary
Guild of America, 1938), 10.

Trembling Earth

# Twilight Ground

## *The Okefenokee Swamp and Ecolocalism*

The best way to get to know a swamp is to wander around in it for a while. The last time I wandered the Okefenokee, a large swamp that sits in southern Georgia and northern Florida, I did so in a canoe. It was April, an ideal time to go swamping – warm enough for migratory birds and alligators to frolic in the swamp's waters and early enough to avoid the yellow flies that in the summer months would bite through even the thickest layers of clothing. I helped my guide, Chip, push the canoe into the Suwanee Canal, a thirteen-mile-long gash cut into the eastern Okefenokee in the 1890s as part of a misguided attempt to drain it. We paddled out into the channel, and after twenty minutes of awkwardly but enthusiastically digging into the water, my shoulders began to ache.

The pace slowed as we turned from the canal southward into Grand Prairie, an expanse of aquatic plants, sphagnum moss, and peat islands anchored in water that was in constant, languid motion. Its depths were difficult to judge – tannin from cypress trees stains it to a coppery black that reflects trees and clouds like a mirror. This element of Okefenokee ecology has always disturbed visitors; one cannot see what lies beneath, and the prairie waters seem bottomless. Every now and again the surface would break and a pair of eyes would emerge and survey the scene. As we drifted closer, the gator would object to our presence by submerging itself again, lost to our sight as it navigated waterways that were, it turned out, about two feet deep.

We made our way through multiple watercourses within Grand Prairie, and I lost all sense of direction. The sky had begun to cloud over, so I could not even use the sun to position myself. But then I was distracted by a group of five sandhill cranes that stalked the prairie in front of our canoe, bobbing and bowing, looking for choice tidbits of grass shoots or insects to feed on. We tracked them as they moved in a group around a clump of aquatic plants until a motorboat's loud report from the canal startled them and they took off into the air, their dun-colored wings beating slowly and their legs dangling below them. Turning back in a direction Chip assured me was northward, we paddled over to a group of baby alligators gathered on the edge of a hammock, a small peat island in the midst of the prairie. They snapped at one another with needlelike teeth; such ferociousness was almost comical when performed by such tiny creatures. One foot long and vulnerable to all kinds of swamp predators, they nudged curiously at the side of our canoe until their much larger mother swam over with surprising speed to chase us away.

As we rounded the hammock, tall stands of trees loomed on the horizon, some twice as high as those surrounding them. I thought that some might be longleaf pines, but others, obscured by long, gray strands of hanging moss and the large nests of migratory birds, were unfamiliar to me. This part of the Okefenokee, the eastern half, is quite different from the western side. There swampland around the Pocket is dominated by riverlike waterways rather than shallow prairies, large soil islands instead of low-lying hammocks, and dense stands of cypress trees instead of pines. The Okefenokee's 660 square miles, carved 250,000 years ago by Pleistocene glaciers, are an ecological mosaic; the swamp contains six different kinds of swamp ecosystems, each defined and differentiated by its tree growth. This diversity draws hundreds of species of migratory birds, and in their wake, bird enthusiasts, all of whom converge on the Okefenokee every spring. While most ornithologists believe that one of these migrating birds, the ivory-billed woodpecker, is extinct, it continues to haunt the imaginations of Okefenokee visitors. Almost every year at least one birdwatcher stumbles to the Wildlife Refuge Center from Chesser Prairie or Honey Island and reports a glimpse of the bird's white bill or a snippet of its call. But it often happens that humans see in the swamp those things they desire rather than those things that truly exist.

From the hard seat of the canoe, I gazed around at the towering trees, tangled vines, and sharp-edged saw palmettos and noticed that the black water was beginning to reflect darker, angrier clouds. At this moment I began to understand why those who encountered the swamp often noted their dual feelings of admiration and fear. It was so easy to get lost in this morass, to feel alone and abandoned, despite the beauty all around. As a soaking rain began to fall, the light dimmed and created a kind of twilight in the swamp. It seemed fitting, for the Okefenokee is a twilight place – an ecosystem that is both dark and bright, water and land, beautiful and dangerous. It is a place of overlap, of blurred lines, and of ambiguity.

The Okefenokee is an edge space, the kind of environment, as the writer Barbara Hurd has noted, that is defined by "transition and diversity and abundance." It is a marginal space, and "things in the margins, including humans who wander there, are often on the brink of becoming something else, or someone else."[1] This promise of alteration, of "becoming," is what local communities embraced in their interaction with the Okefenokee Swamp over time. In their desire to become something else (wealthy or famous or independent), local inhabitants often came into conflict with others who also sought change in the depths of the swamp. The peculiar ecology of the Okefenokee – its twilight duality – created discord as human groups attempted to draw in it firm lines that topography did not provide. I believe that such desires to alter the Okefenokee resulted in the alteration of the communities that grew within and around it.

The role of the Okefenokee and its hinterlands (which extend forty miles from the swamp's rather murky borders) in the creation of local cultures is the subject of *Trembling Earth*. In the following chapters I argue that the swamp provoked people to develop a constellation of competing ideas rooted in beliefs about land use and value and shot through with convictions about race, gender, and class distinctions. These ideas and beliefs determined a particular pattern of action that communities took within swamplands, and thus shaped local cultures. This process of cultural development in swamplands is an example of what I call "ecolocalism."

Ecolocalism emerged in the Okefenokee hinterlands out of several kinds of encounters. Most communities developed a web of related ideas about the Okefenokee due to both direct experiences with it and secondary contact via written or visual media. As they encountered the Okefenokee, the groups who are the focus of this study responded in ways that were varied and complex. Members of each community saw the swamp differently and desired multiple things (both material and abstract) they thought this environment could provide for them. For example, rice planters saw southeastern swamplands not for what they were but what they could become – a gridded landscape of rice fields fed by the power of tides and river currents controlled by man-made technologies. To the slaves who actually built these hydraulic systems, by contrast, the Okefenokee and other swamps were sites of work but also places in which they could assert their independence and improve their lives. Both planters and slaves saw these ecosystems as places in which they could change their own status, but their swamp desires were adverse. Ecolocalism emerged out of conflicts like these between communities within local ecosystems.

Because groups inhabiting the Okefenokee hinterlands saw the swamp as something that *could* provide what they desired, they acted within or through it in order to fulfill these desires. In doing so, these communities encountered resistance in two forms: from other residents in the locality and from Okefenokee ecology itself. The United States military's experience in the Okefenokee and other southeastern swamplands during the 1830s and 1840s exemplifies this interaction. At this time the U.S. government sought control over the Okefenokee hinterlands and over Native Americans who lived there. In response to encroachments on their agricultural, hunting, and battle sites, Seminoles resisted forced removal and attacked U.S. forts in the area in 1835. The Second Seminole War ensued, and U.S. soldiers found themselves defeated by both Seminole ecolocalism and swamp ecology. The muck and mire of the Okefenokee hinterlands were not conducive to "regular" military action, and the U.S. military withdrew from the area in 1842, broken by its battles with Seminoles, saw palmettos, and yellow flies.

Such encounters between communities and between groups and swamp ecology often thwarted community desires. Because successful manipulation of the Okefenokee was ultimately untenable for most of these groups, a distinctive cultural pattern emerged in which people initially coveted control over nature and power over other people, then encountered resistance, and ultimately failed to achieve the ambitions envisioned in and through the Okefenokee. This pattern was cyclical: multiple failures begat different desires that subsequently provoked new conflicts. These failures and their repetition reveal that many assumptions and beliefs about the Okefenokee (and swamps in general) were flawed and that actions local communities took within them, therefore, had multiple unintended consequences. These ironies are fundamental to swamp ecolocalism and illuminate the complexity of human interactions with the Okefenokee between 1732 and 1940.

Ecolocalism is a concept that provides an alternative way of thinking about the creation of culture in relation to natural environments. Unlike regionalism – which emphasizes a unifying identity across generations and geographic boundaries – ecolocalism conceives of cultural identity as rooted in a locale oriented to a specific ecosystem and as divisive and variable over time. Additionally, rather than conceiving of these locales and their cultures as emerging in the context of nationalism, ecolocalism allows an opportunity to compare local cultures transnationally.[2] The pattern of belief and action revealed in the Okefenokee hinterlands has parallels in swampland ecosystems outside of North America. The novelist Amitav Ghosh, for example, has begun to study a lowland mangrove landscape in India that has provoked economic and spiritual desires in the communities that encountered it throughout the twentieth century.[3] The similarities between cultural production (the creation of ideas, images, and institutions within a particular community) and conflict in the Okefenokee hinterlands and in India's mangrove swamps suggest that ecolocalism may offer an intriguing paradox: a theory of local cultural production that transcends national boundaries and is potentially global in nature.

Ecolocalism in a swamp context is also expansive in the ways it uncovers the multiracial nature of the American Southeast. Most narratives of the development of southern racial discourses have focused on the relationships and conflicts between white masters and black slaves. Yet Seminoles and other Native Americans also resided in Okefenokee hinterlands until the 1850s; their encounters with the swamp have a long history. And although the Okefenokee became the domain of poor whites after 1865, these groups were often described as "savages," and some Swampers, in turn, claimed "Indian blood" to explain their exemplary hunting skills. Also, some poor whites in Georgia and Florida were Confederate deserters, hiding out in the Okefenokee in the 1860s just as fugitive slaves had for a century before them. As Gael Sweeney has noted, "there is something not quite 'white' about White Trash."[4] By shifting the focus of southeastern cultural history from plantations, port cities, and coastal landscapes to the lowland interior, ecolocalism illuminates the elusive quality of racial categories. It also allows for the voices of inhabitants previously thought to be marginal – fugitive slaves, Seminoles, and Swampers – to be heard.

This idea that communities on the margins shape culture not only belies any claims for a monolithic southeastern experience but also challenges dominant regional narratives of the United States that have privileged stories of western conquest, manifest destiny, and agricultural expansion. The Okefenokee offers no hilltop prospect, no comfortable wilderness aesthetic; it plays host to no linear march of "civilizing" hunters and farmers. The Okefenokee's inhabitants have been combative and mobile, resistant to the cultivation of small farms and responsible citizenship, and wary of the expectations that "civilization" entails. And although scholars of both environmental and new western history have found fault with Frederick Jackson Turner's promotion of the "frontier" as a justification for conquest, they have continued the tradition in cultural history and American studies of making the West the primary landscape in the creation of an American culture.[5] An investigation of swamp ecolocalism challenges the assumptions ingrained in national narratives of mountains, forests, and movement westward and presents a vision of cultural production that is not orderly, unified, or defined by mastery.

As disorderly landscapes, the Okefenokee and other swamplands have never captivated a national, admiring audience. Visitors have more often reacted with horror and disgust to swamplands' suffocating vegetation, poisonous snakes, and ravenous alligators. After experiencing myself the multiple ways that the Okefenokee makes humans uncomfortable – through labyrinthine waterways, oppressive humidity, or mosquito bites – I can understand why it is so hard to love a swamp. And yet there is a fascination that swamplands also provoke that renders them, as Harriet Beecher Stowe called them, "a glorious, bewildering impropriety."[6] The fluctuations, circulations, and confrontations embedded in the swamp muck reveal an American historical narrative that is not a neat, organized (and thus, appealing) trajectory. Instead, it is messy, befuddling, and often difficult to pin down. It is, in short, the muck of history.

Although *Trembling Earth* is the first cultural study of the Okefenokee and its hinterlands, it is not the first book to make connections between swamps, communities, and culture. Previously, David C. Miller, Ann Vileisis, Hugh Prince, Jack Temple Kirby, and Mart Stewart have turned their attention to North American lowlands and the ways that these ecosystems provoked changes in environmental perception, populations, and policy.[7] Two historiographical issues encompassed in these scholars' studies are particularly important to my arguments: when American perceptions of swamplands changed and which communities found what they desired in this ecosystem. While Miller and Vileisis have argued that Americans began to appreciate swamps just as the pace of lowland destruction began to quicken in the 1850s, Prince argues for a more variable trend in attitudes toward lowlands; *Trembling Earth* reveals that in the Okefenokee context, ideas about the swamp did not evolve from disgust to delight in a linear fashion but have been more mercurial. Various Okefenokee communities saw the swamp as beautiful or dangerous or worthless in response to a variety of exigencies – legislative decisions, economic need, or literary production – at different moments in time. Perceptions of the swamp also differed from community to community. Georgia boosters, for example, saw the Okefenokee as valuable only if converted to agricultural land, while surveyors found that adventures undertaken in the undeveloped "primeval" Okefenokee made them into masculine men. This variable group of ideas about the Okefenokee provoked different actions within it; the Okefenokee's cultural history thus uncovers a wide variety of attempts that communities made to achieve their dreams of transformation in the midst of this ecosystem.

The character of these groups that have interacted with swamplands has also been at issue in previous studies. For Miller, emergent nineteenth-century middle-class writers and artists seized control of swamp images as a way to express their changing view of nature, while for Kirby, the Great Dismal Swamp in Virginia and North Carolina became home to "hinterlanders" – poorer white residents, mulatto freed people, and fugitive slaves. Alternatively, Stewart proposes in his study that Georgia's coastal lowlands changed hands multiple times over three centuries; the Native American landscape gave way to the plantation, which gave way to the lumber kings, the military, and the tourist industry. Like Kirby's Great Dismal, the Okefenokee is a site of refuge for raced and classed "others." And like Stewart, I argue in *Trembling Earth* that the Okefenokee was a contested site that resisted sustained human control or manipulation and attracted different communities over time. But ecolocalism in the Okefenokee hinterlands suggests that successive waves of community control were not common. Rather, groups confronted one another in the swamp, and some communities disappeared from the area and then reemerged at a later date. Human control of environments is thus not a dominant theme or trend in this ecolocale; instead, fluctuation and complexity have characterized ecosystem development and local culture in Okefenokee history.

*Trembling Earth,* then, reveals a swamp culture that is multiracial, nonlinear, consistently contested, and complex. The ecolocal ideas with which the Trustees of Georgia, rice planters, slaves, fugitive slaves, antebellum writers, Seminoles, the U.S. military, surveyors, lumber companies, Swampers, and scientific preservationists engaged have often been unstable and contradictory. All of these groups have had ambivalent relationships with the Okefenokee and its hinterlands. This study thus proceeds chronologically but not successively. Each chapter focuses on the experiences of at least two communities in the Okefenokee hinterlands, their conflicts with one another, the often unintended consequences of these relationships, and the swamp ecolocalism that emerges in the course of these conflicts.

Each chapter also exhibits overlap with those that precede and succeed it. Sometimes this overlap is temporal, sometimes it is thematic. In both cases, this imbrication reinforces my argument that human interactions with swamplands have always been dynamic and fluctuating. It also renders the swamp a kind of palimpsest, a text in which several communities have inscribed themselves and their desires, replacing but never totally erasing the identities of other communities or the ecology of the Okefenokee Swamp. Some elements of swamp ecolocalism appear, seem to be erased, and then reemerge over time. This is the irony of ecolocalism itself: its unstable nature has provoked a relatively stable (and therefore somewhat predictable) pattern of responses.

It is another irony of swamp ecolocalism that its motifs often point to instability. The changeable nature of race and racial difference is one such theme that pervades community encounters with swamp muck. In the early eighteenth century the Okefenokee was relegated to Africans, African Americans, and Seminoles. Over time, however, it ceased to be linked to or provide refuge for people of color; during the decades of Reconstruction and thereafter, the Okefenokee hinterlands became a bastion of whiteness. But the swamp of the late nineteenth and early twentieth century bears some of the markings of its previous racial associations. As noted earlier, white Swampers were often fugitives, and their ways of life came under fire, just as the cultures of runaway slaves and Seminoles were criticized; these connections reveal that the Okefenokee has rarely been a space of racial privilege and social power.

Swamp ecolocalism is also shot through with shifting but ever-present class and professional anxieties. Many men of uncertain professional status – inexperienced planters, military men, and scientists – came to see the Okefenokee as a place in which they could improve their socio-economic standing. Others, however, developed relationships with the swamp based on their perception of the ecosystem's ability to free them from such social and economic delineations of success: fugitive slaves, Seminoles, and Swampers sought to live where and how they chose, preferably on the edges or within the depths of the Okefenokee Swamp.

Although the Okefenokee has not been universally admired, it has consistently captured the human imagination. The Okefenokee's "greens too green – the green of living things that feed upon death and destruction," and exotic wildlife have always appealed to observers' flights of fancy.[8] Those who encountered it were always moved to wax dramatic: strands of sphagnum moss were "the beards of druids," and the prolific foliage seemed to strangle with special malevolence. But the Okefenokee does not exist only within the imagination. The reality of inundated soils and dense tree stands was a constant force against which many communities felt the need to push. But since the first contact humans made with the Okefenokee, the swamp has been extremely difficult for humans to infiltrate or destroy. Because of its size, the Okefenokee has survived extensive droughts in addition to drainage and ditching projects. Thus both the Okefenokee's imaginative and tangible histories are the subjects of this book. The swamp's persistence is another theme of ecolocalism in the Okefenokee context; it contradicts more traditional American environmental narratives of abuse and destruction.

The interplay of persistence and instability is, as noted earlier, an ironic element of ecolocalism. Other ironies also abound, for the actions communities took within this environment often had unexpected consequences. Swamp ecology itself reflects this aspect of ecolocalism. Most humans who depicted the Okefenokee in words continually recorded their surprise when they stepped on undulating peat moss – earth that moved and thus was not quite earth – or when traversing multiple microenvironments in what had seemed a homogenous landscape. Although I did not walk on peat islands or canoe the entire width of the Okefenokee during my April trip, I did witness the shifting nature of the swamp – its darkness during daylight, alligator tracks filling with water, beautiful flowers bursting with poison. It is this aspect of the swamp, its trembling earth, that is the most striking and revelatory element of swamp ecolocalism. It reminds us that while we do much to shape natural environments, this shape often takes on different dimensions than what we had imagined.

By investigating the ways that swamp ecolocalism shaped cultures of combativeness in the Okefenokee hinterlands between 1732 and 1940, *Trembling Earth* brings the diversity of human experience into narratives of America's environmental history. This book is a study of the American Southeast conceived in terms of the hinterland and swamp rather than the port city and plantation. As such, it also reveals that culture – a web of ideas, beliefs, and actions – and its narratives emerge from community conflict and through encounters with local ecosystems. Ecolocalism, then, does not frame cultural history from above or below. It conceives of cultures as generated from the spaces between, the margins that have been at the center all along.

# 1 A Path to Freedom
## Slavery and Resistance

In the fall of 1838 Frances Anne (Fanny) Kemble made her way with her husband, Pierce Butler, her children, and a coterie of servants from Philadelphia to Georgia. She was to visit her husband's rice and cotton plantations – the source of the Butler family wealth – for six weeks. As they passed the Great Dismal Swamp in southern Virginia, Kemble was horrified, writing in her journal, "It looked like some blasted region lying under an enchanter's ban, such as one reads of in old stories. Nothing lived or moved throughout the lonesome solitude, and the sunbeams themselves seemed to sicken and grow pale as they glided like ghosts through these watery woods. Into this wilderness it seems impossible that the hand of human industry, or the foot of human wayfaring should ever penetrate; no wholesome growth can take root in its slimy depths; a wild jungle chokes up parts of it with a reedy, rattling covert for venomous reptiles; the rest is a succession of black ponds, sweltering under black cypress boughs – a place forbid."[1] Kemble saw nothing glorious or beautiful in these swampy climes. They were slimy, sweltering, and solitary – a "place forbid."

And yet, when she arrived at the family's plantations in Georgia, Kemble came to admire the riotous swamp growth on the margins of the rice fields: "Thickets of the most beautiful and various evergreen growth . . . beckoned my inexperience most irresistibly . . . the wood paths are as tempting as paths into Paradise." One of the Butler plantation slaves, Jack, on hearing her exultations, warned her against venturing into the wooded swamps. Rattlesnakes, bottomless sandpits, and other untold horrors awaited her there, he argued.[2] But Jack could have had more than Kemble's safety in mind, for the swamps surrounding the Butler cotton plantation and the Butler's Island rice plantation on the Altamaha River were the landscapes of slaves and fugitives during the antebellum era. In warning Kemble away from the Butler hinterlands, Jack may have been preventing her from trespassing on his community's property.

In the eighteenth and nineteenth centuries, European and European American communities struggled with African and African American slaves for control over the Okefenokee hinterlands and other southeastern lowlands. While European American communities saw swamps as sites of agricultural production and slave labor, slaves saw them as places in which they could potentially lead independent lives. Investigation of conflicts over slavery in Georgia and the use of the Okefenokee and other hinterland swamps as places of independence and freedom by slave communities uncovers the ways that slavery and resistance to it shaped swamp ecolocalism in the Okefenokee hinterlands and other southeastern lowlands before the Civil War.

When European explorers and colonists arrived on the southeastern coast of North America in the early sixteenth century, the area had been inhabited and used by Native American groups for more than ten thousand years. But as these communities came into contact with newly arrived English, Spanish, and French inhabitants, disease decimated them; Native groups in the area suffered near extinction. By 1733, when the English philanthropist (and trustee of the Colony of Georgia in America) James Oglethorpe landed eighteen miles east of Yamacraw Bluff along the Savannah River with 114 of England's "worthy poor," very few Native American towns existed along the Georgia coast. Thus no competing desires initially interfered with the colonial trustees' Georgia Plan, which aimed to create an agricultural paradise in the area.[3]

The Georgia trustees, a group of wealthy Englishmen whose aims for the colony were philanthropic, economic, and military, granted each of the colonists fifty acres for the purpose of silk production. Landowners could pass on these acreages only to male heirs, could not abandon them without the trustees' permission, and were required to cultivate them within ten years. The trustees also demanded that colonists plant and raise one hundred mulberry trees on their acreage (silkworms would feast on the trees and then produce their threads). Other colonists who traveled to Georgia without the trustees' aid, labeled "adventurers," received five hundred acres from the trustees. The plan required that these adventurers bring at least ten servants, cultivate at least one hundred acres in ten years, and plant a minimum of one thousand mulberry trees per one hundred acres. The Georgia Plan forbade land speculation, trade with the West Indies (to prevent consumption of rum), and in an unusual move, the use or importation of African slaves.[4]

Underpinning these decisions was not only the philanthropic ideology of cultivating character but also the widely held assumption that working the land oneself was intimately connected to public virtue, community stability, and good government. The trustees knew that Georgia's lowlands would be difficult to wrestle – they had read enough travelers' accounts to assure them that much of the area was choked with trees and inundated (flooded) at least seasonally. They were not dissuaded from their plan, however; an easily tilled soil and an Edenic climate more closely matched the desires of workers, not the needs of trustees. To the designers of the Georgia Plan, the work that created the landscape of small farms from the chaos of swamplands shaped the moral character of the community.

But within months of the initial clearing and building, colonists were already grumbling about the trustees' restrictions. The weather had not cooperated. Sixty of the original 114 colonists were ill with dysentery, and constrictive rules regarding alcohol use frustrated the new inhabitants. By 1738 many of the original colonists who had survived the first summers of illness and malnutrition had emigrated illegally to South Carolina; those who remained were anxious about their futures.[5] A group of "Mutinous Malcontents" (as Oglethorpe deemed them) voiced their discontent through petitions and pamphlets in the late 1730s and early 1740s, focusing their complaints on the sharp disparity between the trustees' promises of fertile, tillable land and the reality of vast expanses of swamp in Georgia. They called for a restructuring of land policies and the introduction of slavery. Integral to these arguments was a web of ideas connecting race, labor, and swamplands.

The trustees explicitly outlawed slavery in Georgia, but Carolina slave owners had continually crossed the Savannah River to take up residence south of the border since 1733. Only three years after Oglethorpe landed on Yamacraw Bluff, he found it necessary to declare that slaves discovered in the new colony would henceforth be considered property of the trust, any person found to be a slave owner or a transporter of slaves would be fined fifty pounds, and fugitive slaves from Carolina would be returned to their proper owners.[6] In the pamphlet war that erupted in the early 1740s, Georgia's swamplands and their suitability to slavery was a central issue.

In a satirical protest booklet called *A True and Historical Narrative of the Colony of Georgia in America* (1741), the malcontents Patrick Tailfer, Hugh Anderson, and David Douglas mobilized long-accepted ideas about the connections between climate and illness and manipulated the image of Georgia's swamplands in order to bolster their arguments for the introduction of slavery to the colony in the 1740s.[7] They complained that the extreme preponderance of sickness in the European community during the summer months demonstrated the inability of white laborers to work in Georgia's climate; attempts to cultivate lowlands with white servants, they argued, had proven "vain and fruitless."[8] The malcontents depicted Georgia's swamps as sources of pestilence; this belief was as old as medical theory itself. The Greek physician Hippocrates had noted in the fifth century B.C. that inundated landscapes were poisonous and that strangers to lowland areas should avoid them at all costs. During the eighteenth century doctors in Europe and in the Americas agreed that both endemic and epidemic diseases emerged from a combination of "insalubrious conditions of the atmosphere," high humidity, strong winds, hot temperatures, and a preponderance of landscapes dominated by standing water.[9] These conditions created miasmas – poisoned air that caused a range of illnesses, from mild recurrent bilious fevers to fatal attacks of typhoid and yellow fever. People would become infected through inhalation or absorption of these miasmatic poisons – disease thus passed through the air, not through contact with neighbors, nurses, or family members.

While miasmas were often quite difficult to see, the swamplands from which they were believed to emanate were not invisible. The medical theory of disease etiology popular in the eighteenth century, therefore, gave doctors and their patients a disease origin they could witness. As one Georgia doctor wrote later in 1806, "It is the opinion of many authors, that putrid matter, whether animal or vegetable, propagates fever; and it is evident, that the margin of a dead swamp can do it equally well."[10] The malcontents, informed by long-held beliefs in the pestilent nature of swamps and in response to the high mortality rates among colonists, argued that these lands were literally killing them.

The medical theories that connected swamps and disease also made links between a person's native latitudes and the ability to withstand the effects of swamp miasmas. Africans, eighteenth-century physicians argued, were acclimatized to the epidemic atmospheres created by the lowlands of west and central Africa. In North America, Africans seemed almost immune to endemic fevers like malaria and survived yellow fever epidemics at a much higher rate than Europeans. Although doctors acknowledged that these perceived immunities were not absolute, the lower susceptibility to disease among Africans suggested that they were ideal sources of labor in the swampy lands of colonial Georgia. John Brickell, a natural historian who wrote about the landscapes and peoples of the American Southeast, noted in 1737 that Africans could labor even in the warmest and wettest months, "being better able to undergo fatigues in the extremity of the hot Weather than any *Europeans*."[11]

This theory that Africans resisted miasmatic diseases like malaria and yellow fever in greater numbers than Europeans was, for the most part, correct. Efficient resistance to yellow fever among Africans and African Americans was due to a combination of genetic traits, acquired immunities, and geographic circumstances. A large number of eighteenth-century Africans and African Americans lacked the Duffy antigen (the enzyme glucose-6-phosphate dehydrogenase), which rendered them less susceptible to the more mild *vivax* malaria strain. Others also had a hemoglobin condition, a form of anemia (sickle cell disease) that provided some measure of resistance to the more virulent *falciparum* malaria strain in addition to yellow fever. The medical historian Todd Savitt has suggested that roughly 30 to 40 percent of the enslaved and free black population in nineteenth-century America expressed one or more of these genetic conditions and passed them on to their children.[12]

In addition to having some genetic protections against malaria and yellow fever, those Africans and their descendents who were forced to labor in the American Southeast had acquired immunities to miasmatic diseases during their lifetimes. In West Africa malarial diseases were endemic, and adults were a population of survivors. Where populations were stable and families lived in one area for several years consecutively, chances were good that children, who usually survived first attacks of yellow fever, would grow into immune adults. Western communities, which tended to be more stable than others, were also more likely to be raided by slave traders; immunities thus crossed the Atlantic with African captives.[13]

In the case of yellow fever, the vagaries of the slave system and a lack of mobility could also have helped Africans in America to survive the epidemics that killed thousands of white inhabitants of the southeastern lowlands. Yellow fever was primarily an urban disease, a fact that eighteenth- and nineteenth-century physicians noted with puzzlement and could not fully explain.[14] Because slavery in the Southeast was primarily contained in rural hinterland areas and on large rice plantations, only a small fraction of the slave population would come into contact with the yellow fever virus during epidemic summers. These patterns of disease resistance revealed doubled ironies: that slaves' restriction of freedom may have protected them against some epidemic diseases and that this perceived protection entrenched them further into slavery.

The malcontents noted miasmatic disease resistance among African slaves working on South Carolina rice plantations and promoted the association of swamps, rice, and black labor in a defense of slavery: "If they had swamp that would bear rice, white people are unable to clear them if they are covered with trees . . . it were simply impossible to manufacture the rice by white men." The introduction of slavery as a system of labor in Georgia, according to the malcontents, not only would prevent white mortality but also would woo migrants and increase rice production and profits. Black labor "would both occasion great numbers of white people to come here, and also render us capable to subsist ourselves, by raising provisions upon our lands, until we could make sure produce fit for export."[15]

Although these arguments promoting African slavery provoked some resistance among inhabitants of the most southern reaches of the colony (who had to contend with Spanish offers of freedom for British slaves, as discussed later), the malcontents nonetheless succeeded in their quest.[16] Ecolocal ideas promoting the close relationship between Africans and swamps ultimately wore down trustee resistance on the subject of slave labor. Shortly before they surrendered their dominion over Georgia to the British Crown in 1750, the trustees repealed their prohibition on slavery.[17] Over the next ten years the population of whites increased 300 percent and the black population increased tenfold. By 1776 the number of black slaves in Georgia had grown to sixteen thousand, 48 percent of the population of the colony.[18]

The Georgia Plan failed not only because the reality of mucky, overgrown tracts did not measure up to the ideal the trustees had created in their promotional pamphlets but also because European colonists increasingly separated themselves from swamplands and placed Africans within them. Colonists had come to Georgia hoping to demonstrate their power over nature. In their failure to subdue swamplands completely, they relegated swamps to slaves and, ironically, nurtured the relationship that would undermine the stability of white society in the American Southeast.

The influx of Carolina planters and their slaves into Georgia after the trustees' repeal halted the colony's meager production of silk and introduced staple crop agriculture to the lowlands between the Savannah and Altamaha rivers. Carolina planters had already established successful rice culture along the northern coastal plain, and they expanded southward after 1750, seeking profit and power in the swamplands of Georgia.[19] Between 1750 and 1790 the Georgia Low Country (including outlying areas of the Okefenokee hinterlands) morphed into a region of sculpted rice plantations. These new rice lands were established either along inland freshwater swamps or perched on the banks of coastal rivers, in estuarine swamps a few miles from the ocean.

Inland rice plantations dominated the southeastern landscape from 1750 until the 1780s. Their networks of ditches transported water from springs or ponds (formed by the construction of dams) to inland swamp areas; the water then drained through ditches into area streams. Rice cultivation required successive "flows" of water to cover the growing rice plants—the water simultaneously nourished the young plants, protected them from predators, and killed weeds. Early irrigation works were not very elaborate, and cultivation consisted of intensive hoeing and hand-weeding. Slaves cleared the area of cypress trees and underbrush, built banks on the bottom and top of new fields, and constructed an impoundment pond above them. Inland swamp cultivation necessitated two flows per season; slaves then hoed the fields after draining the water off the plants. When the crop was ripe, slaves cut the plants with a sickle, dried them, bound them into bundles with straw, and carried the bundles or rafted them along rice field canals to storage barns. They then threshed,

winnowed, husked, and packed the harvested rice in plantation outbuildings and stacked bundles on barges for transport to port cities. When confined to inland swamps, Georgia rice lands were small in acreage and the
crop yields were low.[20]

Although this inland system was relatively simple, as Mart Stewart has
argued, the construction of this kind of plantation "still required substantial modifications of the swampy environment and large investments in
wrenching labor."[21] It was intensive and risky. Planters who used these areas conformed their fields to geographic features (rivers, hammocks, and
hills) and were vulnerable to sudden freshets (rising streams) that destroyed
dikes and submerged fields at inopportune moments. By the late eighteenth century southeastern planters, attuned to technological innovations
and the main chance, turned their attention to more coastal ventures.

After the chaos of the Revolutionary War had subsided, planters made
forays into Georgia's tidewater river swamps to experiment with a different approach to rice cultivation. By 1790 the tidal rice method prevailed
along the coastal plain and involved major alterations of the southeastern
environment. As Joyce Chaplin has argued, the transformation of the
physical landscape gave the area distinctive features and entrenched slavery deeper in the Southeast, permanently altering the region.[22] To create
their giant tidal estates, planters moving into Georgia had to invest large
amounts of capital in technology and slaves. Medium to heavy surface
soils such as clay and swamp muck were ideal for a good rice crop, but
these lands required an immense amount of labor for clearing and cultivation. With hand tools, slaves rooted out undergrowth of tangled
swamps filled with deep-rooted foliage and jungle timber, leveled the
fields and smoothed them out, and constructed systems of banks, canals,
ditches, drains, and trunks.[23]

This system of cultivation was more labor intensive at every stage –
clearing, cultivating, and harvesting – than inland swamp processes but
provided greater control over water flow. Large-scale rice plantations
were giant hydraulic machines that were much more dynamic than inland
swamp plantations. Tidal cultivation demanded rivers with long water-
sheds and with channels deep enough for the layering of salt and fresh
waters: an elaborate irrigation system extracted fresh water from the top
layer of estuarine rivers, using the power of the tide to force the water
through canals, ditches, and trunks. Planters thus had to create rice fields
far enough from the sea to avoid a greater salt "push" and far enough
downriver to avoid flooding from the uplands. A variety of systems

evolved along Georgia's coastal plain as planters responded to specific local conditions along the Savannah, Ogeechee, Altamaha, Satilla, and St. Marys rivers, but most established a geometric grid of fields and irrigation ditches.

The rice grid was always defined in some part by the rivers and swamplands from which it emerged. The resultant contrasting aesthetics (the straight lines interrupted by the curves) struck many observers forcefully. The naturalist William Bartram found river swamp fields to be "charming and animating" when he visited plantations in the 1770s; he noted with satisfaction that "these swamps are daily clearing and improving into large fruitful rice plantations."[24] Fanny Kemble did not think so highly of the rice grid or its permanence, however. Initially, she found the Butler's Island rice plantation to be decidedly unpicturesque and constrictive: "my walks were rather circumscribed, inasmuch as the dikes are the only promenades. On all sides of these lie either the marshy rice fields, the brimming river, or the swampy patches of yet unreclaimed forest." Because she was not able to walk or take horseback rides along the narrow dikes, Kemble learned to like canoes and discovered that there was much to see from her low perspective. The banks of canals seemed to her both symbolic of human endeavor and indicative of nature's enduring power:

> The banks of this canal, when they are thus laid bare, present a singular appearance enough – two walls of solid mud, through which matted, twisted, twined, and tangled, like the natural veins of wood, runs an everlasting net of indestructible roots, the thousand toes of huge cypress feet. The trees have been cut down long ago from the soil, but these fangs remain in the earth without decaying for an incredible space of time. This long endurance of immersion is one of the valuable properties of these cypress roots; but, though excellent binding stuff for the sides of the canal, they must be pernicious growth in any land used for cultivation that requires deep tillage.[25]

Kemble expresses here a vision rarely noted in antebellum literature and painting: the antiprospect, the view from below. From her canoe, she can see the earth below its surface and notice the "indestructible roots" of the cypress, a tree indigenous to swamplands. Kemble's observation reveals the planter's desire and ability to incorporate swamp ecology as an anchor for his hydraulic machine. Yet her perspective simultaneously affirms the obstinate nature – the "fangs" – of the swamp ecosystem.

The rice plantation grid, despite its relative permanence, was not infallible. Threat of natural disaster – freshets and surges caused by strong storms – was always present in tidal rice swamps. Hurricanes did not frequently make landfall on the Georgia coast; the sharp "scoop" of land westward below Savannah diverted most storms northward. But the Okefenokee hinterlands often felt the impact of hurricanes making their way up the Atlantic coast or moving across northern Florida from the Gulf of Mexico. As Fanny Kemble wrote, even in winter, thunder and lightning "appear neither astonishing nor unseasonable, and I should think in summer . . . lightning must be as familiar to these sweltering lands and slimy waters as sunlight itself."[26] Planters had to choose the sites for trunks carefully; these were weak spots in banks that were most vulnerable to blowouts. Trunks, in addition to floodgates, were meant to direct and control water flow, but the network hinged on these points, and the smallest structural weakness could mean disaster. Strong winds could burst trunks, bring river water over the banks into the fields, fell machinery and buildings, and drive tree limbs through canal banks.

Hugh Fraser Grant, one of Kemble's neighbors on the Altamaha River and owner of Elizafield Plantation, noted in his journal entry for September 18, 1841, that his banks had sustained "Breaks by Gale. tide & freshct in the 27, Lower 20, 22, 17, 18 & 3 Acre squares the rice in the above been in water (Stacked) since Wednesday the 15th." In October Grant's slaves had finished cutting the rice that had survived the September gale, but his harvest was a month late and he lost many barrels due to "high tides, freshets and incessant rains." A strong hurricane that hit Georgia in September 1854 devastated Grant's plantation: "Blowing a gale from N.E. tides very high but no damage yet – Look for trouble this night. . . . Dreadful Gale. Everything under water break in 16, 22, 18 & Kesia Scipio Square Every stack in the field blown and washed away. Loss entire 110 Acres of Rice about 6,000 bushels."[27]

To wrest their plantations out of the muck and protect them from meteorological exigencies, planters had to invest large amounts of capital in the hydraulic machine. It was Kemble's belief that creating the grid was too expensive and exhausting: "it is a very obvious thing that [planters] must all very soon be eaten up by their own property."[28] Indeed, planters faced unexpected resistance from their own property, from both the swamplands out of which they shaped the grid, and the slaves who built it.

By constructing rice plantations and relegating slaves to swamps along the southern Atlantic coast and in the Okefenokee hinterlands, planters simultaneously bolstered and destabilized their economic and social hegemony during the eighteenth and nineteenth centuries. Planters were dependent on large numbers of slaves to cultivate their landholdings; the Rice Belt averaged 226 slaves per plantation between 1750 and 1860.[29] Consequently, a black majority characterized much of the coastal landscape; this majority was often the context for an emergent creolized slave culture on large rice plantations that adapted African styles of dress, food, religion, music, and oral narration to life in the slave quarters.[30] Slaves also adapted African methods in agriculture to inundated landscapes and, in so doing, developed their own ecolocal culture.

As Judith Carney has recently pointed out, Africans who inhabited the Upper Guinea Coast of West Africa during the eighteenth century were rice farmers. The floodplains, coastal estuaries, and mangrove swamps extending from Senegal to Liberia provided rich soils for rice agriculture. The Upper Guinea region also included several coastal port cities in which African farmers bought and sold various products. Ironically, this proximity to the coast and its ports made Upper Guinea farmers more successful but also more visible to European slave traders; they were thus primary victims of the transatlantic slave trade.[31]

Rice culture, a sophisticated, "underlying knowledge system" that shaped the cultivation, milling, and preparation of rice, accompanied Africans across the Atlantic. As it was "central to subsistence and cultural identity over a broad area of West Africa; it was to become equally so in communities of the Americas settled by slaves from the rice region and their descendents." Abundant evidence shows that South Carolina and Georgia planters knew of the rice expertise of certain African ethnic groups and deliberately purchased slaves from these groups in order to exploit their experience.[32] On American plantations, before and even after the cessation of the Atlantic slave trade in 1808, large numbers of slaves in the American Southeast not only applied their knowledge to shaping rice fields but also recognized and used their hinterlands — forested, swampy lowlands – as sites of cultural formation and resistance against slavery.

Familiarity with the general ecology of inundated lands (although West African swamplands are significantly more saline than North American swamps – the growth of mangroves is indicative of this salinity) and the prevalence of the task system on rice plantations gave these slaves opportunities for independence that may not have been available to those residing and working on plantations in more northern climes. The American version of the task system, which Carney has argued is probably of African origin, may have been shaped by both slaves and planters, for slaves "provided critical expertise in exchange for a labor regime that would improve the conditions of their bondage."[33] As such, this negotiated labor system offered a more technical, varied, and flexible work schedule. Overseers or drivers assigned individual slaves tasks, usually measured spatially: anywhere from one-quarter acre to a full acre of tilling, planting, or hoeing. When the slave finished the task, he or she could spend the rest of the day in his or her house or garden. Slaves shaped the task system to suit their needs, using their posttask time to develop other skills and often, individual garden plots that augmented diets and created a local provision economy in the slave quarters.[34]

This relative flexibility in the task system does not mean that life on a rice plantation was pleasant or enjoyable. Hours were long, sickness prevalent, and the labor arduous. Mortality rates, as William Dusinberre has shown, were horrifyingly high.[35] But the presence of swamplands and many slaves' familiarity with them, in addition to the sporadic free time that slaves carved out for themselves, prompted many slaves to use the plantation hinterlands for their own benefit.

Use of outlying inundated landscapes provided many slaves with better diets and a sense of independence. It also prompted flight from slavery, either for short periods of time or permanently. In swamps, slaves and fugitive slaves found a refuge from the horrors of bondage; the ecolocal ideas that propagated enslavement in the Southeast put slaves into contact with an environment that increased their chances for freedom between 1750 and 1850.

When Fanny Kemble arrived in Georgia, both her husband and the slave Jack warned her away from hinterland paths. And although she reported that St. Simons slaves "seem to me to have a holy horror of ever setting their foot near either tree or bush, or anywhere but on the open road and the fields where they labor," many enslaved men and women came to the Butler plantation infirmary with rattlesnake bites in 1838. This indicates that reported fears were either exaggerated or were not enough of a deterrent to keep slaves out of the swampy hinterlands.[36]

Throughout the Southeast, slaves entered swamps, creating paths through clearing and consistent use. They gathered herbs and edible plants and hunted wild game that supplemented their meager diets. While Kemble's husband, Pierce Butler, did not allow his slaves to carry firearms, other planters did and expected their slaves to hunt for birds and other wild game in the lowland forests surrounding the plantation. When Frederick Law Olmsted traveled through Georgia in 1853, he stayed with "Mr. X," a planter who allowed his slaves to store guns and ammunition in their own cabins. Mr. X expected that slaves would hunt "for their own sport."[37] Some slaves procured as much as half the meat in their diet from hinterland hunting excursions, while the other half came from weekly provisions, fishing, or domesticated animals (fowl, cattle, hogs) that some slaves kept on the edges of the plantation.[38] Wood was also plentiful on the margins, and slaves cut firewood for their own use or for sale and felled trees to shape into canoes they would later use to navigate the intricate waterways of lowland swamps. In addition, slaves made use of products unique to the swamp environment. As Fanny Kemble reported, "the people collect moss from the trees and sell it to the shopkeepers in Darien for the purpose of stuffing furniture."[39]

It is clear from the architecture of southeastern plantations that planters themselves expected slaves to be "closer" to the surrounding swamplands than to white residents. Planters usually arranged slave quarters in a block pattern away from the Big House, sometimes far beyond plantation outbuildings. Such physical distance from the seat of white power often allowed slaves to exert domestic control and take possession of lands for their own benefit. As John Michael Vlach has shown, slaves laid claim to portions of the plantation landscape – some of those spaces were ceded to them and others were not. Forest paths and trails, like those that appealed to Fanny Kemble on St. Simons, were central elements of the slave landscape that provided slaves with a means to escape their masters' control, if but briefly. The slave environment, as Vlach has argued, was "marked by few overt boundaries and fixed sites, an environment open to and characterized by movement."[40] Swamps were such open, poorly marked landscapes; their boundaries shifted constantly and offered concealment and abundant resources.

Plantations were places of work, as were the hinterlands, but slave appropriation of surrounding swamplands was a direct material expression of both their experience with lowland ecosystems and their desire for power over their own lives.[41] Slaves were the threads creating a web of social, economic, and environmental relationships on southeastern plantations. Their relationship with both plantation lands and hinterlands was socially prescribed through ecolocal ideas connecting race, labor, and environment, yet it was also socially destabilizing. By developing their own ecolocalist sensibilities – seeing the swamp as a source of freedom – and then acting according to these ideas by using the products of the swamplands surrounding plantations, southeastern slaves shaped an ecolocal culture and created some measure of independence for themselves in these spaces. No act was more subversive in this landscape of slaves than flight. Fugitives fled southeastern rice plantations in large numbers between 1750 and 1850, and they used the Okefenokee and other southeastern swamps as conduits to freedom.

Slaves were both human and property, and this unique doubleness meant they could use their status as chattel as a weapon against their masters. Resistance reduced the fugitive's worth and robbed his owner of labor and resultant revenue. Also, planters forced to advertise for their runaways acknowledged publicly that they could not fully control their laborers. Slave resistance challenged the tightly administered social, economic, and environmental world rice planters attempted to shape and had both political and environmental implications.[42] Planters coveted control over their property while slaves desired freedom; these adverse aims clashed within the fluctuating boundaries of swamplands and shaped ecolocalism in the eighteenth and nineteenth centuries. Using the Okefenokee and other southeastern swamps, fugitive slaves sometimes joined maroon communities on the margins of American cities but more often engaged in *petit marronage* (or lying out) for months at a time or made a run for the Georgia-Florida border to achieve permanent freedom in colonial Spain.

Although maroons populated and destabilized every slave society in which mountains, swamps, or other terrain provided hinterlands, few viable maroon groups emerged in the American Southeast. Those that did exist formed in the eighteenth century and were small and fragmented communities supported by agricultural subsistence, hunting, and theft.[43] In October 1786 the *Charleston Morning Post* reported that more than one hundred South Carolina runaways had established a camp on a swampy island seventeen miles up the Savannah River, "and for some time past committed robberies on the neighboring Planters." The state's political leaders found it "necessary to attempt to dislodge them."[44] The attempt worked, but only after a bloody battle between the Savannah Light Infantry, the South Carolina militia, and the maroons.

The outskirts of Savannah were a popular gathering place for fugitive slaves in the eighteenth century; the area was still relatively unpopulated but, most important, the Forest City was surrounded on three sides by swampy lowlands during this time. These river swamps, however, were not viable for permanent maroon inhabitation; the encroachment of white migrants and aggressive drainage plans in the nineteenth century prevented sustained maroon activity in the area. Also, it was difficult for gangs of runaways to maintain cohesive communities for long periods of time in swamps, particularly if they had not yet obtained guns for hunting the abundant game that roamed these ecosystems. Fugitives looking to join already established rebel communities in the Okefenokee hinterlands often made their way to the Seminole towns of central and northern Florida. These maroon towns provoked much fear in European communities on both sides of the Georgia-Florida border, and with good reason — maroons joined Seminoles in raids on American and Spanish plantations and homesteads throughout the eighteenth and nineteenth centuries. But these maroon groups were not sustainable, and after the first Seminole War (1817–18), they were scattered and nomadic. Maroon communities were rare in North America, but those few that did exist reveal the importance of swamp ecosystems in the act of running away.[45] Flight was a political and economic feat but also an act of environmental knowledge and use.

Fugitives who took advantage of the protection that southeastern swamps like the Okefenokee offered most often used them as havens for a short period *(petit marronage)* or as conduits to other counties, states, or territories. Those slaves engaging in *petit marronage* stayed away from the plantation for weeks or even months but remained in the neighborhood, harboring in swamps and pillaging or looting local homesteads. Many slave owners saw this fugitive behavior as somewhat acceptable and different from actually running away; some owners did not advertise for a runaway until he or she had been gone for more than a month. Roderick McIver, a planter from Pedee Island, South Carolina, advertised four missing slaves in the *Georgia Gazette* on September 1, 1763, and noted that three of the four (Whan, Isaac, and Christopher) had been gone for one and a half months, while Jack, presumably the ringleader, had been gone for three years.[46] Some slaves experimented with lying out before attempting permanent escape. A slave named Sampson, who fled from his Georgia plantation in 1844, had run away earlier that year when "his master undertook to whip him." He stayed in the area and "no one knew where he was, except for a trusted few of his faithful companions. He kept hid during the day, only venturing out at night, in order to procure necessary supplies." Sampson lay out for about three months before he approached Lewis Paine, a northern white factory manager, to help him flee to Alabama.[47]

John Brown, a Georgia slave who escaped to Ohio and then to England in the 1840s, also had a past of *petit marronage*: "During my old master's lifetime, I had frequently hidden away in the woods and swamps; sometimes for a few days only; at others for a fortnight at a stretch; and once for a whole month. I used to sneak out at night from my hiding-place to steal corn, fruit and such like. As long as it lasted, the release from the severe labour put upon me was quite grateful; and though I always got cruelly flogged on my return, the temptation to get rest this way was too great to be resisted."[48] Brown snuck away to gain a "release from severe labour," a motive common among slaves lying out. While some historians have argued that lying out bolstered slavery by giving slaves an opportunity to "rest" within the context of their servitude (thereby making it more palatable to return), it is clear that the presence of slaves lying out tried masters' patience and disconcerted the white community. Swamps were dark, mysterious, dangerous places, and the fugitives within them challenged white assumptions about their slaves' "happy" dispositions and racial inferiority. Also, fugitives in the swamps served as a reminder to their owners that their ecolocal ideas connecting race and labor had been undermined. Slaves used their relationship with swamplands to escape from, not to bolster, slavery in the American Southeast. Fugitive slaves created chaos as they fulfilled their desires for freedom in the Okefenokee hinterlands. They also exploited imperial rivalries during the eighteenth and nineteenth centuries to reach their goals.

Runaways who were neither hiding out in groups nor lying out but who were seeking permanent freedom were likely to use the Okefenokee and other swamps to shield them from pursuers and inclement weather while they were on the move. They were aided in their quest for freedom by the unstable geopolitical situation in the Southeast between 1750 and 1821. Most Georgia slaves lived within 150 miles of the Florida border, and both the Spanish and Loyalist British presence in Florida offered southeastern slaves unique opportunities. Many slaves took advantage of tensions evolving between Spain and Britain, the United States and Britain, and the United States and Spain to achieve freedom.

In 1739 a group of Scots-Irish farmers who disagreed with the malcontents' call for slavery in Georgia wrote a petition from Darien arguing that the "Liberty of having Slaves" would be "dangerous" and lead to "bad Consequence." The petitioners listed five reasons for these dangers; the first of these was even more persuasive in light of the commencement of the War of Jenkins Ear later that year, which pitted England against Spain in the New World: "The Nearness of the Spaniards, who have proclaimed Freedom to all Slaves who run away from their Masters, makes it impossible for us to keep them without more Labour in guarding them, than what we would be at to do their Work."[49] The Darien petitioners were justified in their fears. The Spanish Crown had granted freedom to all African runaways in 1693, "the men as well as the women . . . so that by their example and by my liberality, others will do the same." The king reiterated his offer in 1739.[50] That year officials also commenced construction on a fort to house runaways and to provide a Spanish outpost in northeastern Florida.

James Oglethorpe understood the point of these actions, writing to the trustees on June 19, 1741, "The Spanish Emissarys are very busy in stirring up Discontents amongst the People hence their Principal Point is Negroes since as many Slaves as there are [in the Carolinas], are so many Enemys to the Government, and consequently Friends to the Spaniards. Another great Point is to Discourage the Planters, since they think if planting don't go forward England will grow tired of supporting the Colony & then of course the Spaniards will gain their ends."[51] Oglethorpe clearly linked Spanish legislative seductions to both slave escape and rebellion. He argued in 1742 that the Spanish reiteration of amnesty had undoubtedly encouraged the Stono Rebellion in South Carolina three years earlier.[52] Spain offered slaves freedom, homesteads, and the opportunity to take up arms against their former owners. Their offers of freedom presumably spread to British American plantations through the channels of conversation; some literate slaves may also have read of Spain's policies in local newspapers. Whatever the route of information, written documents produced on both sides of the international border attest to the fact that hundreds of slaves living and laboring in the Southeast heard of Spain's amnesty proclamation and took advantage of local swamplands to achieve freedom in Spanish Florida.

Britain's brief tenure in Florida (1763–84), as Jane Landers has noted, temporarily eliminated the international border and subsequently, black freedom in Florida became only a remote possibility. With the restoration of Spanish rule in Florida in 1784, however, the Okefenokee hinterlands again became a site of American slave society's instability. The Spanish Crown repeated its offer of sanctuary to runaway slaves, enticing them with land grants, royal subsidies, tax relief, and other privileges and exemptions.[53] But Georgia planters complained loudly to the American federal government, and in 1790 Spain finally abrogated its sanctuary policy. The Spanish governors insisted, however, that all fugitives who had already claimed freedom in Florida remained free.[54]

Even without an official sanctuary policy after 1790, slaves still ran. They crossed the border in family groups or by themselves, but they continued to seek freedom in Florida until its annexation to the United States in 1821. The Spanish governors of Florida did what they could to stave off slave catchers and angry owners and provided some measure of protection to those runaways arriving in St. Augustine after the sanctuary abrogation. Many Georgia slaves took advantage of the geopolitical turbulence, using the dark and tangled passageways of the Okefenokee and other southeastern swamps to achieve freedom. Their actions shaped swamp ecolocalism in the eighteenth and nineteenth centuries.

Fugitive slaves with an eye toward permanent self-determination most likely used the Okefenokee as a conduit to liberty, but direct evidence of their use of this ecosystem is sparse. No maroon communities or permanent fugitive shelters sprang up within its depths until black runaways and Seminoles joined forces in the 1830s and 1840s. Few slave narratives from the eighteenth or nineteenth centuries illuminate the multiple roles the Okefenokee or other southeastern swamp ecosystems played in the runaway's fight for freedom. But newspaper advertisements for runaway slaves in middle and southern Georgia (1760 to 1845) and the letters sent between Georgia and St. Augustine (1784 to 1821) reveal that substantial numbers of slaves fled from Georgia and South Carolina in a southerly direction and that the Okefenokee Swamp was in the perfect geographical position to provide shelter, food, and protection for those fugitives who fled southward to freedom.

Investigations of runaway slave advertisements, "brought to jail" notices, and letters between Georgia officials and various governors of East Florida between 1760 and 1845 reveal that of the 349 runaway slaves known to have headed southward from South Carolina and Georgia, 83 percent were men, and 57 percent of all runaways traveled in groups.[55]

Spanish sanctuary was a powerful impetus to flight: 140 (40 percent – the largest percentage) ran south to Florida when Spain offered sanctuary between 1784 and 1821.

A precise count of fugitive slaves is, of course, impossible to achieve. The 349 slaves advertised as running southward in the *Georgia Gazette*, *Milledgeville (Ga.) Reflector*, and the *Milledgeville (Ga.) Federal Union* between 1760 and 1845 are only a small percentage of the total advertised runaways in the state of Georgia. And, as Philip Morgan has put it, "advertised runaways represent only the most visible tip of an otherwise indeterminate iceberg."[56] Some owners did not advertise at all, for many reasons: they thought the slave would return of his or her own accord; they could not afford to place an ad; their distance from a city center or access to mails to place the ad could present an obstacle; or embarrassment about their failure to control their slaves might deter them. And even if they did manage to advertise, owners or overseers could have also made many misjudgments about their slaves. But most historians agree that it was in the owner's best interest to be honest about his runaways. Otherwise, the advertisement was misleading to readers, and the chances of catching the runaway would decrease significantly.[57]

While newspaper advertisements might be a bit vague, the letters that darted over the border between Georgia officials and slave owners and the Spanish governors of East Florida between 1751 and 1821 are clear and specific. They detail the numbers and names of those fugitives who had fled from Georgia plantations (and sometimes American plantations established illegally in Florida) to cross the border. They also make very clear that many slaves ran to Spanish Florida and lived to claim sanctuary. These slaves must have encountered the Okefenokee hinterlands at some point during their travels, and it is likely that they used the swamp along their route.

Runaways to East Florida during these years took minimal possessions with them and traveled by canoe, by horse, or on foot – sometimes they used all three methods of transportation at different points during their journeys. The most striking fact gleaned from runaway slave advertisements, brought to jail notices, and international letters is that of the 140 fugitives who crossed the border into East Florida between 1783 and 1819, when Spanish sanctuary was their goal, 109 (78 percent) traveled in groups. In comparison, between 1763 and 1770, during part of the British occupation of Florida, 56 percent of runaways ran in groups; after Florida's annexation, between 1830 and 1845, only 35 percent of fugitives ran together. The dramatic decrease in the percentages of groups traveling southward after annexation suggests that Spanish freedom was a more attractive option to families than to individuals. Most runaways in groups heading for Spanish sanctuary consisted of between two and four members – most often men and women and their children.

One fugitive family from South Carolina, the Wittens, took advantage of wartime chaos and the reversion of East Florida to Spanish possession in 1783 to gain freedom. Sometime during the Revolutionary War, British soldiers plundered Prince Witten; his wife, Judy; and their children, Glasgow and Polly, from their proprietor's estate in South Carolina. American troops then recaptured the family, but they escaped from these U.S. soldiers in June or July 1785, making their way across the border and requesting sanctuary in St. Augustine in 1786. They ultimately became property holders, were baptized into the Catholic Church, and took Spanish names.[58]

Like the Wittens, the Blackwood family ran to St. Augustine in the 1780s, although their fate is not so clear. According to John Blackwood, their former owner, Amos Blackwood; and his wife, Silvia; and their two children, Aron and Dolley, were stolen from his southern Georgia plantation and taken to St. Augustine. John Blackwood spent much of the year 1792 trying to track down this family. Their labor meant a good deal to him and his finances were suffering; in August 1792, Blackwood could not afford to hire a lawyer or travel to St. Augustine to file the appropriate paperwork and claim his property. In a letter to Captain Howard, the fort captain on Amelia Island, Blackwood wrote anxiously that "unless I do Something Shortly I Should Loose them." While a Spanish official from St. Augustine wrote to Blackwood and assured him that "Justice would be done," it is unclear whether this planter was ever successful in recapturing Amos Blackwood and his family.[59]

Groups of runaways to East Florida were not always composed of family members, however. In May 1797 southern Georgia slave owners compiled a list of runaway slaves that included a group of twelve fugitives who had fled together: Titus, Tice, Jeffry, John, Summer, Lester, Sue, Beck, Beck's child, D., Rose, and Rose's child. It is possible that two of the men in the group were the fathers of Beck's and Rose's children, but the list did not make note of any other familial relationships.[60] Some groups formed and reformed over the border. In 1797 a fugitive named Titus (a different man from the Titus mentioned earlier) gathered a band of runaways together in Florida and traveled northward to wreak havoc on the plantations of their former owners. They made their way along the seacoast until they reached Savannah, where they absorbed some fugitive slaves hiding out in the surrounding swamps. They "became very troublesome to the people," as James Seagrove (the commissioner of Indian Affairs in Georgia) put it, as they traveled up and down the coastal plain, plundering rice plantations. Titus's band was then outlawed, and a party of armed men pursued them in Savannah's hinterland swamps. "It being a very thick Swamp, most of them escaped," but rumors of some deaths (due to the amount of blood on the ground) circulated. Seagrove was unsettled but not too disturbed at Titus's getaway. "Parties are constantly after them," he wrote, "and there is little doubt they will be taken or killed."[61]

Fugitives running to East Florida most likely made the trip in large numbers because it was easier to move larger groups the relatively short distance between southeastern Georgia plantations and the St. Marys River, rather than north to Canada. Group running also provided protection, more numbers for hunting and provision gathering, and sociability in a time of great stress. Fugitives probably also considered the knowledge they had that the Spanish Crown would grant them land. Greater numbers meant more labor to develop such land grants in addition to an instant community providing psychological and emotional support during the transition to a life of freedom in Florida. But perhaps the most meaningful suggestion that this data provides is that fugitives in groups were planning for long-term freedom – they cultivated a vision of the future that included family members and friends.

Several slaves did strike out for freedom alone, however, and most were young men. Of the thirty-one individual runaways known to have crossed into East Florida between 1783 and 1819, 84 percent were male. One such runaway was Emanuel McGillis, who "eloped" from his master's service in July 1803. Emanuel had been captured by the British during the Revolutionary War and changed hands several times in the postwar years. When he made his escape from the St. Marys district, he passed into Florida "under a pretence he is not the property of Mr. McGillis." Emanuel may have not remembered his former master's name; most likely, he lied to gain admittance to Florida. The guards at Amelia Island let him through, and James Seagrove subsequently petitioned Governor White of St. Augustine to return the fugitive to the border so that his owner could retrieve him. It is unknown whether White or Seagrove was ever successful in capturing Emanuel.[62]

Only one female fugitive is known to have run alone between 1783 and 1817: Nelly Pooler appeared on the list of forty-three slaves that Georgia slave owners compiled for claiming purposes in 1797. But more women took advantage of imperial rivalries during the First Seminole War of 1817–18 to seek their freedom. Of the six women advertised as running southward alone from South Georgia in 1817, one was advertised as a runaway (Priss Spradlin). The other five were brought to jails in Savannah, Augusta, and in Jacksonborough and Baldwin counties, all having been headed in a southerly direction. Individual fugitives traveling southward were not as numerous as runaways in groups, but most fugitives were likely to have traversed or taken refuge in the Okefenokee and other southeastern swamps during their flight to Florida. The landscape of slaves became an environment of fugitives in these cases.

As slaves ran through the Okefenokee and other swamps, their owners and public officials bickered over their capture. Seagrove and the slave owners in southern Georgia expected their slaves to be returned to them. A treaty between the United States and Spain, signed in May 1797, stipulated that "all Fugitive Slaves, who have taken shelter in his Catholic Majesty's province of East Florida, since the Second day of September, in the year one thousand Seven hundred & Ninety, belonging to Citizens or Inhabitants of the United States (those belonging to His Catholic Majesty's Rebellious subjects excepted) shall without delay be delivered to the said Commissioner to be by him convey'd into the United States, in order to be delivered, to their respective owners – or in the case of failure in delivery of any part of such fugitives, that the Government of Spain pay a reasonable price for the same."[63] The Treaty of 1797 was meant to codify custom, but Spanish landowners and Seminoles were more than happy to welcome new workers, warriors, and soldiers to their communities in Florida. The attempts of Georgia slave owners to retrieve runaways, therefore, were most often frustrated. James Spalding, a Georgian who owned a plantation on the St. Marys River and lost ten slaves to East Florida from 1789 to 1794, was particularly chagrined. Not only did he and his family suffer from the lack of labor – he claimed that "their detention is a greater loss than their death on my plantation would be" – but the fugitives' success damaged his hopes of keeping his other slaves in line: "it shows the slaves yet remaining with me that they can change their situation when they please and as this knowledge spreads amongst the slaves of my neighbours many of whome they have already lost and if you shall persist in retaining our slaves no doubt many now will be lost."[64]

Hundreds of slaves took advantage of the geopolitical chaos and the presence of the Okefenokee and other swamplands in the American Southeast in order to flee to Spanish Florida or to Seminole towns between 1750 and 1850. Several slave owners reported the theft of canoes at the same time as runaways; those slaves working on rice plantations on the coast or inland would have had knowledge of the multiple serpentine waterways in the region and the skills to navigate them. It is difficult to determine precise routes, for as Frederick Douglass, John Brown, and many other fugitives-turned-writers have argued, authorial silence kept anyone who aided in the escape alive and kept channels open for those who would subsequently run. It also served to obfuscate the path to freedom itself. Georgia officials suspected that fugitives used swamplands as escape routes, but without concrete information they could not possibly pinpoint particular swamplands and thus could not hope to prevent fully their appropriation by runaways.

Within swamps, fugitive slaves represented not only a loss of labor and capital but also a threat to the white community's carefully constructed social hierarchy. Like swamplands, which are neither entirely water nor entirely land, fugitive slaves led a murky, twilight kind of existence. Neither enslaved nor truly free until they reached a destination that would grant them permanent independence, fugitives on the run were ambiguous and paradoxical symbols of liberty in the American Southeast. Their use of swamplands both confirmed and challenged European American ecolocal ideas – slaves and fugitive slaves cultivated their close relationships with swamps but used them to subvert instead of support the ideologies and infrastructure of the slave system. Just as slave rebellions provoked repressive measures across multiple southern landscapes in the eighteenth and nineteenth centuries, ecolocalism shaped by slaves and fugitive slaves prompted a shift in European American beliefs about swamps during the antebellum period.

As slaves continued to use swamps as sites of potential and actual freedom for themselves, European Americans began to reshape their ecolocal ideas through fiction. As the antebellum period progressed and the supposed connections of race, labor, and swamplands were continually undermined by fugitive slaves and attacked by northern abolitionists, southern white writers began to erase black presence from swamplands almost entirely. The most widely read authors of the antebellum period – plantation novelists, historical fiction writers, and southwestern humorists – took up the image of the swamp but emptied it of potentially disturbing black rebels.

John Pendleton Kennedy, in his 1832 novel *Swallow Barn; or, A Sojourn in the Old Dominion*, depicts swamplands as home only to the ruins of a European settlement and the territory of a white backcountry trapper. As Mark Littleton, a New Yorker and the protagonist of the novel, and his Virginian friend Ned Hazard traverse a local swamp, they imagine many ghosts but only find Hafen Blok, a German mercenary who had deserted the British Army and joined the American cause. Blok is a "short, thickset, bandy-legged personage, bearing all the marks of an old man, with a strangely weather-beaten face, intersected by as many drains as the rugged slope of a sand hill. . . . His trowsers and shoes were covered with the mud of the swamp." He knows the ecosystem well, but he "firmly believed in the stories of the Goblin Swamp" and thus is only a sporadic inhabitant.[65] Littleton, Hazard, and Blok stay only a short time in Goblin Swamp and then hurry home to Swallow Barn, a warm fire, and a tasty dinner. The image of the swamp here is one of an abandoned landscape, an ecosystem of ghosts. It ceases to be a material space and exists almost solely within the imagination; it is delineated by myth and resists any kind of inhabitation or use. And it is certainly not a conduit to freedom for Virginia slaves.

The inhabitants of William Gilmore Simms's swamplands are more varied than those visitors to Kennedy's Goblin Swamp, but most of them belong to banditti groups and all of them are white. In *Helen Halsey; or, The Swamp State of Conelachita* (1845), Simms portrays the river swamps of Mississippi as home to backcountry hooligans. The protagonist, Henry Meadows, is a good-natured young man who falls in love with a girl (Helen Halsey) at a tavern and follows her home to a vast morass. Here he runs into a fleeing revenue collector who warns him away from the place: "He gave it as his opinion, that the whole region, which he had fancied a *quasi* wilderness, was alive with rogues – that the settlement was quite a numerous one – that they occupied every fastness and place of cover, and retreat – hammocks and islets – in the swamps and river. . . . They were a vast community, kept together by the common object and necessity, roving always in concert, and sworn against all laws and all honesty." The "Swamp State of Conelachita" is a thriving community, made up of white outlaws who have created a commonwealth dedicated to lawlessness and social disorder. It is internally hierarchical and organized, however, and has a long history. Meadows stumbles into the outlaws' town and is taken prisoner by Helen Halsey's father, who confirms the revenue collector's impressions. The region in which he had wandered "was possessed by a community of rogues. They were numerous and extensively connected throughout the country. Some of them had absolute wealth; and children, born in this American Alsatia – so long had it been a realm of outlawry – were now grown to manhood."[66] Although some of the bandits, including Halsey, are somewhat repentant, they see nothing wrong with their mode or place of living. The swamp is understood to be a site in which a poor white man could make his way and make a home. Fugitive slaves merit nary a mention.

Simms wrote several other novels with swamp settings, including his narratives of the Revolutionary War, *The Scout; or, The Black Riders of the Congaree* (1841) and *The Forayers; or, The Raid of the Dog-Days* (1855). Both narratives begin with a description of swampland homesites and the men who live within them. In *The Scout*, the swamps of Carolina welcome partisan troops who fight on both sides of the Revolutionary War. They "furnished a place of refuge to the patriot and the fugitive, when the dwelling and the temple yielded none. The more dense the wall of briers upon the edge of the swamp, the more dismal the avenues within, the more acceptable to those who, preferring Liberty over all things, could there build her altars and tend her sacred fires, without being betrayed by their smokes."[67] The Carolina swamps in the novel host both the Black Riders of the Congaree, troops who fight for the British and enjoy the liberty of wreaking havoc on the countryside, and the Congaree Blues, a band of men who fight for American liberty and defend local plantations from marauders. The swamp's ambiguity makes it a perfect site to provide these conflicted groups with shelter and nourishment. Simms pushes the duality further by pitting brother against brother within the swamp: Edward Conway, the darker and older brother, was born in the Caribbean and is a Black Rider, while Clarence Conway, fair and American born, battles the British. It is possible that Edward is biracial (his mother's Caribbean lineage is as murky as the swamp), but Simms does not elaborate on his genealogy, and thus the swamps of *The Scout* remain free of black fugitives. Those who prefer "Liberty over all things" are unambiguously white.

One of the only antebellum southern writers to depict black figures within swamplands was Henry Clay Lewis, a physician and humorist who wrote *Odd Leaves from the Life of a Louisiana Swamp Doctor* (1850), based on his experiences as a bayou physician. While other southern humor writers such as Augustus Baldwin Longstreet told tales only of backcountry Crackers and traveling preachers, Lewis's swamps are populated with a variety of characters – rich, poor, black, white, and nonhuman (panthers and bears feature most prominently). In "A Struggle for Life," the tale that concludes the collection, the narrator recounts his nearly fatal struggle with a "negro dwarf of the most frightful appearance" who was "the nearest resemblance to the ourang outang mixed with the devil that human eyes ever dwelt upon." The man is a slave, the only property of a Cracker with planter pretensions who lives in the swamps. He is not exactly a fugitive, but he does take advantage of his own swamp expertise and the physician's gullibility and attempts to kill him for his brandy: "'I will kill you,' he again screamed, his fangs clashing and foam flying from his mouth, his long arms extended as if to clutch me, and the fingers quivering nervously." The slave is full of "maniacal fury" when the narrator refuses to give up his alcohol, and "with a yell like a wild beast's, he precipitated himself upon me." The physician passes out, and when he awakens, he discovers that the mad slave has thrown himself into the fire and "nothing of the human remained; he had died the murderer's death and been buried in his grave."[68] His bones, the physician reports, "were left to bleach where they lay." This slave, then, under the influence of the swamp, attempts to bring himself some form of liberty through murder but then throws himself into a hellfire. Ultimately, he turns white, his bones bleaching in the Louisiana swamps. Lewis's vision of the swamp did include African Americans, but only grotesque and violent caricatures. In "A Struggle for Life," the slave's freedom is deemed murderous and mad; Lewis whitewashes his body and erases his struggle for liberty in swamplands.

As white southern writers reshaped ecolocal beliefs and images to deny black freedom in swamps, an emergent African American literary tradition reconfirmed this community's knowledge and use of swamplands during the antebellum period. These authors also made the link between swamplands, ambiguity, and wildness, yet they made a point of locating fugitive slaves in this space as well. These authors focus primarily on the Great Dismal Swamp, a large lowland in southern Virginia and northern North Carolina. The reasons for this focus are multiple: most slave narratives depicted flight northward, and the Great Dismal was in the path of the many fugitives from slavery. Also, the reference to Nat Turner, a slave who led a slave revolt in Virginia in 1831 and had planned to establish a black community in the Great Dismal, was a symbol too powerful to resist. By depicting the Great Dismal in their novels, African American writers linked their imaginative fugitives to a tangible past of resistance to slavery.

In their narratives, as in many northern abolitionist novels and paintings, black runaways become part of the swamp itself during their transition from slavery to freedom.[69] This wildness, to writers Frederick Douglass and Martin Delany, was not indicative of racial inferiority but of the complexities involved in the fight for human dignity and freedom. In Frederick Douglass's novella *The Heroic Slave* (1853), Madison Washington, named after two great white Virginian leaders, initially escapes from a plantation in southern Virginia and hides out in the Great Dismal Swamp: "In the dismal swamps I lived, sir, five long years, – a cave for my home during the day. I wandered about at night with the wolf and the bear."[70] Washington becomes part of the swamp and a beast of prey, wandering at night "with the wolf and the bear." He lies out in this swamp (he calls it a "city of refuge"), maintaining contact with the plantation world through weekly meetings with his wife and leaving this transitional ecosystem only when fire destroys part of it. Washington is ultimately recaptured, escapes again, travels to Canada, is recaptured, and goes on to lead a successful slave revolt on the ship *Creole*. But it is in the Great Dismal Swamp that he ceases to be a slave (though he is not yet completely free) and lives immersed in nature. He is not the victim of predatory, carnivorous animals but is their compatriot: an aggressor, a hunter, a powerful force of the natural world. Washington lives for five years in the Great Dismal Swamp; it is here that he metamorphoses from slave to hero.

Douglass's portrayal of the Great Dismal Swamp as the site for the development of a leadership instinct finds its analogue in Martin Delany's *Blake; or, The Huts of America* (1861–62). Like Douglass, Delany locates the source of fugitive slave power in the heart of a swamp. Blake, having run away from a Mississippi plantation, travels through the southern states, sleeping through the days and traveling by night, "always keeping to the woods." He seeks protection and solace in South Carolina forests and holds meetings in their dark recesses in order to plan a widespread, regional slave uprising. Most of the attendees at these meetings are "the much-dreaded runaways of the woods, a class of outlawed slaves, who continually seek the lives of their masters." As Blake makes his way to the Great Dismal Swamp, he meets up with "a number of the old confederates of the noted Nat Turner" who "hailed the daring young runaway as the harbinger of better days." In the swamps of the Carolinas, then, Blake assumes the legacy of Turner, whose rebellion in 1831 greatly unsettled Virginia whites and made the Great Dismal Swamp famous. In the Great Dismal, Blake finds "a different atmosphere, an entirely new element." In this landscape he discovers a large band of maroons ripe for his revolutionary message, storytellers who are willing to write him into their narratives of black (rebel) history. This swamp is a marginal space in which former slaves come to inscribe their own stories and dictate their futures. In the depths of the morass, Blake meets with the High Conjurers, who in a secret meeting anoint him a priest of their order. Blake leaves the Great Dismal "well refreshed" and fortified by the support and safety of the swamp and its inhabitants.[71] His heroic character has grown in the Great Dismal, has been anointed by an unseen power – he, like Washington, emerges from this ecosystem as a hero.

Through these antebellum fictions, Douglass and Delany depicted Africans and African Americans creating ecolocal culture in the southeastern United States. And although neither they nor any other African American authors of this period depicted the Okefenokee and swamps of the Southeast in their tales of liberty, they nevertheless acknowledged the role that American swamplands played in the achievement of black freedom. They thus bolstered their claim to power as shapers of swamp ecolocalism in their own right.

Both planters and slaves sought change within southeastern swamplands. Planters wanted to become wealthy, respected, and powerful within white society through their domination and control of both black slaves and the environment. Slaves sought to improve their lives or change their status completely, often using swamplands to negotiate the terms of their bondage or to become free in Spanish Florida. Even as southern white fiction writers attempted to whitewash southeastern swamps, they were never fully able to mask black action within them. And as African American writers began to render swamps and the slaves within them as powerful, heroic figures in the South, they reconfirmed their community's ecolocal culture. Fugitive actions within these environments, however transient, reveal that swamps were contested spaces through time, places that evoked desire as much as disgust and provided freedom as much as they frustrated ambition.

These initial struggles for control of local lowland ecologies established a pattern of action and reaction that later communities would follow when they stepped on the trembling earth of the Okefenokee Swamp. While studies of slavery and rice cultivation along the coastal plain are numerous, fugitives' use of swamplands to resist slavery in the Okefenokee hinterlands has been largely unexplored. One exception is Louis Pendleton's *King Tom and the Runaways* (1891), a juvenile novel that chronicles the misadventures of a young white boy and a slave his age who has "fugitive blood."[72] This lack of serious attention may be due to a paucity of written materials that would indicate this development of African American ecolocal culture. But it is also due to a willful historical amnesia. Local historians rarely acknowledge the prevalence of slave-holding or lying out in the Okefenokee hinterlands; children living in southern Georgia and northern Florida today are more likely to hear about the area's long history of cattle herding than about slavery and resistance to it in the Okefenokee hinterlands. And while I have yet to come across a resident of Ware or Charlton County who boasts of fugitives from slavery as ancestors, the mark of another group of Okefenokee hinterland rebels is boldly claimed in local histories and genealogies: the Seminoles.

# 2 Battleground
## *The Seminole Swamp*

In September 1812 the former fugitive Prince Witten waited with a group of Seminole and Spanish allies for an American wagon train in Twelve Mile Swamp, outside of St. Augustine. The transports belonged to supporters of the Patriot War, a ragtag and unofficial American attempt to overthrow the Spanish in Florida. As the wagons rumbled past them, Witten and his compatriots rose out of the swamp's underbrush, fired on the officers first to maximize chaos, captured the wagons, and retreated. The Patriots would not formally withdraw from Florida until 1813, but the combined forces of Spanish troops, Seminoles, and former slaves kept Americans from establishing a military foothold in swampy northeastern Florida.[1]

Fugitive slaves using the Okefenokee and other swamps to escape from slavery in Georgia and the Carolinas after 1750 often found homes with Seminole bands in the Okefenokee hinterlands. While Seminole treatment of these runaways was not always benevolent – fugitives sometimes traded one kind of New World slavery for another in Seminole towns – and while the two groups did not always have identical interests, they did work together to defend the Okefenokee hinterlands from white American incursions throughout the antebellum period.[2] Former slaves brought their allies knowledge of the English language, agricultural expertise, and formidable and uncompromising battle skills. They also brought an ecolocal culture with them across the border, a shared cache of ecological beliefs and experiences that shaped their lives.

The Seminole towns they joined assembled in the Okefenokee hinterlands between 1700 and 1858, shaping an ecolocal culture rooted in swamps. Seminoles' use of swamplands for agriculture, hunting, and battle directly contradicted European American beliefs in land development and national expansionism. The conflicts between these ecolocal cultures resulted in skirmishes that exploded into war during the antebellum period and brought European Americans into these ecosystems for the first time, reorienting their gaze of development.[3] An investigation of the First and Second Seminole Wars and the role the Okefenokee played in them reveals the ways that divergent ecolocalist cultures both emerged out of and created conflict in the Okefenokee hinterlands between 1715 and 1842.

By the time European colonists arrived in North America in the early sixteenth century, Native peoples had been using the Okefenokee and other southeastern swamplands as sites of hunting, agriculture, and seasonal settlement for thousands of years. Archaeological evidence suggests that Native American inhabitation of this area was semipermanent beginning in 3000 B.C. Both the Suwannee and St. Marys rivers emerge out of the Okefenokee, and hunting groups followed these rivers to the fertile swamp that sheltered deer, bears, turtles, and abundant birds and fish. As Native populations stabilized, they began to grow crops in the Okefenokee hinterlands; archeologists have found evidence of cultivation of garden crops in addition to maize and sweet potatoes.[4]

As communities began to rely more on cultivation, settlement sites increased in size and number in the Okefenokee hinterlands. Site locations changed as Native American groups increasingly sought out better agricultural soils, communities became more socially and economically complex, and trade networks began to evolve. Around 1150 A.D., a dominant Mississippian culture emerged in the Southeast, characterized by subsistence agriculture and semipermanent towns. It was these Mississippian groups Europeans encountered, recorded, and decimated in the sixteenth century.[5]

Although the sparsely settled Okefenokee hinterlands were not as conducive to the spread of European pathogens as was the Atlantic Northeast, exploration and colonization resulted in as much as an 80 percent decline in southeastern Native populations within the first century of contact.[6] Surviving Native communities were unstable as a result of such major demographic shifts, and in the eighteenth century many clans began to disintegrate. In 1702 small bands began to splinter off from Oconee, Yuchi, Alabama, Choctaw, Shawnee, and Creek nations and to migrate into the Okefenokee hinterlands. Bands of Lower Creeks drifted into northern Florida during the early 1700s, and although they acquired knowledge of local lowland ecosystems during their travels, they did not establish any significant settlement networks in the Okefenokee hinterlands at this time.[7]

After the Yamassee uprising against European colonists failed in 1715, however, fugitive bands of Yamassees and Ochesee Creeks settled in various towns around the Okefenokee; by 1738 an Oconee Creek chief named Cowkeeper had established a large town, Cuscowilla, on the Alachua Savanna west of St. Augustine and directly south of the Okefenokee Swamp. In the 1740s a colonial traveler reported that a band of Mikasukis had settled in Tallahassee.[8]

These disparate bands without much in common but geography began to hunt, fish, farm, and herd livestock in the Okefenokee hinterlands. Their numbers increased as they developed disease immunities and absorbed groups of fugitive slaves fleeing from Carolina, Georgia, and Florida plantations. Towns began to form along the Suwannee River in northern Florida, linked to other Native American towns and to villages founded by escaped slaves through infrastructure (roads and shared outbuildings) and intermarriage. After 1767 Upper Creeks began to move into northern Florida, increasing the Native population in the Okefenokee hinterlands to about two thousand in 1790.[9] It was at this point that Spanish and British-American colonists commenced identifying all of these clans as "Seminoles."

There is some dispute about the origin of the term "Seminole" to identify these diverse, loosely connected clans of Native Americans and runaways. J. Leitch Wright and Kevin Mulroy have argued that the term originates from *cimarrones,* a Spanish word meaning "rebel" or "nonwhite aggressor," and was used to identify both fugitive slaves and Seminole bands ("maroon" also emerges linguistically from this root). Wright has pointed out that there is no *r* in the Muskogean languages used by Okefenokee hinterland clans, and therefore, *cimallone* became *Siminole* and then *Seminole.* James Covington has argued that other definitive possibilities of the name Seminole include "wild people," "adventurer," or "wanderer." M. M. Cohen, a soldier writing about his experiences in the Second Seminole War in the 1830s, noted that "the word Seminole signifies wanderer or runaway, or it means a wild people or Outsettlers," and most nineteenth-century Americans shared an understanding of a Seminole as a rebel or runaway.[10]

It is unclear whether these Okefenokee hinterland Native communities thought of themselves as a united entity. Instead of representing a single group, the Seminoles, like the Muskogees (Creeks) to the north, consisted of "many peoples involved in a dynamic process of coalescence."[11] It is evident, however, that these clans (including escaped slaves) shared the experience of relocation and community reorganization. They also shared a developing ecolocal culture rooted in the Okefenokee hinterlands. And as Wright has argued, these Muskogean-speaking groups absorbed the term into their oral culture and thus claimed some part of it as their own.[12] I will therefore refer to all of these clans, including groups of freedmen and freedwomen who allied with them, as Seminoles. Implicit in my use of this term is an understanding of this community's status as a confederacy – a complex, politically integrated community that came together to achieve larger objectives, usually wars to gain territories and hunting rights – and an acknowledgement of this confederacy's internal diversity.[13]

Both the Spanish and the Americans began to see the Seminoles as possible buffers between the two nations, and each established commercial connections with the scattered bands. By 1812 the Seminole confederation was a rather loose organization of associated towns that exercised local autonomy, elected their own chiefs, and established their own trade relationships with American and Spanish emissaries. Cultural diversity among the towns remained stable even as their numbers burgeoned as a result of the Lower Creeks' migration into northern Florida after their loss to Andrew Jackson in the Red Stick War of 1813–14. By 1822 American census takers estimated the Seminole population in the Okefenokee hinterlands at five thousand.[14]

Multiple Native American communities used the Okefenokee Swamp as a hunting ground or homesite before the Seminoles took shape as a community in its hinterlands. Through their pursuit of wild game and extractive gathering practices, they learned the land and named it, exerting a sense of ownership and control over this ecosystem. "Okefenokee" is a word of Muskogee linguistic origin and would have been understood by multiple tribes residing around or within its mucky borders. Its meanings were various, but all denoted the swamp's peculiar ecology. An American map drawn in 1766 and published in William Stork's *A Description of East-Florida* (1769) labels the area as "the great swamp called by the Indians Owa-qua-phe-no-gaw," and Samuel Savery's map of the Southeast in 1769 gives this translation: "[it] is called by the Indians Ekanphaenoka or Terrible Ground."[15] In a conversation with the Indian agent Benjamin Hawkins in February 1797, the Chehaw chief Tustunnagau Haujo suggested two variations of the term: "'I have been a hunter and know the situation of the ground. . . . I have hunted many years about the Okefinaocau (quivering water) or Akinfinocau (quivering earth), the first a Choctaw word Okewah.'"[16] Hawkins later wrote that the swamp was sometimes "called E-cun-fin-o-cau, from E-cun-nau, earth; and Fin-o-cau, quivering. The first is the most common amongst the Creeks. It is from Ooka, a Chactau word for water, and Fin-o-cau, quivering."[17]

The term "Okefenokee" therefore reveals that Native American communities traversed the Okefenokee enough to recognize its distinctive ecology. Methane in Okefenokee's slow-moving water regularly releases globs of peat from waterway bottoms; these blocks float to the surface, and after some years vegetation begins to grow on them. These floating islands (also known as hammocks) are scattered throughout the Okefenokee Swamp, and when one walks on them, the earth seems to pitch and roll — both earth and water quiver. The swamp's Muskogee name has survived while other waterways in the Okefenokee hinterlands were renamed in Spanish and English: the St. Marys, the Suwannee (St. Juans), and the St. Johns. Whenever the Okefenokee Swamp is identified in historical writings and maps from the seventeenth century to the present day, therefore, Native American knowledge of its ecology is clearly communicated.

Southeastern Native Americans claimed the Okefenokee through naming and also through their incorporation of its ecologies into their imaginative storytelling. In *Travels* (1790), his journal of his adventures in Georgia and Florida, the naturalist William Bartram relates an Okefenokee ecolocal narrative that Creeks had shared with him:

The river St. Mary has its source from a vast lake, or marsh, called Ouaqua-phenogaw, which lies between Flint and Oakmulge rivers, and occupies a space of near three hundred miles in circuit. This vast accumulation of waters, in the wet season, appears as a lake, and contains some large islands or knolls, of rich high land; one of which the present generation of Creeks represent as the most blissful spot on earth: they say it is inhabited by a peculiar race of Indians, whose women are incomparably beautiful; they also tell you, that this terrestrial paradise has been seen by some of their enterprising hunters, when in pursuit of game, who being lost in inextricable swamps and bogs, and on the point of perishing, were unexpectedly relieved by a company of beautiful women, whom they call daughters of the sun, who kindly gave them such provisions as they had with them, which were chiefly fruit, oranges, dates, &c., and some corn cakes, and then enjoined them to fly for safety to their own country; for that their husbands were fierce men, and cruel to strangers: they further say, that these hunters had a view of their settlements, situated on the elevated banks of an island, or promontory, in a beautiful lake; but that in their endeavors to approach it, they were involved in perpetual labyrinths, and, like enchanted land, still as they imagined they had gained it, it seemed to fly before them, alternately appearing and disappearing. They resolved, at length, to leave the delusive pursuit, and to return; which, after a number of inexpressible difficulties, they effected. When they reported their adventures to their country-men, their young warriors were inflamed with an irresistible desire to invade, and make a conquest of, so charming a country; but all their attempts have hitherto proved abortive, never having been able again to find that enchanting spot, nor even any road or pathway to it, yet they say that they frequently meet with certain signs of its being inhabited, as the buildings of canoes, footsteps of men, &c.[18]

This tale frames Creeks as both strangers to the Okefenokee and inheritors of it. They are lost within its depths but are saved by their ancestors – a small band of Yamassees, Bartram later conjectures, who took refuge in the Okefenokee after their defeat in 1715.[19] In this narrative, the Creeks do not reside in the swamp but hold it in reverence as a sort of ghost town that offers both danger (the threat of the warriors' imminent return and the labyrinthine quality of the morass) and fertility (in the form of the oranges, dates, and corn cakes the women offer and the wild game the men have entered the Okefenokee to hunt). The swamp appears and then disappears, teasing the Creek warriors with its abundance – it is an "enchanted land." Rendered here, the Okefenokee is both a paradise and a site of potential violence; the Creeks recognized the swamp's dual ability to provoke desire and create strife.

This tale also reveals the extent to which Creeks embraced the Oke-fenokee in their imaginative culture. The swamp was a hunting ground for them, but it was also an enormous environmental mosaic that changed shape every season as rain did or did not fall and as peat gurgled up from its depths. Creeks and other Native American groups knew the Okefeno-kee and other southeastern swamps well, but they did not know them completely. Thus they imbued these environments with meaning beyond fecundity. The Creek Okefenokee narrative reveals the extent to which it was a landscape of mystery to Native American groups and thus captured their imaginations as much as it drew their hunting parties.

Because Native American groups controlled traffic on the Okefenokee margins and in its hinterlands, this landscape was a mystery also to initial European observers. Early European and European American cartogra-phers and explorers thus aligned enigmatic swamplands with occult Native American knowledge. Captain B. Romans's *A General Map of the Southern British Colonies in America* (1776) expresses this alignment by de-picting the Okefenokee as "The Great Swamp of Owaquaphenoga whose Pass is a Secret. Highland Inhabited by an Apalachean Tribe."[20] Most writers of the eighteenth and nineteenth century noted in their descrip-tions of Okefenokee that no white man had ever set foot within its bound-aries. The swamp's ecology often prevented incursions by large European American parties; the Okefenokee was therefore generally understood to be a site of Native and not colonial power.

The visual and narrative connections that eighteenth-century explorers and cartographers made between Native Americans and the Okefenokee hinterlands, however, were the expressive tools of colonialism.[21] By de-picting the Okefenokee and Native Americans as linked "others," colonial observers framed them in opposition to European civilization. Both of these others were to be controlled through words, images, or military ac-tion. As Seminoles began to gather into a confederacy in the Okefenokee hinterlands during the eighteenth century, their ecolocal culture clashed with European and American imperialist ideals of land development and expansionism. Between 1790 and 1842 these cultural differences pro-voked small-scale conflicts that led to full-blown war fought in the heat and muck of the Okefenokee and other southeastern swamplands.

In the late eighteenth and early nineteenth centuries, a loosely defined and completely uncontained type of border warfare destabilized life in the Okefenokee hinterlands. Georgians continually crossed into Seminole lands to steal cattle, provisions, and slaves from Seminole towns, forming bands of about a dozen each that "threatened to hurl the Georgia frontier into a full-scale Indian war."[22] In response, Seminoles burned houses and stole slaves from American inhabitants. These depredations were recorded in American newspapers, depositions, letters, and in Seminole speeches at council negotiations. In 1789 the Georgian John Twiggs wrote to Governor George Walton from "Rebel Town, Georgia," that "from the appearance of the hostile Intentions of the Indians on the whole line of frontier we have not a moment to loos in Collecting a force Sufficient to Check the progress of the Enemy."[23]

American inhabitants of the Okefenokee hinterlands became increasingly paranoid about state and federal commitment to their protection in the 1780s and 1790s and often formed vigilante groups to engage in small-scale warfare with Seminoles. On September 6, 1793, Henry Carvel of Washington County, Georgia, testified that he and thirteen men had given chase to some Seminole horse thieves four days before:

> There were two horses stolen from Capt'n Stokes volunteer troop station & at the long bluff, on the 2nd the Capt'n with 13 men (this deponent being one) crossed the Oconee River and pursued on the trail of the horses, and by the appearance of a sign, there were four persons, we came up with them on the bank of the Oakmulga, discovered three Indians, fired on them, their fire was return'd, Capt'n Stokes [fired] upon them, and took the ground immediately, by the appearance of blood, two were mortally wounded and one certainly killed on the River, we recovered our own two horses, and one other, three rifles, and one smooth-bore gun, with sundry other articles, and return'd to our station without damage, except hunger and fatigue.[24]

Constant skirmishes like this firefight on the banks of the Ocmulgee River kept the Okefenokee hinterlands filled with tension and nearly emptied the area of permanent inhabitants. When word of Seminole attacks or movements reached their houses, Americans fled to Savannah, Charleston, or Mobile. The Okefenokee hinterlands began to take on a desolate quality that served to strike even more fear into the hearts of travelers and residents as Seminoles moved throughout the area. Vast tracts of vacant lands meant speedy travel for Seminoles and indefensible positions for those Americans who stayed.

The Okefenokee hinterlands became so unstable that social, economic, and racial categories often blurred – one could not tell the European or colonial "adventurer" from the Seminole. Louis Leclerc Milfort, a Frenchman who traveled to America in 1775, wrote in his journal that he despised southern Georgia colonists, who he found to be indistinguishable from their foes: "These robbers wear their hair cut very close to the head and paint their bodies and faces with different colors in the same manner as the savages; with the result that their appearance is truly terrible."[25] The Okefenokee hinterlands, according to "civilized" white observers, tended to turn everyone who resided there into "savages." The swampy backwoods Milfort visited seemed almost impenetrable to him, and any entrance into these ecosystems promised only danger and potential death. Seminole migrations into the Okefenokee hinterlands coincided with European movements into the same area, and the contests between the two groups prompted much confusion and fear. In a landscape in which enemies could appear out of nowhere, towns were few and far between, and the line between the "savage" and the "civilized" blurred, everyday life became extremely unsettled.

During the late eighteenth century the Okefenokee hinterlands became a vital crossroads of Spanish, American, and Seminole communities. In 1792 the Indian agent James Seagrove argued that construction of a fort on the southeastern edge of the swamp for purposes of defense and negotiation was a necessary expense: "If St. Mary's is approved of as the place to communicate with the Indians I would advise a respectable force be kept at the head of this river, and some good works erected; the situation is commanding should we be involved in a war with the Indians, and will be a great check to Spanish insolence."[26] Despite increasing numbers of European migrants, the area was still a Native American stronghold at the turn of the century. Lower Creeks and later, Seminoles, considered the Okefenokee to be theirs because it was their ancestral hunting ground and seasonal settlement site. In 1797 the Indian agent Benjamin Hawkins explained to a colleague that the Creeks would never sell the Okefenokee to Americans: "the nation is not disposed to sell. On the contrary, it requires that a man should be high in the confidence of the Indians to be able to mention the subject in the public square without being insulted."[27]

Continual Seminole migration through the Okefenokee hinterlands in the 1810s prompted the American inhabitant Archibald Clarke to write to the U.S. Army general Edmund Gaines to "appeal for some protection.

A small detachment of troops upon the head of the St. Marys would answer a most valuable purpose, by at once checking the inroads of the savages, and preventing our abandoned and unprotected citizens from adventuring into Indian country, and driving in herds of cattle."[28] The Okefenokee hinterlands were a popular Seminole thoroughfare and were thus a contested space between 1750 and 1842. This area played a major role in instigating and prolonging the two major Seminole Wars of the antebellum period.

The Okefenokee hinterlands were a place of continual chaos and minor skirmishes since the first years of European exploration. The Okefenokee and other swamps were sites of inhabitation and hunting but served their most important purpose to Native American communities in their function as battlegrounds or spaces of postwar retreat. Archaeological evidence – arrowheads and other weapons – at swampland dig sites, in addition to colonial and exploration literature, indicates that Native Americans used these environments militarily. In 1528 Panfilo de Narvaez landed at Tampa Bay with a group of Spanish soldiers and proceeded to march northeastward into the Apalache region (about forty miles south of Okefenokee). One of his compatriots, Alvar Nunez Cabeza de Vaca, wrote of the "adventure" on which they had embarked and its singular miseries:

> They [natives] conducted us through a country very difficult to travel and wonderful to look upon. In it are vast forests of trees being astonishingly high. So many were fallen on the ground as to obstruct our way in such a manner that we could not advance without going about a considerable increase of toil. . . . In view of the poverty of the land, the unfavorable accounts of the population and of everything else we heard, the Indians making continual wars upon us, wounding our people, and horses at the places where they went to drink, shooting from the lakes, with such safety to themselves that we could not retaliate . . . we determined to leave that place and go in quest of the sea.[29]

Cabeza de Vaca's report reveals that even as some Native Americans guided the Spanish explorers through southeastern swamps, others attacked them within "vast forests of trees." Native Americans thus used their ecological knowledge doubly – to both aid and undermine European efforts to explore and control swampland ecologies. Narvaez and his men had most likely never before encountered this type of ecosystem or battle within it and found themselves unable to respond. They could only "leave that place and go in search of the sea."

One year later Hernando de Soto followed his countryman into peninsular Florida and entered into much of the same kind of warfare with the Native Americans that Narvaez's men had endured. The account that Garcilaso de la Vega wrote of de Soto's expedition echoes Cabeza de Vaca's narrative. According to de la Vega, this second group of Spanish explorer-soldiers was picking its way through a dense forest of trees and underbrush along a narrow path when "they were opposed by Indian warriors. The passage, however, was so narrow, and so completely walled on each side by thorny and impervious forest, that not more than the two foremost of each vanguard could come to blows. . . . Both armies fought to their waist in water, stumbling about among thorns and brambles, and twisted roots, and the sunken trunks of fallen trees."[30] Battle in southeastern swamplands was a messy affair; these ecosystems precluded most strategies of conventional warfare. Narrow passageways did not allow for multiple-front offenses, and the tangled undergrowth made flanking maneuvers difficult. The soggy ground, sinkholes, and waist-deep waters of the Okefenokee and other southeastern swamplands were a far cry from the mowed fields or cleared forests of European battlefields, and in these boggy places the force of Spanish numbers was actually a detriment. The Natives "made continual war upon" the explorers, shooting at both men and horses from within the "thorny and impervious forest." The Europeans could not retaliate quickly or easily, if at all. These early accounts of Native American military strategy are echoed in narratives of the Seminole Wars two centuries later.

These sixteenth-century descriptions of Native American war strategy reveal that swamplands were integral to Native American culture and to their protest against European colonization. The accounts also depict plans of action that fit the profile of guerrilla warfare: a set of "irregular" military tactics used by a minority group or indigenous population to oppose a foreign occupying or trespassing force. Guerrilla groups often operate in difficult terrain; within these environments individuals possess and use knowledge often denied their opponents. Their power lies in maneuvers instead of numbers, and they often attack at night or from overgrown places with surprise as their ally. Their numbers are small, and therefore guerrilla groups are more mobile than conventional armies —

they plan and execute hit-and-run raids that enable soldiers to damage and evade, prolonging the overall struggle. Guerrilla bands also tend to acquire legendary status in their own communities and in the lore of their opponents. Their strategies and goals fit well into popular and global cultural narratives of the quest and the underdog.[31]

The environments in which these guerrilla actions take place also often acquire a legendary status. The Okefenokee and other swamps were suitable sites for dramatic battles and thus have played major roles in Seminole War literary and visual culture.[32] But swamps often did not fare well in the midst or aftermath of battle. During the ambushes and skirmishes of the Seminole Wars, Seminoles cut notches into trees to hold guns steady for firing; they also cut down tree stands for defense purposes and burned sections of undergrowth to provide a clear line of fire. American soldiers burned interior towns, makeshift fortifications, and swamp vegetation in their pursuit of Seminoles. The Okefenokee and other swamps were ecologically compromised when they served as battlegrounds, and the confrontations between ecolocal cultures that took place within them ultimately opened them up to more devastating depredations.

By 1815 Native Americans had a long history of warfare in the swamplands of the American Southeast. Nineteenth-century European Americans could not boast such extensive experience, but they did have some familiarity with guerrilla tactics. American soldiers had initiated partisan warfare – the use of irregular tactics by regular or organized irregular troops in support of conventional operations – in the French and Indian War and more extensively during the American Revolution.[33] Militia generals such as Francis Marion used their knowledge of swamplands in the Carolinas and Georgia to capture loyalist property and to harass British soldiers.[34] But despite colonial successes with use of swamplands and partisan warfare, nineteenth-century U.S. military officers did not understand the importance of these skirmishes or the ecosystems in which they were waged.[35] Their refusal to consider the tactical benefits of guerrilla and partisan warfare, in addition to their ignorance of swamp ecology, left them poorly prepared to meet the challenges of Seminole warfare between 1817 and 1842.

The First Seminole War was a result of movements of the Okefenokee hinterland's European Americans and Seminoles against one another during the late eighteenth and early nineteenth centuries. The Seminoles, according to the Indian agent Benjamin Hawkins, controlled more than three hundred square miles of the Okefenokee hinterlands in 1807. They considered any encroachment on the part of hunting or scavenging whites to be a hostile act.[36] But American inhabitants of the Okefenokee hinterlands did not consider this area to belong to the Seminoles. They had developed ecolocal beliefs that framed the area only as a possible conquest.

Skirmishes erupted in the Okefenokee hinterlands on a regular basis and escalated into wars in the nineteenth century. As part of the machinations of the War of 1812, a group of Georgian farmers followed the lead of the former Georgia governor General George Mathews and marched to St. Augustine in an effort to conquer and annex Spanish East Florida in what became known as the Patriot War. Mathews had encouraged Okefenokee hinterland inhabitants to create their own governments and assured them that U.S. troops would support their actions. In response, Seminoles used swamplands and guerrilla tactics to destroy property and interrupt Patriot supply lines. In July 1812 a group of Seminole warriors struck the St. Johns River plantations of Patriot sympathizers, destroying houses and stealing slaves before retreating back into the swamps of northeastern Florida. Two months later Prince Witten orchestrated and commanded the assault on a Patriot wagon train in Twelve Mile Swamp.[37] The Patriot movement soon fell apart, and the pattern of small-scale clashes in the Okefenokee hinterlands resumed.[38]

The U.S. military again confronted Seminole warfare tactics during the Red Stick War of 1813, in which a militant antiwhite faction of Upper Creeks fought against both conciliatory Creeks and Andrew Jackson's American troops. These battles took many Creek lives but did not result in definitive U.S. government control of Native groups. Both Creeks and Seminoles in the area ignored the terms of the treaty and reacted to American encroachments with violence. These confrontations continued without pause in the second decade of the nineteenth century. The situation came to crisis in October 1817, when a detachment of soldiers stationed at Fort Scott in southern Georgia traveled to the Seminole village of Fowl Town, fifteen miles away and just north of the Florida (Spanish) border. The soldiers demanded that the Fowl Town chief Neamathla surrender warriors who American military officials believed to be responsible for the murder of several Georgia families. Neamathla refused. In response, the soldiers drove the Seminoles into the surrounding swamps and killed about twenty men before plundering and burning Fowl Town. Both Seminoles and Georgians living in the Okefenokee hinterlands immediately arose, and the First Seminole War began.[39]

This first full-scale war between Seminoles and the United States consisted of Seminole raids on farms and plantations and daylong chases through the Okefenokee and other southeastern swamps. The situation for American inhabitants of the Okefenokee hinterlands was precarious. In March 1818 one such resident wrote to the editor of the *Savannah Museum,* "such is the state of alarm in this county, on account of these savage invaders, . . . that people are constantly moving from the frontiers into the centre of the county, and unless the depredations of the savages are soon put an end to, more than one half of Camden county will be deserted."[40] U.S. military retaliation was sluggish until Andrew Jackson took control of the American campaign in the spring of 1818. He recruited fifteen hundred Americans and eighteen hundred Creeks and brought his troops from the St. Marks River to Bowlegs Town and the freedmen's villages along the Suwannee River in April.

Jackson's strategy was to "penetrate immediately into the centre of the Seminole towns," but he was unaware that runners had already informed the Suwannee villages that American troops were on the move.[41] Nero, an escaped slave and leader in Old Suwannee Town, placed his men in the village facing the American soldiers, with their backs to the river.[42] But Bowlegs, the Suwannee Town chief, withdrew immediately and fell back with his fellow warriors to Pinhook Swamp, the southern side of the Okefenokee that sits in Florida. Nero and his men remained for the skirmish, which Jackson's troops won, but most escaped safely to join their Seminole allies. In response, Jackson chased the Seminoles up the Suwannee to the edge of the Okefenokee: "On the morning of the 12th, near Econfinnacu . . . a party of Indians were discovered on the margin of the swamp, and attacked by General McIntosh, and about fifty Tennessee Volunteers, who routed them, killing thirty-seven warriors, and capturing six men and ninety-seven women and children."[43] This battle, fought along the margins of the Okefenokee Swamp, was costly to the Seminoles but not debilitating. Most of the former inhabitants of the Suwannee towns established a new village on an island in the Okefenokee interior. It remained a Seminole refuge for fifty more years.

The brief battles of the First Seminole War seem on the surface to be decisive American victories. But most Seminoles escaped into swamplands and ignored the treaty that concluded the war and demanded they transfer the Okefenokee to American control. "The *children of the sun*," as one American observer put it, "would not be divested of Bartram's Paradise." In 1821 American Okefenokee hinterland inhabitants still reported Seminole movement in the area, and John H. Bell, the Indian agent in southern Georgia, listed "O-ke-a-fenoke Swamp, south side" as the site of a Coweta town.[44]

The years between the cessation of the First Seminole War in 1818 and the commencement of the Second Seminole War in 1835 were not years of peace in the Okefenokee hinterlands. American attempts to relocate Seminole men and women as part of the Indian Removal Act of 1830 were met with resistance, and warriors began buying ammunition in large quantities in October 1834. Relations between local Indian agents and Seminole chiefs began to disintegrate. In November 1835 the Seminole leader Osceola brought his clan from southern Georgia to the Withlacoochee River swamps on the northwestern gulf coast of Florida. Returning to the area, he was moving back home – his mother was a Creek who had settled in the vicinity of the Okefenokee Swamp in 1808 when Osceola was four years old and then moved to a hammock near the Withlacoochee River.[45] From his stronghold deep in the swamps of north-central Florida (called Powell's Town), Osceola orchestrated the events that launched the Seminoles into armed conflict with the U.S. Army in 1835. These events demonstrated the widely held American belief that, in the Indian agent Gad Humphreys' words, Seminoles' "proceedings of a hostile kind are always *covert* and *unadvertised*" and that this community had developed an ecolocal culture in which swamps were places of military action.[46]

On December 18, 1835, Seminoles captured a baggage train led by Colonel John Warren near Alachua, cutting off a major supply source to both Fort Brooke (Tampa Bay) and Fort King, an Indian Agency in northern Florida.[47] On December 23 a relief unit of five officers and one hundred enlisted men, under the command of Brevet Major Francis L. Dade, left Fort Brooke for Fort King. On December 27 a group of Seminoles and maroons hid in the canebrake on the edge of the Wahoo Swamp (just east of the Withlacoochee Bend), awaiting the unit's arrival. As Dade's troops entered the swamp margins, they were distracted by the landscape around them and slowed by the transport of supply wagons and a six-pound cannon. The Seminoles waited behind thick screens of foliage, propping their guns against trees and taking aim at the officers. A signal sounded and the Seminoles began to fire, killing Dade and his second in command immediately. Although the remaining American soldiers built a barricade to try and defend themselves, fifty mounted Seminoles ambushed them from behind and cut them all down.[48]

Alligator, one of the commanders of the Seminole offensive, later described what whites called the Dade Massacre: "Just as day was breaking we moved out of the swamp into the pine barren. . . . Every warrior was protected by a tree, or secreted in the high palmettos. . . . We returned to the swamp about noon."[49] As J. T. Sprague noted in 1836, Alligator was a tremendous leader in the Seminole nation, due to his familiarity with the environment: "His knowledge of the country, and tactics in the field of battle, as displayed in advancing and retreating, in diverting the enemy and outflanking their extended lines, gave him an ascendancy, and made him a dangerous foe."[50] Alligator's Town was only twenty miles from the Okefenokee Swamp—his clan probably used the giant forested wetland as a hunting ground and battle site and through it and other smaller swamp systems, became familiar with lowland ecologies. Due to Alligator's and Osceola's precision and aggression, only three Americans survived the Dade Massacre, and one of these died as the soldiers crawled through swamp and scrub on the way to Tampa Bay.[51]

Meanwhile, there were developments in another part of the Okefenokee hinterlands. The Indian agent Wiley Thompson, who was stationed at Fort King, had written to Secretary of War Lewis Cass on December 11, 1835, that "The Indians in this section of the nation . . . assembled at the towns of Big and Long Swamp. . . . I have no doubt that the object of the whole body of the disaffected is to retire to the wild region of the peninsula of Florida, in the neighborhood of what is called the Everglades."[52] Thompson was observant in this case, but he often misjudged and mistreated Seminole chiefs. While he served as agent to the Seminoles in north Florida, he insulted them at almost every meeting. His refusal to sell Osceola gunpowder earlier that year provoked the Seminole chief's ire. The day after the Dade Massacre, little more than two weeks after writing his letter to Lewis Cass, Thompson was ambushed by forty Seminole warriors while on his nightly walk. The warriors shot him fifteen times, scalped him, and escaped into the Wahoo Swamp.[53] After these carefully planned attacks, Alligator and Osceola took their warriors back to the Withlacoochee to await the American response and to plan their next move.

The Cove of the Withlacoochee, one hundred square miles of swamp, hammock, and prairie formed by a big bend in the Withlacoochee River, became the major battleground of the Second Seminole War. The cove, as James Covington has argued, made an excellent center of operations for the Seminoles. Americans knew little about the cove because it was unmapped and its "numerous swampy islands and heavily wooded hammocks provided wonderful places of concealment."[54] The Seminoles, by contrast, knew Okefenokee hinterland swamps like the Withlacoochee well. They understood how to traverse them efficiently and silently, gathering food and water from surprising locations. They had expertise in guerrilla war tactics particularly suited to the dense, vine-strewn swamp forests of northern Florida.

Swamplands became a dominant part of the Seminole plan of attack during the Second Seminole War. The Seminoles camouflaged themselves with mud and plant dyes, covered their tracks, cut notches in trees to hold their guns, burned grass for better viewing and firing, and established defensive posts behind bogs, deep streams, and quagmires. Seminole ecolocal culture – their understanding of swamps as places of diverse use – included judgments about swampland's suitability to battle. This ecolocal culture tested the strength, determination, and longevity of the U.S. Army, engaging the soldiers in a war increasingly unpopular among American citizens.

Standard U.S. Army procedure in previous wars against Native Americans had been to assemble and mobilize an overwhelming force of regulars, militia, and Native American allies, to build forts and roads leading into enemy territories, and to direct the main thrust of the army against Native towns and villages. But in northern Florida, vast stretches of land were unmapped, roads were extremely difficult to cut, and supply routes were long and full of sinkholes. In addition, most American soldiers were unused to southeastern ecosystems and the diseases that resulted from time spent in hot, wet, insect-ridden places.[55] U.S. Army leaders, for the most part, were unable or unwilling to translate any kind of geographic knowledge or experience with partisan warfare into militarily useful information in the 1830s. Nineteenth-century military leaders preferred to contemplate only modified guerrilla strategies in combating insurgents and paid little attention to unconventional patterns of war.[56] Seminoles easily cut off the Americans' supply routes and recognized their officers from uniforms military leaders insisted their soldiers wear. U.S. troops, often mired in swampy muck, were continually frustrated by their inability to force their way through swamps in pursuit of small bands of Seminoles. Their reactions to area swamplands and the Seminole advantage in the Okefenokee hinterlands are most evident in reports of the battles of Withlacoochee during the first campaign of 1836–37.

In response to the Dade Massacre and the ambush of Wiley Thompson at Fort King, General Duncan Clinch and three companies of American troops followed the Seminoles to the Cove of the Withlacoochee in early January 1836. As the Americans attempted to cross the river into the swamps, Seminoles rose out of the scrub and fired, repulsing the troops and initiating a consistent pattern of ambush, skirmish, and retreat that would continue for the next four months. In February a lieutenant named Henry Prince joined Clinch's troops at Withlacoochee and wrote a journal about his experiences that is one of the most vivid accounts of swampland warfare in existence. Prince was born in Eastport, Maine, graduated from West Point in 1835, and was assigned to the Fourth Infantry Regiment, which saw action in most of the early battles of the Second Seminole War.[57] He was wounded in the hip during the battles of Withlacoochee, but not badly enough to be evacuated.[58] Prince's diary reveals the frustration and paranoia that resulted from bunking in swamplands and from the Seminoles' unorthodox tactics, disclosing that guerrilla warfare in the swamplands took a physical toll and had a deleterious psychological impact on American troops.

In March 1836 the Seminoles retreated into the cove, and Prince's regiment returned to Fort Brooke: "Thus, backs out a baffled army. Baffled not through want of numbers or the true spirit or a good leader – but for want of means & by the seduction of a subtle enemy." Swampland ecology allowed Seminoles to be subtle and seductive in war – they drew soldiers into mucky traps and disappeared into dark, vine-choked passageways. The army returned to the Withlacoochee later that month after resting and restocking provisions at Tampa Bay. On March 31 the U.S. troops were finally able to penetrate the Withlacoochee, and Prince described the action in his diary: "What a day. We started across the Praire. Left in front first on the lead was Lt. Graham's company, next Reeves' &

then mine. There are Islands of hammock in the Praire impenetrable to day light. Some officers on horse attempted but could not get along. I saw one horse sink so that his face only was out of water. The men all cross the place though – horses left behind. Emerging from the praire onto green oak scrub, the Indians fired out of scrub. . . . The right flank of the line was then thrown forward and all advanced – through briar & bush & pond & praire & marsh till we came to swamp – cypress swamp. 'O God who can describe that scene.'" U.S. troops, with their heavy supply wagons, cannons, and horses, were unprepared to deal effectively with swamplands. Their horses sank in waters whose depths they could not judge, and marches were slow and disorganized. Struggling through "briar & bush & pond & praire & marsh" was physically exhausting for fully outfitted men with little experience in swamplands. Prince's repetitive use of the ampersand in his description of the swamp topography reveals his sense of being overwhelmed (swamped?) by the physical challenges of swamp bogging. In addition, all of the elements that provoked cartographers to envision swamplands as "secret" – the black reflective waters and the lush, claustrophobia-inducing vegetation – generated paranoia and suspicion among the American troops. By April 4, Prince noted, "Quantities of men are broken down."[59]

U.S. soldiers faced the unknown, constant fear of ambush, unbearable heat, disease, great quantities of flies and mosquitoes, and Seminole ridicule during their tours of duty in the Withlacoochee. In October 1836 Prince reported, "Alligator said that he had been fighting and fighting successfully and that he should continue to fight. . . . He admires our mounted men *because they run away so easily.*"[60] Although Prince despised this verbal abuse and depicted Seminoles as enemies of the United States and deadly foes "to the helpless woman & child" in his journal, he could not help but admire their fighting style: "The Siminoles & niggers are decidedly the best fighters. Jumpers', Powel's or Alligators' band would whip the whole 500 Creeks."[61] The Seminoles had experience as warriors and the emotional courage of defenders of their own land on their side, but they benefited from an ecolocal culture that valued swamplands as battlegrounds.

Swamp environments provided shelter and a psychological edge for Seminoles, while these ecosystems slowed U.S. troops and often led them astray. On a march to the Wahoo Swamp (which Prince described as "a vast place – secluded from the world – & a world in itself") in February

1837, two men disappeared from his company. They returned three days later: "The two men lost on the 11th arrived at Ft. Clinch last night without their horses they had been bewildered in the woods & met with several adventures. They were out 3 days & nearly 3 nights without anything to eat – on one occasion were followed by Indians but succeeded in eluding them."[62] It was not difficult to lose one's sense of direction in swamplands. Trees towered all around, and many soldiers kept their eyes on the ground, wary of snakes and sinkholes. U.S. troops "bewildered" in the swamps often fired on their own men or on phantasms conjured in their minds out of loneliness and desperation. They felt completely discombobulated and, like Prince's lost men, became the hunted instead of the hunters in swampland battlefields. As M. M. Cohen put it, "we are 'strangers in a *very* strange land.'"[63]

Swamps confused and depressed U.S. soldiers, who conceived of these ecosystems not as fabulous hunting grounds or refuges for freedom fighters and perhaps not even as fields of battle, but as a "sepulcher."[64] Secretary of War Joel R. Poinsett wrote to General Jesup in 1837, "From the severe duty which has been imposed on the troops of Florida, and their suffering, under circumstances of peculiar privation, in a climate little congenial to the health of most of them, [I] feel much concerned in their behalf."[65] Soldiers could not help but be exhausted from hard marching in deep muck, paranoid about the Seminole attack that could be launched at any second, and depressed by a lack of successful action and victory. M. M. Cohen and his fellow soldiers found no solace in the swamps, whose "vines woo us most lovingly, and clasp us with so tenacious [an] embrace, as to render parting scarce practicable."[66] Troops were desperate to escape from the swamplands but found themselves entangled and psychologically beaten.

By the time Henry Prince had seen action in the Withlacoochee, the Wahoo Swamp, and the Okeechobee, he was fed up with Florida and with the U.S. Army's inability to make any inroads in the mucky wilderness. On May 31, 1838, Prince left Florida for an assignment in the western Indian Territory and bid the area a contemptuous adieu: "Waked at one o'clock to see the last end of Florida. Vile country! I have risked my life three years for you!"[67] Other observers were just as disillusioned. John T. Sprague, a Massachusetts soldier commissioned into the Eighth Infantry Regiment, wrote that "the progress of the Florida War from the 1st of January, 1836, was attended with large expenditures of money, and se-

rious embarrassments. The climate, ignorance of the swamps and hammocks, and the treachery and activity of the enemy, baffled the skill of the
most zealous and intelligent officers."[68]

The northern Florida theater during the Second Seminole War was "bewildering," and U.S. military commanders did not convert any of their
knowledge gained from previous experiences with either Native American wartime tactics or swamplands into a solid counterinsurgency plan.
European American ecolocal beliefs had separated white men from
swamplands and placed people of color within them, yet they also conceived of both swamps and Seminoles as dangers to be erased. Despite
the attempts of antebellum southern writers to whitewash the swamp in
fiction, soldiers and officers could not imagine their place in swamps
much less develop military strategies within them.

Most U.S. generals in charge of the Florida campaigns blamed their
failures on a lack of topographical knowledge. General Winfield Scott,
who was appointed to lead the Florida offensive after the Withlacoochee
debacle of 1836, argued that the forested wetlands of northern Florida
were available to him only in "booksellers' maps," which, like early cartography, provided only an outline "filled up with unlucky guesses." While
topographical engineers were present in the army and in the battles in the
Southeast, they often were not able to remain long enough to draw up any
usable maps, for the summer and early fall brought sickness, and the
army had to withdraw from northern Florida for nearly five months of the
year. The Court of Inquiry that investigated Scott's failed campaigns during the Second Seminole War understood these problems and ascribed
the failure of the campaign to the following: "the want of time to operate;
the insalubrity of the climate after the middle of April; the impervious
swamps and hammocks . . . ; an absence of all knowledge of the country;
together with the difficulty of obtaining, in time, the means of transport-
ing supplies for an army."[69] For the U.S. Army in the 1830s, the Withlacoochee, Okefenokee, and other southeastern swamps were outlines on
maps filled with empty space. As the war progressed, however, American
incursions into swampland interiors served not only to weaken Seminole
strongholds but also to render the Okefenokee hinterlands more visible –
and thus available for encroachment – to European Americans.

The wartime engagements that commenced this process of making the
Okefenokee Swamp visible and available for development occurred be-

tween 1836 and 1839. Even as the swamp battles moved farther and farther southward into peninsular Florida over the course of the Second Seminole War, bands of Seminoles continued to befuddle their enemies by backtracking up into the Okefenokee. Newspapers reported the capture of "A Creek mother and her two children making their way into Florida via the Okefenokee" in September 1836, and regular articles appeared in local dailies and weeklies concerning Seminole "depredations" in the area.[70] Octiarche, a Creek leader who pledged to "die upon the soil," participated in many skirmishes along the edges of the Okefenokee and was rumored to have taken up residence in the swamp in 1836.[71] Wild Cat (Coacoochee) was also thought to be in the Okefenokee in 1837, "encamping in its fastnesses, sally[ing] forth, as occasion permitted, and spread[ing] death and devastation in the southern settlements of Georgia."[72] The Seminole chiefs Halpatter Tustenuggee and Cotzar-fixico-chopco also roamed the area, keeping "the country around the Okefinokee Swamp constantly in arms."[73]

In July 1836 Colonel Thomas Hilliard, an officer in the Ware County militia, wrote to the Georgia governor, William Schley, to inform him "from undoubted information that several strolling Partis of the Creek Tribe of Indians are now within the limits of this County and are Generally supposed to be making thare way to the okefenoke swamp Under these circumstances Grat alarm prevails amongst the Inhabitants of this County being daily under the apprehension of an attack from the savage foe."[74] "Strolling parties" of Seminoles had used the Okefenokee as hunting and battlegrounds for centuries and had established a stronghold there after the First Seminole War. In the 1830s, however, American banditti and militia groups organized to meet them. Hilliard and his company of militia patrolled the northern and southeastern parts of the Okefenokee, and throughout the summer of 1836 they engaged in chases and clashes with small bands of Seminoles. According to Hilliard, Seminole warriors, women, and children had been passing through Ware County almost every day that August. "They Go consealed as much as possible," he wrote, "and are committing depredations continually robbing our corn fields and killing our stock."[75]

Several engagements that took place in late September and early October prompted the first European American incursion into the Okefenokee Swamp, by Hilliard and Captain William Beall of the Ware Militia. Beall, along with sixteen men from the Ware County and Florida militias, tracked a party of Seminoles up the Suwannee River to the edge of the Okefenokee. When Hilliard and his reinforcements joined them the next day, Beall led them along a Native trail, "through the dismal and almost impassable bays of the Okefenoke for about four miles, when we came upon a very large Encampment situated in a large island, which had been abandoned only a few days (not more than four or five) and had all the appearance of having been occupied for some length of time. . . . After sometime spent in fruitless attempts to trail them, we returned to our horses, and made our way for the settlements, being very short of provisions. It is strongly believed that a considerable number of Indians remained concealed in the swamps and bays with which this country abounds."[76] Beall's entrance into the Okefenokee interior with his soldiers was most likely the first European American expedition into the swamp's "dismal and almost impassable bays." But the militiamen found only abandoned towns and were never able to track, capture, or engage the Okefenokee Seminoles fully in large-scale battles. After the skirmishes in the summer and fall of 1836, the area seemed to quiet down a bit, despite Wild Cat's rumored settlement in the Okefenokee hinterlands. But in May 1838 Seminoles resurfaced along the swamp's margins and provoked what would be the first large-scale European American invasion of the Okefenokee Swamp, which in turn prompted the Okefenokee's initial emergence into the European American developmental consciousness.

On May 27 and 28, 1838, a large band of Seminoles engaged in battle with the Ware County militia along the eastern Okefenokee edge. On June 4 Thomas Hilliard wrote again to the governor of Georgia (now George R. Gilmer) for aid: "I have Received information that a considerable Number of Indians have left Florida and are at this time in the limits of this county the Number I have not bin able to correctly assertain but are supposed to be one hundred warriors by those who have been engaged with them it appears thare are different ages of thare sign and it is believed other companys have come before them and have taken up thare Residence in the Okafanoka Swamp two Battles have been [fought] by them and our citizens on the 27th and 28th May last the particulars of which I have not bin able to assertain."[77] Hilliard further reported that citizens of Ware County were leaving their homes and land; these desertions rendered the Okefenokee hinterlands even more unstable and made it hard for the militia to procure provisions. Hilliard had five companies in the field and was forced more than once to purchase supplies for them out of his own pocket. The Seminoles burned down houses and barns and killed livestock, reducing opportunities for the Americans to find shelter and food.[78] The many letters Hilliard sent to Gilmer and the desperation of the situation for the Americans along the Okefenokee rim in 1838 prompted the governor to write to General Zachary Taylor, who was serving for one year as commander of the Florida War. In response, Taylor promised to send two companies of dragoons and two infantry battalions to the Okefenokee and ordered Captain Waite of the U.S. Navy (moored in the St. Marys River) to provide regular supplies to the troops garrisoned around the swamp.[79]

As the army bureaucracy sorted itself out, the situation along the Okefenokee's margins intensified. Within two days in late July, small groups of Seminoles ambushed and killed the Wild and Tiffin families, who had lived on the edge of the swamp; those American inhabitants still residing in the area fled to Savannah. The American Robert Brown wrote to the governor of Florida from Okefenokee, "We are most critically situated. The Indians in the north of us, on the Okefenokee, and on the south in the nation; our market-road, leading from this to any market accessible to us, passes through their 'gangway.' We are here exposed from the Okefenokee down both sides of their 'passway' to the nation, and no protection whatever from the army."[80] Brown and his neighbors felt trapped and threatened in this ecological vise. In late October 1838 Americans living on the Okefenokee's margins finally received some protection, and the swamp simultaneously became vulnerable to American incursion.

On November 6, 1838, Governor George Gilmer announced in a message to the Georgia House of Representatives that he had given orders to raise an Okefenokee regiment to operate under the command of General Charles Rinaldo Floyd in order to destroy or drive away "the savage enemy."[81] Floyd was the son of the famed Red Stick War general John Floyd, and he had accompanied his father on several engagements in the course of his military training.[82] Although Okefenokee lore and some histories of Georgia place General John Floyd at the scene of the Okefenokee campaign of 1838, none of the reports of the events (nor Charles Floyd's diary) mention his presence. Charles Floyd was a talented painter with a love of antique guns and dueling. He was a decent militia leader whose obituary lauded his military prowess, his intellectual attainments, and "a peculiar sensitiveness of nature."[83] Floyd had ample opportunity to observe and write about the peculiar nature of the Okefenokee during his three months of commanding duty on the swamp's edge and in its interior. His actions during the winter of 1838 were deemed a success, not because he had forced the Seminoles out of the Okefenokee but because he had, in effect, brought the white man inside its borders and thus helped to re-shape European American ecolocal culture.

Floyd was notified of his commission in early October and started for the Okefenokee to take command of the Georgia Regiment and other troops in the field on Saturday, October 27, 1838. When he arrived on the rim to the southwest of the Okefenokee on November 2, he found five companies waiting for him, a total of three hundred noncommissioned officers and privates. His trip had gone smoothly and captains were elected without incident, but once Floyd announced to his troops that only three regiments would travel on horseback, "Capt. Lasseters Company *mutined*, in consequence of *dismounting* them. . . . I had the ringleaders put in irons." This protest against the loss of social and military status through dismounting did not stop Floyd's march – the five companies left for the Okefenokee the next day. Six days later, on November 10, 1838, Floyd arrived and "encamped on the edge of the *great monster*, the Okefinokee Swamp, in a bend called the 'pocket.'"[84]

The next morning Floyd marched into the swamp to "Chepucky's Island" (most likely Billy's Island). Floyd established camp and sent his soldiers back for provisions, which they transported into the swamp on their shoulders – "a very arduous duty." Floyd spent the rest of the day planning his march, which he hoped would take him to an "*Island*, described in Indian traditions, as near its centre, and as being a most lovely place inhabited either by the ghosts of Indians, or by a race of Indians of singular beauty. This Island has never been seen by white men, and its existence is problematical."[85] Floyd, it seems, had also read Bartram's *Travels* – the Creek narrative included in the naturalist's account evidently informed the general's assumptions about the swamp and its contents. This comment in Floyd's diary makes it clear that the general's mission in the Okefenokee did not solely involve eradicating the Seminoles suspected of hiding there. He was to be a soldier and explorer, a ghost hunter and dispeller of myths, the first white man to traverse the "great monster." He was to make the swamp visible to all European Americans – and devoid of disruptive people of color – by seeing and recording the Okefenokee in its entirety.

On November 13 Floyd and his troops advanced into the Okefenokee Swamp from Chepucky's Island in search of Bartram's paradise. What they found was less mystical than they had imagined, but a productive "discovery" in any case:

> Our course was N.E. and on an old Indian trail followed about 3 miles last August by Capt. B. Beall of the 2nd Dragoons at the head of 2 companies. Each man carried 5 days provisions & his arms & accoutrements – nothing else. For 8½ hours we struggled through one of the most formidable swamps in the World, sometimes waist deep in mud & water, and reached the famed Island, never before seen by white men. It is indeed a beautiful place, – high and dry, with magnificent Oak & Laurel trees. Discovered a large Indian Camp, & an Indian town with 14 or 15 very comfortable houses – but *no Indians*. By the signs they had left the Island about 2 months, and were in number about 150.

Floyd and his troops may not have found paradise, but they had discovered the site that had been rumored to be a Seminole town within the Okefenokee. That the Seminoles had turned out to be "ghosts" did not seem to worry Floyd, and he was delighted to hear that his officers had named the former Seminole town site "Floyd's Island," by which name "it will hereafter be known."[86] Thus began a tradition of identifying the islands within the Okefenokee with American names, an assertion of linguistic control over the unruly, "savage" environment.

Floyd's troops stayed on the island the next day, burned the town, and left another mark in the form of a tin can top nailed to a tree announcing, "Georgia Reg't commanded by Gen'l Chas. Floyd, Nov'r 14, 1838."[87] His troops in good spirits and high on the adrenaline of exploration, Floyd took his men and left the island the next day. In the course of their march eastward through the swamp, however, their spirits took a beating:

> We had no trail to follow, but went by a small compass, which I carried with me. For 11½ hours we marched through the most infernal places – thickets of vines, briars & bushes; and bogs & lakes about waist deep – and emerged from the swamp after night, about 12 or 14 miles north of Trader's Hill, having by our computation marched about 18 or 20 miles. The troops were worn down with fatigue, and many were without shoes, hats, & pantaloons, these articles having been destroyed by the obstacles in the swamp. Camped in a pine barren – and although hungry, wet & cold, & in rags, we slept soundly in the palmettos. The immense fatigue we had endured acted like an opiate. This day's march will never be forgotten through life by those who performed it. I would rather have crossed the Alps *several times*.[88]

Floyd and his soldiers had entered the Okefenokee well-fed, fully clothed, and energetic. They left it "hungry, wet and cold," nearly naked, and exhausted. This experience affected Floyd and his men profoundly; it was a march that "will never be forgotten through life." Floyd wrote in his diary that he was impressed with both the horror and the beauty of the swamp environment. He admired the magnificent oaks of Floyd's Island but soon forgot those pleasing scenes while he and his men slogged through mud and vines that tore their clothes to ribbons. He alternately described the swamp as Edenic and a "great monster," a "most beautiful" and an "infernal" place. The many faces of the Okefenokee often befuddled those humans who encountered it – the ecological mosaic of swamplands promised both delights and dangers. Floyd and his men had endured the Okefenokee, survived it, and at this point the general paused to record his impressions.

Floyd was to be a soldier and an explorer within the Okefenokee, but his additional duty as commander of the militia and the campaign was to report his wartime actions in words for his superiors and for the general public. After each major engagement (every two weeks or so), Floyd spent an entire day transferring the immediate impressions of his diary into a more contemplative report of the action in the Okefenokee for newspaper readers all over the Southeast. In his first letter of the campaign to the *Savannah Georgian,* which was reprinted in the *Savannah Daily Republican* (among other newspapers), Floyd narrated his soldiering adventures within the Okefenokee. In his initial report, he emphasizes the challenges swamp ecology posed to the march to Floyd's Island, elaborating on his diary entry noted earlier: "our course was N.E. with very little variation for 8½ hours through one of the most horrible swamps on the face of the earth." He also extends his physical description of Floyd's Island: "The island . . . is about twenty miles long, very high and shaped like a crescent, one end pointing to the west and the other to the north, the concave side fronting N.W. On this side of the island is an extensive praire, level as a lake, and covered with short grass, and adorned with beautiful islands from which (over the praire) the woods on the border of the swamp may be seen about 20 miles distant to the S.W. and N.W. The Okefenokee instead of being a barren waste, contains some of the best land in Georgia."[89] In the letter Floyd's Island is an oasis – it is beautiful and large and, most important, *high* – the island has a prospect (one can see for twenty miles) and thus can be understood as having financial prospects. Floyd

writes the valuable Okefenokee into the southeastern public consciousness at this moment, and his vision of it is deliberately both negative and
positive. The negative aspects (the boggy mud, the gloomy cypress trees,
and the vicious briars) serve to justify the incursion and his gaze of development. Here, a new motif in European American ecolocal culture
emerges, shaped by a man who was both artist and soldier.

Floyd was proud of the literary aspect of his military duty. At this point
he was less concerned with eradicating the Seminole presence in the
swamp than with his pioneering achievement: "it is a satisfaction to me to
have performed what all other men have deemed impossible; *to cross the
Okefenokee with an army.*" In his letters, Floyd asserts the multiple effects
this trip will have on the inhabitants of the Okefenokee: "Our discoveries
of the swamp will be of great utility – they will enable us hereafter to ex-
clude the Indians from the Okefenokee, [and] open to the citizens of
Georgia new sources of wealth in the rich lands of the swamp."[90] The Okefenokee, seen by a white man and rid of obstreperous people of color, was
made visible to the American public in Floyd's newspaper reports. By seeing and interpreting the value of the Okefenokee, Floyd helped to reshape
European American ecolocal culture and provoke a period of developmental incursions in the "great monster."

For three months Floyd remained in the Okefenokee and on its margins.
He established interior posts, exterior mobile units, and scouting squads
in the swamp and was thus the only military leader in the first phase of the
Seminole War to attempt to employ partisan warfare tactics. If these maneuvers had been more popular with the leaders of the conventional army,
the U.S. military's actions in the Seminole Wars would have been more decisive and successful. But despite Floyd's embrace of more environmentally mindful strategies, his troops did not capture any Seminoles. The
Okefenokee foiled most of his plans and provided the Seminoles with sites
of refuge. The mystery of the swamp, however, continued to appeal to his
sense of adventure and conquest: "The Okefenokee is one of the wonders
of the world – it is a complete labyrinth, and many of its recesses are yet to
be explored."[91] His admiration for the Okefenokee's beauty extended to
the attractiveness of its future utility and the excitement of exploration. In
traversing the Okefenokee, Floyd and his men mapped out its future and
secured its availability to Georgia's residents.

Seminole depredations continued in and around the Okefenokee during the winter of 1838–39 despite Floyd's presence there. By early Janu-

ary most of his companies' tours of duty had ended, and none were mustered back into service. It was Floyd's contention that the Okefenokee area needed at least five hundred men kept in service for the protection of people and property, eight hundred if the commanding officer wanted to build forts and roads for complete access to the swamp.[92] On January 17, 1839, the *Savannah Daily Republican* published a muster call for five hundred troops to serve three months in the Okefenokee area, but these troops never materialized. Thus Floyd left the Okefenokee on February 2, 1839, and rode home to his plantations in Camden County.[93] After his departure, Captain Thomas Hilliard continued to write to Governor Gilmer to request troops to defend the Okefenokee. He offered to serve as commander of a regiment of volunteers from the frontier, but his offer went unrecognized. Brigadier General Leigh Reid did command a militia unit at Trader's Hill after Floyd's departure, but U.S. Army commanders agreed that the Okefenokee was not a permanent stronghold for the Seminoles, and Reid was discharged in April 1841.[94] Local militia groups continued to police the Okefenokee's mucky margins, but no Seminoles were ever captured there during the Second Seminole War. Rumors circulated among local communities that Seminoles were still living on the northeastern edge of Okefenokee in 1862.[95]

By 1841 the U.S. military finally acknowledged the success of the Seminoles' guerrilla tactics and moved to gain more ecological knowledge and initiate appropriate counterinsurgent campaigns and technologies. Army leaders vowed to fight throughout the summer, formed small units of soldiers that could move quickly through swamplands, and drafted naval forces to fight Seminoles in the Everglades and other Florida lowlands. These military developments succeeded in surprising the Seminoles but took a major toll on the U.S. Army and Navy. Almost all of the soldiers on active duty during the summer of 1841 campaign were felled by sickness at one point or another. Two thousand men were able to return to the action, but many soldiers died or had to be evacuated in order to recover from their illnesses.[96] The summer campaign of 1841 turned the tide of the Second Seminole War, but it did not bring it to an end.

As much as they may have adapted to their surroundings, the soldiers could not fully expel the Seminoles from Florida. The futile searches for rebels and fugitives were exhausting. As the soldier J. T. Sprague put it, "Wading through swamps and hammocks, in search of six, eight, or ten

Indians, was like hunting a wolf, who at night would look into your camp, and follow your footsteps at noonday."[97] The First Seminole War had ended with a treaty that the vast majority of Seminoles had ignored. The Second Seminole War ended as President John Tyler, exasperated, declared a cease-fire on May 10, 1842. One of the reasons he cited for halting operations was the swamp ecosystem and its suitability to Seminole strategies: "the very smallness of their numbers . . . increases the difficulty of finding them, in the abundant and almost inaccessible hiding-places of the territory, render any further attempts to secure them by force, impracticable, except by employment of the most expensive means."[98]

The Second Seminole War was costly for both sides. It was one of the most expensive and time-consuming wars the United States has ever waged. The Seminoles lost almost 90 percent of their population to death or capture; only six hundred Seminoles out of five thousand remained in Florida after 1842. But under the peace terms, these six hundred men, women, and children were allowed to remain on their lands in southern Florida. The Seminole chief Halleck Tustenuggee explained this outcome in a talk with Colonel Worth in April 1842. "My people," he said, "are wild, and start at the cracking of a bush; they live in the swamp and will always live there as long as your troops pursue them."[99]

Between 1700 and 1842 the Okefenokee hinterlands were a contact zone, a site of ecolocal encounters that were often bloody and violent. Multiple communities met and clashed in these places; the destruction and death that resulted from these conflicts in the Okefenokee hinterlands make for a dark chapter in this area's history. The U.S. Army's ecologically misinformed campaigns during the First and Second Seminole Wars could not bring about a victory and thus aided small communities of Seminoles in their fight to stay on their lands. But Okefenokee hinterland battles with American soldiers did not result in complete victory for Seminoles either; they lost the freedom to travel, hunt, and cultivate the Okefenokee hinterlands as they chose.

Ultimately, Seminole ecolocal culture prompted southeastern European Americans to reshape their own ideas about swampland ecologies. American inhabitants of the Okefenokee hinterlands, as they read in local newspapers Charles Floyd's letters regarding his swampland battles, came to see the Okefenokee as a potentially valuable space in which white men could affirm their masculinity and social status, improve their economic situations, and change their lives. The importance of Beall's and then Floyd's incursions into the Okefenokee lies in the entrance of white Americans into a landscape that had been marked previously as nonwhite. The irony of this turn of events is that Seminoles, in using the Okefenokee and other southeastern swamplands to protest European invasions, made these ecosystems visible to white Americans. What followed was a period of American exploration of the Okefenokee and its subsequent transition from a blank space on local maps to a landscape marked by the chains and lines of surveyors, engineers, and lumber kings.

# 3 El Dorado

*The Okefenokee and Dreams of Development*

In April 1851 an article by the Georgia entrepreneur W. W. Starke, titled "Drainage of the Savannah Bottoms: An Amusing Sketch," appeared in the *Savannah Republican.* In their preface to the article, the editors of the *Republican* remarked, "Major STARKE deserves the thanks of the public . . . for having transformed a prolific source of pestilence – worse than a barren waste – into a salubrious and most productive plantation. There are thousands of acres in the southern Atlantic States now worthless which are equally susceptible of reclamation by proper drainage." Swamplands were, according to the editors of the *Republican,* "worse than a barren waste" – they were unhealthy and unproductive of agriculture and therefore "worthless." The reclaimed plantation, by contrast, was not only salubrious and fertile but also beautiful. Before drainage, Starke's inundated land was "covered with cypress, whose rich foliage and drooping moss, intercepting the sun's rays and overshadowing the waters, presented to the view a dismal canopy *above* and a horrible landscape *beneath.*" After reclamation, Starke reported that his land is "no longer an *eye-sore,* but Pygmalion's clay metamorphosed into a beautiful woman."[1] In the nineteenth and early twentieth centuries, the Okefenokee Swamp was an environmental Cinderella. Its exploration, survey, reclamation, and conversion were plot points in a European American ecolocal narrative that enticed and intrigued inhabitants and outside investors for nearly eighty years.

But these developers, like rice planters and the U.S. military, misunderstood the complexities of the Okefenokee Swamp. They saw it only for what its exploration and conversion would provide for them: manliness, civic virtue, and great wealth. Because they could not see or understand the true nature of the Okefenokee's ecology, they failed to establish long-term and renewable industry within the Okefenokee's depths. Like all dreamers, these developers were stymied by reality when they attempted to force on the Okefenokee a mode of production that swamp ecology would not sustain. Investigation of the entrepreneurial Okefenokee illuminates how the narrative of swamp adventure and development shaped ecolocal culture in the Okefenokee hinterlands between 1850 and 1927.

During the late eighteenth and early nineteenth centuries, the state of Georgia acquired most of its lands through Cherokee, Creek, and Seminole cessions, and subsequent surveys shaped entrepreneurial desires by measuring, bounding, and pricing these tracts. American surveyors first encountered the Okefenokee Swamp and the surrounding area in the late eighteenth century; most agreed that the Okefenokee hinterlands were extremely difficult to traverse, hopelessly entangled, and of little monetary value. Andrew Ellicott, who was assigned to establish the Georgia-Florida boundary in 1798, abandoned the line west of the Okefenokee and sailed around the Florida peninsula to continue the survey from eastern Florida. The westward march toward the Okefenokee in January 1800, wrote Ellicott, "was extremely disagreeable, owing to bad weather, cold rains, and the wet marshy ground on which we were encamped." After completing the line and exploring the southeastern edge of the Okefenokee, Ellicott opined that the swamp and other lowlands in the area were too inundated to till and were therefore worthless; his journal entries reverberated with pessimism regarding Okefenokee development.[2]

Despite Ellicott's painstaking survey, the Georgia-Florida boundary line continued to be a matter of vigorous disputes between 1800 and 1859; these conflicts resulted in several survey trips to the Okefenokee area. Those surveyors who followed Ellicott experienced similar frustrations during what they called their "mud cruises." William Green, who was appointed to mark the line in 1818, wrote to Governor William Rabun of

Georgia in June 1819, "Indeed the country along the line is so much occupied with swamp & ponds & marsh that it is nearly impossible to get pack horses thro." The claustrophobic vegetation and uncertain footing gave many surveyors nightmares, and several parties gave up due to the "difficulties to the passage . . . beyond the conception of any who [had] not visited it."[3]

But swamp ecology was not the only impediment to surveyors and settlement in the Okefenokee hinterlands. Many Creeks and Seminoles resisted the terms of the multiple land cessions that augmented Georgia's territory in the late eighteenth and early nineteenth centuries. Seminole clans in particular did not recognize the annexation of Florida to the United States in 1821 (or Spanish, French, and British claims that came before, for that matter) as legitimate. They roamed the Okefenokee hinterlands and provoked skirmishes with United States survey teams that were mapping a grid onto the southern Georgia and northern Florida landscape. Sometimes Seminoles did not directly engage surveyors in battle but acted indirectly to subvert their goals. In 1835, for example, when the surveyor R. B. Ker arrived in Marion County (midcentral), Florida, to begin a replatting of its lands, he found "only a hole where the post had been. It was destroyed, I suppose by Indians, and the numbers erased from the trees."[4] This kind of Seminole subterfuge was common; European American landowners often arrived on their Okefenokee hinterland tracts to find that boundary stakes had been uprooted and tree markings scraped away. The presence of surveyors, their actions, and the marks they left on the landscape and in print were powerful symbols of European American social order that marginalized groups found oppressive. As long as they remained in the Okefenokee hinterlands, Seminoles fought back by erasing such marks and harassing the surveyors who attempted to make them.

As Seminoles retreated from the Okefenokee hinterlands after 1842 and migrated to southern Florida, Georgia and Florida businessmen and politicians began to focus on the Okefenokee as a site of land development. Charles Floyd's traverse of the swamp and his written accounts of the "great monster" and its potential whetted their appetites. Additionally, the entrance of Florida into the United States in 1845, the Armed Occupation Act (which provided free land to European Americans willing to inhabit and defend the Okefenokee hinterlands), federal legislation promoting the drainage of swamplands, high rates of mobility, and the pressures of soil exhaustion in many areas of the Southeast prompted Georgia's governing men to look to the Okefenokee and the resources that lay buried in its muck as a developmental El Dorado. At this point, the European American ecolocal narrative began to depict the Okefenokee not as a stronghold of people of color but as the agricultural domain of whites.

Central to developers' plans for swamp reclamation and conversion were assessments of swamp fertility. As "muck," inundated lowlands had been traditionally understood to be public domain: large acreages of open range that were assessed as worthless. Increasingly in the nineteenth century, however, residents of the Okefenokee hinterlands began to note that "muck" was actually extremely fertile and that its agricultural potential was great. But it was clear to all those who took part in nineteenth-century debates about land value that the Okefenokee's ability to create wealth depended on successful drainage and reclamation. The health benefits of drainage had been widely publicized – ecolocal ideas that connected swamps and disease called for eradication in the name of public health – and entrepreneurs increasingly recognized the feasibility and profitability of swamp reclamation in the 1840s.[5] Congress passed the first Swamp Land Act in 1849, which provided for government funding of drainage projects, and Okefenokee hinterland residents began to dream of the financial benefits of draining the Land of Trembling Earth.[6]

The Okefenokee Swamp emerged into the American public consciousness slowly between 1800 and 1850. In 1805 the southeastern corner of the Okefenokee was surveyed into rectangular lots, platted, and offered up for sale, but the Georgia Bend did not attract many buyers. The rest of Appling County (now Ware County) was surveyed as part of the Florida annexation furor between 1819 and 1821. After the annexation, surveyors divided the Appling County lots into 490-acre sections. This platting decision reveals that the early developmental narrative of the Okefenokee devalued its lands, for the larger the tract size, the lower the quality (and thus the value) in the opinion of the surveyor. In comparison, surveyors divided potential rice lands along the Altamaha River into lots of 202½ acres and gold lands in northern Georgia into 40-acre tracts.[7] While they judged Appling lands to be nearly worthless, surveyors did not even bother to mark lines in districts ten and eleven – the Okefenokee Swamp. Interest in the investigation and division of these lands increased, however, in the late 1830s. The narrative of General Charles Floyd's march

into the Okefenokee was widely publicized and became a legendary local adventure story. Floyd's tales also prepared readers for the possibility
of Okefenokee development, for the general had written that his expul-
sion of the Seminoles would "open to the citizens of Georgia new sources
of wealth in the rich lands of the swamp."[8]

By the late 1840s members of the Georgia legislature, who were also
the state's business leaders, became more and more interested in the Okefenokee Swamp. In December 1849 the legislature authorized a weekly
mail route from Waresboro (Ware County) to Center Village (Camden
County) and to Blount's Ferry, Florida – a route that skirted the eastern
edge of the Okefenokee. In the same session, the legislature passed an act
to sell unclaimed lots on the west side of the swamp and created the St.
Illa Plank Road Company, a corporation that it authorized to construct
a plank road or canal from the Satilla or the St. Marys rivers westward
across the Okefenokee to any point on the Flint River.[9] These acts reveal
the shift in the ecolocal narrative of development in the Okefenokee hinterlands. Swamps may be useless in and of themselves, officials reasoned,
but drainage could change Floyd's monster into an agricultural Eden.

These legislative actions also indicate governmental approbation of
swamp reclamation. Growing interest in the Okefenokee led, in 1850, to
the passage of a bill to survey and dispose of the unsurveyed districts ten
and eleven; the lands would be sold to the highest bidder at the Waresboro Court House immediately after the plats had been mapped.[10] The
governor acted within four days of the bill's passage and appointed Mansfield Torrance, a fifty-five-year-old land speculator, to "survey all the
unsurveyed lands . . . which in his opinion it may be practicable to survey . . . and enter upon the discharge of the duties hereby assigned him so
soon as the Nature of the country to be surveyed will permit."[11] Torrance
was to make a full report to the legislature, draw a map of the entire
acreage surveyed, and create a separate plat for each lot. He accepted the
appointment and left for the Okefenokee Swamp with four surveyors
(who acted also as chain carriers) and a guide in May 1850.

Over forty days Torrance's survey team measured, marked, and mapped
as many lots as possible on the northern, eastern, and southern perimeter
of the Okefenokee Swamp. When they returned, Torrance wrote up his
field notes, and Surveyor General James Butts compiled maps of districts
ten and eleven. A fragment of the large map remains, but the notes were

lost, and only individual plat maps, an account of the survey by "One of the Surveyors" published in the *Milledgeville (Ga.) Southern Recorder* in July, and a letter from Torrance to the editor of the *Columbus (Ga.) Southern Sentinel* in August 1850 have survived. The identity of "One of the Surveyors" is unknown, but he could have been any one of Torrance's team members. This lengthy Okefenokee account provided for readers thrilling details of the "far-famed Swamp" and the "gratification" the surveyors experienced on investigating its interior.[12] The Torrance survey's intent was clear: to determine drainage feasibility so that the Okefenokee land could become productive (and therefore useful) to the citizens of Georgia. Published accounts of this 1850 survey brought the Okefenokee into the European American gaze of development.

Torrance's survey team entered the Okefenokee on the northeast side and entered an open prairie (most likely Sapling Prairie). The "shaking earth" of the prairie's peat islands was fascinating to "One of the Surveyors": "Standing still a few minutes causes the water to ooze through the moss and make puddles at each foot – evidently a hydraulic bed that no art can imitate." But before long, the Okefenokee became much more unpleasant than awe inspiring. While carrying the chains, the men would often lose their footing and plunge "knee-deep among the roots and hard tortuous stems of the tie-tie. . . . In this situation a man's foot is apt to be associated in imagination with snakes, scorpions and black ants."[13] In a landscape of black water and spongy peat, the surveyors could only guess at the dangers lurking under their feet. The survey was thus both physically and mentally difficult; it seemed to both Torrance and "One of the Surveyors" that the swamp purposefully thwarted their efforts. Torrance found it confounding to describe the Okefenokee's ecology but wrote to the editor of the *Columbus Southern Sentinel,* "You may form some idea of the undergrowth when I tell you that it is not an uncommon thing for two hands, with huge hooks, hatchets and large knives, to be a whole day cutting a mile open enough for the chain carriers to pass."[14] The surveyors, who had initially hoped to become nature's conquerors in the Okefenokee, were exhausted by their labors and continually harassed by water moccasins, yellow flies, and centipedes.

Okefenokee ecology physically and psychologically tormented the Torrance surveyors, as it had Floyd and his troops. It also rendered the survey itself superficial and uninformative. Because of the Okefenokee's dense foliage and unpredictable water depth, Torrance and his team kept to the edges on the north, east, and part of the south side of the swamp. Forty days in the Okefenokee left both Torrance and his survey members with no sense of the feasibility of drainage, and Torrance decided that an additional survey was not worth the time or the money to conduct. In response to Torrance's advice, the governor of Georgia discontinued the Okefenokee project and offered the lands Torrance had surveyed to the public at the price of two dollars per lot – .004 cents per acre – in 1852. But sales were sluggish, and the land sold brought the Georgia legislature little more than one thousand dollars.[15] Why developers passed up the chance to buy these lands at such a low price is mystifying; perhaps some of them thought that even .004 cents an acre was too expensive for untested swamp muck. But entrepreneurial attention had been turned to the Okefenokee; several more surveys of its interior shaped public perception of the swamp over the next twenty-five years.

In 1854 developers who had scorned the 1852 sale clamored for an Okefenokee giveaway: several railroad companies petitioned the Georgia legislature to grant them the unsurveyed Okefenokee lands for free. But government officials were clearly wary of these companies' demands. The request prompted a two-year legislative debate over the assessment and sale of the swamp and the lands along its edges. In January 1856 the House offered a bill to provide for a survey of the swamp, and the action was approved during the spring session.[16] Governor Herschel Johnson appointed Richard L. Hunter, a civil engineer with experience working for railroad companies and newspapers – two entrepreneurial powers that continued to have a hand in Okefenokee surveys for thirty years – to head the survey.[17]

The Georgia legislature of 1856 nurtured the vision of a successful, agricultural Okefenokee and argued that reclamation through drainage would make this dream a reality. Therefore, Hunter and his surveyors were told to survey the lands inside the swamp in order to determine drainage feasibility and subsequent potential for agriculture and timber extraction. But the surveyors and the public also considered the 1856 survey to be an exploratory adventure, as revealed by the publication of Hunter's report to the governor in pamphlet form and the appearance of Miller B. Grant's "The Okefenokee – Within and Without" in an 1858 issue of *Frank Leslie's New Family Magazine*. Grant was a surveyor on Hunter's team and the son of Robert Grant, one of Georgia's most powerful railroad and civic boosters.[18] Exploration narratives were popular reading material in the 1850s; Bartram's *Travels,* the *Journals of Lewis and Clark,* and the *Journal of Andrew Ellicott* sold well, and David Livingston had just returned from Africa and would soon write *Missionary Travels,* one of the most popular geography and travel books ever written.[19] Hunter, Grant, and their fellow surveyors and chainmen were conscious of their roles as "adventurers" encountering parts of the Okefenokee that white men may not have ever seen. Both Hunter's report and Grant's article illuminate the desires for profit, public acclaim, and social prestige that drove entrepreneurial development and shaped swamp ecolocalism in the Okefenokee hinterlands between 1850 and 1927.

Whatever their personal motives, the Hunter surveyors never lost sight of their official mission in the Okefenokee: to determine its potential for agricultural or timber development. Grant felt that the conversion of the Okefenokee into productive agricultural lands would contribute to the "civilization" of the state of Georgia: "No part of the country surpasses this section in its adaptation of soil for cotton growing, cane and other productions, and not many years will elapse before, I doubt not, it will rival in productiveness and enlightenment and civilization the more vaunted portions of our Glorious Empire – old Georgia, God bless her!"[20] The Okefenokee's reclamation would create a landscape befitting the Jeffersonian ideal, with small plots given over to agriculture and yeomen farmers who would demonstrate the "productiveness and enlightenment and civilization" of American democratic society. This pastoral vision prompted the Hunter surveyors to read the Okefenokee as they wished it to be, not how it really was. For them, even the tangled undergrowth that Torrance found so trying was indicative of potential productivity: "This vigorous growth is no doubt owing to the rich soil and abundant moisture." Hunter, Grant, and the other surveyors saw luxurious growth and production everywhere, from the moist soil to the sharp palmettos to the towering trees. As Grant wrote in an addendum to his article twenty years later, "This whole country is heavily timbered with the best of yellow pine and probably embraces as large an area of timbered land, in one body, as can be found in the South."[21]

The team's arguments for drainage were full of confidence. The reclamation plan Hunter suggested to the governor involved artificial channels to drain the Suwannee and St. Marys rivers (at flood level, these rivers were higher than the swamp and would not drain the Okefenokee naturally) and a minimum of twenty canals leading from the swamp interior to different outlets. After the Okefenokee had been drained, farmers in the area could cut their own drains into these canals for irrigation purposes. Hunter's proposed drainage project would be expensive, however; he estimated the total cost of the excavation engineering at $1,067,250. This amount likely shocked the members of the Georgia legislature who remembered the paltry sum the state had earned from the sale of Okefenokee lands in the early 1850s – less than 1 percent of this revised estimate of the cost of drainage. But the economic possibilities of drained lands were a different matter entirely. As Hunter concluded in his *Report,* "the soil of the swamp, if it shall ever be drained, will be very valuable."[22]

The legislature balked at Hunter's elaborate drainage project, although they rewarded his work with a bonus of thirty-five hundred dollars beyond his initial fee.[23] Most Georgia newspapermen, however, were strongly in favor of Okefenokee drainage. An editor of the *Savannah Georgian* wrote in 1857 that "aside from the value of the soil, . . . the worth of the cypress with which it so largely abounds, constitutes a strong argument in favor of the undertaking." He went on to convey an even more powerful argument, one to which every Georgian could relate: "And the aesthetic consideration of giving form and beauty to a chaotic and hideous wilderness, pleads loudly in behalf of the enterprise."[24] The Okefenokee was a troubling ecosystem, a "chaotic and hideous wilderness" that offended the economic and aesthetic sensibilities of Georgia's inhabitants during the antebellum era. Swamplands clearly resisted commonly accepted ecolocal ideas about land value and development. Drainage would convert the swamp into an agricultural paradise, a sculpted and beautiful landscape entirely of human construction. Reclamation of the Okefenokee would therefore be a powerful symbol of humans' ability to manipulate and control unruly nature.

As delightful as this vision was to most residents of the Okefenokee hinterlands, efforts to sell the Okefenokee "as is" during the late 1850s and 1860s came to nothing. Investors had dropped out of sight during the depression of 1857, and the Civil War diverted the attention, capital, and manpower of the Georgia state government, railroads, and newspapers. The exigencies of war, emancipation, Reconstruction, Redeemer politics, and economic depression dominated life in the Okefenokee hinterlands in the 1860s and early 1870s. But as northern troops began to pull out of the South, Georgia's politicians, businessmen, and boosters began to perceive of manufacturing and industry as vital to the state's rebirth and re-definition.[25]

Between 1875 and 1890, in the context of the New South's economic diversification and the rise of a business class, interest in the "jungles of South Georgia" resurged and took strength from the arguments of young men looking for postwar adventures and civic boosters focused on encouraging development in the Okefenokee hinterlands. The Okefenokee Swamp became the center of attention for these young explorers and developers. Motivated by curiosity, business interests, and a desire for an escapade, these men launched three excursions into the Okefenokee in 1875 that provoked more public awareness of the Okefenokee Swamp than any other projects before or since.

In the years following the Civil War, groups of young businessmen emerged in southeastern cities and towns, encouraging local entrepreneurialism. Using the print medium of daily and weekly newspapers to advertise their locales and their desire for both agricultural and industrial development, these young men promoted the introduction of factories, corporations, and railroads into the Okefenokee hinterlands. As a result of vigorous boosterism, technological innovations, and Reconstruction policies, the railroad lines that had just begun construction in the 1850s expanded at a rapid pace during the postbellum years. Between 1877 and 1900 the South built railroads faster than the nation as a whole.[26] In the 1870s the Georgia legislature incorporated dozens of railroad and canal companies: the Macon and Brunswick Railroad, the Brunswick and Albany Railroad, the Okefenokee and St. Mary's Canal and Drainage Company, the South Georgia Navigation Company, and the St. Mary's Log-Rafting Company.[27] These were just some of the corporations created and supported to promote industrial construction in the Okefenokee hinterlands.

Boosters were increasingly vocal about the potential of their locales. W. C. Folks, a physician and civic booster from Waycross, a town on the northeastern side of the Okefenokee, depicted the Okefenokee hinterlands as a blooming desert: "This vast Desert was described . . . as being poor beyond redemption, a sterile soil, worthless for agricultural purposes, scarce and inferior timber, few and sluggish streams, bad water, and a hot, sickly climate, a fit abode only for alligators and hooting owls. . . . [But] This desert is [now] yielding the finest timber the world ever saw. . . . Manufactories of various kinds are being put up and either run by steam or these sluggish streams. . . . the forest has and is being cut down, and the soil that was regarded as being so worthless is being made to yield heavy crops of corn, cotton, rice, peas, potatoes, sugar, fruits and many other articles."[28] Folks's language is typical of New South booster rhetoric. The Okefenokee hinterland's products are "the finest the world ever saw," and the soil is "being made to yield" both staple and garden crops. Industry has converted the area from a "fit abode only for alligators and hooting owls" to a landscape of active workers, efficient production, and fertility. New South boosters argued that the pine barrens and swamps in their midst could be reborn as gardens, lush and bountiful. Folks and other boosters hailed agriculture, clear-cutting, railroad development, and factory construction as both indicative and productive of the Okefenokee hinterland's economic health.

The most powerful and vocal boosters were journalists who made names for themselves, their towns, and their newspapers by advocating and defending new industries. The most famous of these journalists was Henry Grady, the editor of the *Atlanta Constitution*, who argued that southerners could partake of the industrial boom without forsaking their self-respect. By the late 1880s Grady's *Constitution* boasted the largest circulation of any weekly paper in the United States; his promotional rhetoric was spread far and wide.[29] Editors of newspapers with more local or regional distribution were also powerful voices for public support of private enterprise. They too called for textile production, timber extraction, land reclamation, and further exploitation of all of the Okefenokee hinterlands' natural resources. These men had a vested interest in the economic diversification of the area and the drainage and conversion of the Okefenokee Swamp, but they also had a personal stake in reclamation. Most of these young editors saw the exploration and development of the Okefenokee as opportunities to display their manliness.

This group of journalists and editors tended to be between the ages of twenty and thirty-five, most of them born before the Civil War but too young to have fought for the Confederacy. They watched their fathers and brothers return from the war defeated, mourning for the excitement and leadership opportunities of the military and telling tales of glories won on the battlefield. For this generation, an accident of timing meant that they had been unable to demonstrate their masculinity through war; therefore, they felt, they could not fully enter southeastern male society.[30]

Furthermore, the immensely influential narrative of the Lost Cause dictated that the defeat of the South in the Civil War emasculated white men. As they lost their mastery over slaves, these men cast about for places of potential conquest, spaces in which they could (re)establish their manhood. Between the extremes of the landscape of battle and the landscape of the pastoral, southeastern men found that their manliness could emerge, alternatively, in the landscape of the "frontier."[31] Conceiving of themselves as the heroes of a new kind of adventure, these young men, who had been born in the Okefenokee hinterlands and had rarely traveled outside of its boundaries, set out to explore their local frontier – the Okefenokee Swamp – in the 1870s. Their conceptualization of the Okefenokee as a site of the production of manliness did not stop these young men from joining the call to drain and develop the swamp. They found that wealth could also demonstrate their manliness, and therefore the exploration *and* prosperous development of the Okefenokee served them equally well.

Two of these businessmen-editors, Charles R. Pendleton of the *Valdosta (Ga.) Times* and George W. Haines of the *Jesup (Ga.) Georgian,* had both grown up in Tebeauville, Georgia, on the northeast side of the Okefenokee Swamp. Familiar with the edges but not the heart of the giant swamp, Pendleton and Haines itched to traverse it, live to tell about it, and in so doing gain fame for themselves and their locales. They were both young men – in their midtwenties, as opposed to Torrance, who had been fifty-five years old during his survey, and Hunter, who had been forty-one. Pendleton and Haines had both money and manliness on their minds when they planned three Okefenokee expeditions in 1875. Their motives were several: they sought to find a dry passage through the swamp and "hunt out" the most practicable route for a timber canal; they desired to demonstrate to the government that the Okefenokee could be "drained, utilized and made valuable to the people and the state"; they aspired to boost the circulation of the *Valdosta Times* and the *Jesup Georgian* through published narratives of their adventures in the Okefenokee; and they sought to bolster their own sense of masculinity by engaging in a series of "pioneering" efforts.[32]

That Pendleton and Haines were newspaper editors exemplifies the powerful role the print media played in shaping civic boosterism, the craze for development, and an ecolocalist narrative of masculine adventure that emerged in the late-nineteenth-century Okefenokee hinterlands.

These young, white business leaders wanted to make their mark in the world, and they were determined to achieve social status through exploration. Businessmen-adventurers like Pendleton and Haines compared themselves, as did their colleagues, to the great explorers of Africa and Asia. The *Valdosta Times* proudly reported on May 8, 1875, that Pendleton "is sloshing his way through mud, water, bamboo, mosquitoes, alligators, snakes, and – gosh! our blood runs cold when we think of it! . . . Be it as it may our readers may be on the look out for something startling – a book like Stanley's, or something of the kind, perhaps."[33] Henry Stanley, who had explored central and southern Africa and "discovered" Dr. Livingston, had been a *New York Herald* reporter before his departure. Pendleton and Haines considered themselves to be, like Stanley, journalist-heroic explorers. They also conceived of the *writing* of the Okefenokee as more important than the actual exploration. By narrating their adventures within the swamp with an eye toward entertainment, boosting circulation revenues, and displaying their masculinity, these newspaper editors continued what Charles Floyd had begun almost forty years before – they wrote the Okefenokee into the New South developmental consciousness.

Haines's and Pendleton's first jaunt into the Okefenokee in May 1875 was not a pleasant one. The late winter and early spring had been tremendously rainy, and wading through the swamp was "trying on the muscles." The group quickly ran out of provisions and was forced to abandon the expedition after just two weeks. The adventurers were disappointed with their accomplishments – the team had not discovered a timber canal route, nor had they found Floyd's Island, the central island in the swamp and, as Pendleton called it, the "El Dorado of our hopes."[34] However, the explorers did manage to publicize their efforts. Multiple newspapers in Georgia and Florida reprinted Pendleton's narrative of this first excursion, which elicited much comment in Okefenokee hinterland communities. The explorers vowed to return to the Okefenokee during the dry season, and W. C. Folks wrote approvingly in early August 1875 that the young men were preparing "another expedition to Southern Georgia's pet swamp."[35]

The second Haines-Pendleton survey, supported by a publishing contract with the *Atlanta Constitution,* got underway in mid-August 1875. During this trip both Pendleton and Haines again wrote of themselves as adventurers seeing "more of the interior of the great *terra incognita* than any set of white men have yet seen."[36] Their desires – to be the first to achieve a feat and to demonstrate their masculinity through responding to nature's challenges – shaped discussion of the Okefenokee and its usefulness to local inhabitants in 1875.

Much of the team's time during this survey was devoted not to making measurements or calculating distances but to stalking and shooting birds, bears, and deer. This hunting excursion in the Okefenokee was not a subsistence activity but a form of leisure that allowed men to escape to a world of male companionship and to exercise an unrestrained will through the destruction of nature. The bird or beast that the triumphant hunter brought back to camp was a material display of his masculinity, an increasingly important symbol to white men living in the postbellum South.[37] Although the survey party did eat some of what Pendleton and others killed, they also shot many animals and then declined to pursue and use them. To Pendleton and Haines, material proof of their prowess was not so necessary because they were writing about their adventures. The act of narrating the killing was a form of display, a new kind of "trophy" for the young editors.

The hunting narratives that dominate the surveyors' letters also reveal that the killing of animals in the Okefenokee was not about subsistence but was instead about control over the swamp environment. This control was vital to the surveyors' sense of their own masculinity and to the developmental plans they cherished. Pendleton's description of his victory over nature during a bear hunt is telling: "once the monarch of all he surveyed, now the victim of the hunter's deadly aim! As I stood over his once powerful frame, now in the cold embrace of death, a supreme satisfaction enthused me, akin, doubtless, to that felt by Gordon Cummings when he killed his first elephant in the wilds of Africa."[38] Pendleton liked to compare himself to African explorers; his reference here is meant to shore up his own sense of manliness and to compare the Okefenokee to colonized Africa. The white hunter would achieve civilization's mastery over barbaric nature in the wilds of southeastern Georgia. As Gail Bederman has argued, a white man seeking to remake his manliness in the 1870s and 1880s "publicly measur[ed] the violent power of his own masculinity against the aggressive predation of 'nature.'"[39]

Pendleton and Haines infused their narratives with the excitement of the chase and the satisfaction produced through the use of violence and demonstration of power within the Okefenokee's depths. The swamp was not an aesthetic landscape to enjoy but a challenging environment to overcome, physically. As Pendleton and his compatriots plunged into the Okefenokee from Billy's Island on the northeastern side, the editor wrote, "Ahead of us was a dark and dense swamp stretching for miles away, and the man who has never ventured upon such an undertaking as was ahead of us knows little of the feeling that stole over me at that moment. . . . We were standing on the margin of the great southern dismal, and various were the thoughts that flashed through my mind as we paused, like Caesar on the banks of the Rubicon."[40] Pendleton and his compatriots clearly relished thinking of and depicting themselves as explorers, part of a small coterie of men with rarified knowledge and experience entering the territory of the enemy that they would soon conquer. In this passage, Pendleton writes both the explorers and the Okefenokee into an ancient adventure tale and connects the Okefenokee hinterlands to the Roman Empire. These adventurers saw themselves as heroic and considered their actions in the Okefenokee to be justified by thousands of years of tradition that framed chaos and disorder as rebellious enemies of the state and of civilized men. Pendleton also depicted the "survey" party as experts in the experience of Okefenokee exploration – "the man who has never ventured upon such an undertaking as was ahead of us knows little" – and this sense of exclusivity served to bolster the explorers' authority within the pages of the *Atlanta Constitution*.[41]

By the time Pendleton and Haines sent in their dispatches from the second survey in late September 1875, the editors of the *Atlanta Constitution* had seen such a jump in revenues that they decided to plan and fund an exploration of the Okefenokee themselves. The newspaper executives took two months to organize their survey, maximizing publicity and bringing together knowledgeable guides (Haines, Pendleton, and "Uncle Ben" Yarborough, a Swamper guide who lived on the southeastern edge of the Okefenokee), *Constitution* staff members (the publisher, W. A. Hemphill, and editor, E. Y. Clarke), Georgia's state geologist (Dr. Little), several members of the Georgia Geological Survey, a civil engineer (C. A. Locke), and a survey artist (Mr. Hyde). The party numbered twenty-two men altogether, the largest single surveying party to enter the Okefenokee Swamp.

The organizers of this third survey strove for a balance between the adventuring expedition and a legitimate scientific survey, turning down applications from "mere seekers of romance." Their goal, they stated, was to explore "the mammoth mystery of Georgia. The interests of science, as well as the progress of the state, loudly call for a thorough knowledge of this great body of land and water on our southern border."[42] The *Constitution* survey was to complete a scientific reconnaissance of the Okefenokee, gain a "thorough knowledge" of the swamp's interior, and expose "the great swamp, its character, its condition," thereby exerting control over its chaos.[43]

Pendleton and Haines had only two weeks to recover from their second expedition, for the *Constitution* survey reached the Okefenokee in the first week of November 1875. The "complete exposure" of the swamp was achieved through weekly letters to the newspaper from Pendleton, Haines, and *Constitution* editor E. Y. Clarke, in addition to a field report from Locke (the civil engineer) and Hyde's visual images (now lost). Clarke's perception of the role the surveying team was to play in the swamp was clear from his first dispatch: "our tents are pitched on Billy's Island. They make quite a martial appearance, stretching in a line fronting the mighty swamp, our pretty little flag floating jauntily from its staff in the centre tent." He reported later that George Haines had reached the rendezvous point "with his force." This martial language recurred in Clarke's letters. The first week of the survey, the editor described how, after a day of marching twenty-five miles, the "order was given to halt and pitch camp," and then sixteen surveyors entered the Okefenokee "fully armed with the necessary implements of warfare against undergrowth and beast."[44] These surveyors, born too late to achieve glory in the Civil War, were making themselves over into an army, crossing a mighty river and entering into battle against a rebellious ecosystem.

The survey organizers expected that this expedition would provide entertaining adventure narratives, but they also wanted to obtain and publicize scientific information critical to the potential development of the Okefenokee. The *Atlanta Constitution* and the other newspapers that reprinted the letters from the fall expedition were invested in the results of the scientific survey and a potential development boom – population and economic growth would translate into increases in newspaper circulation and revenues. Therefore, the trip was to be almost completely devoid of "romance." Clarke lamented that members of the survey team were so busy that "Pendleton and myself will find it no easy task to keep up the adventure part of the programme." While Little, the state geologist, did make time to go fishing, the vast majority of the surveyors had "devoted little time as yet to hunting or sport" during the first week of the expedition.[45]

Articles and letters that survey members produced did address potential Okefenokee drainage and development, but because technical details
lacked a certain drama they were not dominant elements of these exploration narratives. The civil engineer Charles Locke, in his report to George
Little, tried to balance his account by including dramatic scenes of adventure and scientific assessments of the swamp's reclamation prospects.
He wrote that he found the Okefenokee to be a "perfect desert of animal
life" whose silence was almost unbearable: "human nature shrinks from
it in an indescribable manner. Men of known courage who have un-
flinchingly faced artillery & musketry are alarmed by the solitude & feel
the mutiny of bears a relief." For Locke, this excursion in the Okefenokee
was not war – it was worse than war. Survey members, in his view, were
more courageous than soldiers because the solitude of the Okefenokee
was more troubling than artillery fire. When Locke was not describing the
swamp and the surveyors' place within it, he did evaluate the possibilities
of Okefenokee drainage. In his opinion, the soil was demonstrably rich;
it was covered with luxuriant growth that predicted agricultural productivity. Drainage would be relatively easy, he surmised, because the first
layer of sand could be removed quickly, and the red clay below was "easily moved by hydraulic processes when once loosened."[46]

The Haines-Pendleton expeditions of 1875 provoked public interest in
the Okefenokee, its "mysterious" ecology, and its agricultural and extractive potential. They reveal the power of newspapers and journalists in the
dissemination of New South rhetoric and the intensity of civic boosterism
in Okefenokee hinterlands during the 1870s. They also illuminate the
self-perceptions of the explorer-businessmen who made up the survey
teams. Their desire to demonstrate their manliness shaped ecolocal narratives of adventure. The newspapermen did learn more about the Okefenokee's ecology and topography than either Torrance or Hunter had,
but their primary concern was to make names for themselves. Their desire to achieve victory in the battle against nature and their hopes for the
industrial development of their locales shaped the way they saw and narrated the Okefenokee. Their experiences produced little more than a
good read every week in the *Atlanta Constitution* and other Georgia newspapers, but their environmental explorations made it possible for entrepreneurs to visualize the Okefenokee's development.

Okefenokee developmental schemes emerged throughout the 1870s
and 1880s but came to nothing. A survey in 1878–79 interpreted the Oke-

fenokee's usefulness in terms of water instead of land, investigating the feasibility of a barge canal route from the Mississippi River to the Atlantic. Despite widely held beliefs in the "incalculable benefit" of such a scheme, the Okefenokee canal project never got off the ground.[47] During the 1880s the swamp faded from public conversation, but Okefenokee hinterland boosters continued to push for its development. Major Luther C. Bryan of Thomasville, Georgia, attempted to provoke some action in the Okefenokee when he called for its drainage in 1883:

> Okefenokee, as a land investment, presents a magnitude of speculative and industrial enterprise wholly unknown to the people at large, and suspected only by a few, who, as surveying parties, or adventurous hunters, have lifted the veil of mystery hung around it by tradition, and penetrated its fertile interior. . . . for more than a century Okefenokee remained shrouded in the gloom and mystery of swamp, though enclosing within the miry folds of that forbidding exterior a princely reward for the enterprise and industry that shall boldly take the key nature has deposited in the banks of the St. Mary's at Camp Pinckney, and unlock its agricultural and commercial storehouse. . . . it can be drained. . . . The fertility and agricultural value of the lands, when properly drained, could not for a moment be questioned.[48]

It seems obvious to Bryan that the Okefenokee itself wants to be drained, that the essence of "Okefenokee" is not swamp but agricultural land that will produce a "princely reward." The swamp had deposited a key to "unlock its agricultural and commercial storehouse" in the "banks" of the St. Marys River (it was through this river that drainage advocates hoped to channel the swamp's water), and Bryan urged his entrepreneurial compatriots to take possession of that key and convert the Okefenokee into what it was at the core: useful property.

Promoters heeded Bryan's call and continued to agitate for various development schemes in the Okefenokee, but none came to fruition. A group of hunters from Folkston crossed the swamp from east to west in 1887, but the excursion did not garner much press attention and the hunters obtained no ecological data. By 1889 the Georgia legislature was ready to wash its hands of the "mammoth mystery of Georgia," and various entrepreneurial interests encouraged them to do so. When they put the Okefenokee up for auction that year, government officials and boosters referenced all of the surveys launched between 1850 and 1875 and argued for the drainage and development of all 660 square miles of the Okefenokee's "useless land." In 1890 the Georgia legislature made possible the first large-scale entrepreneurial effort in the Okefenokee – one that was focused on drainage – and finally satiated the social and economic appetites that the swamp surveyors had aroused. As a result, the Oke-fenokee shifted from a site of adventure to a place of development. As they envisioned profits, Okefenokee hinterland entrepreneurs mobilized ecolocal narratives that altered the Okefenokee landscape.

The Okefenokee sale came at a time of industrial frenzy in the Okefeno-kee hinterlands. In 1881 the Waycross and Jacksonville Railroad bridged the St. Marys River, making development of the area more feasible.[49] The same year a Florida real estate entrepreneur organized a drainage com-pany that reclaimed nearly four hundred thousand acres of the Ever-glades lowlands in two years. The company's progress was reported in most of Georgia's and Florida's newspapers.[50] Local businessmen like Dr. Frank C. Folks (son of W. C. Folks and a Georgia state senator) and Benjamin Upton of Charlton County pressured the legislature to sell the Okefenokee for the purposes of drainage and development. Senators Folks and Warren Lott authored a pamphlet in 1889 arguing for the sale in the name of the economic health of southeastern Georgia: "It is our opinion that the drainage of the Okefenokee swamp would prove an in-estimable blessing to all our section, whereas it is now a positive injury." The swamp was no longer merely useless, but a "source of damage and injury" to the economy if it remained inundated. The Okefenokee Land and Drainage Company offered to take these injurious lands off of the Georgia legislature's hands at 12½ cents per acre. The company also pro-posed to contribute five thousand dollars for an initial survey and twenty thousand dollars as a guarantee that they would purchase the entire swamp within a year of the survey.[51]

The debate that ensued over the sale of the Okefenokee Swamp to the Okefenokee Land and Drainage Company reveals the paradoxes inher-ent in entrepreneurial ecolocal ideas. Senator W. G. Cooper pointed out to the *Atlanta Constitution* readership in July 1889 that the gentlemen pro-moting the Okefenokee Land and Drainage Company had argued that Okefenokee land "was of so little or no value that the state would do well to sell it for the price they offer," he wrote. "If it is of so little or no value why do they want it?" he replied. Cooper attributed this paradoxical state-ment of value to the peculiar ecology of the Okefenokee itself: "It is admitted that the Okefenokee swamp is a dismal place. Swamps are always so, but the very causes that make them dismal make them fertile, and the noxious influences yield to engineering skill."[52] Like Floyd and Pendleton, Cooper found swamp fertility to be simultaneously attractive and foreboding. What to do with the Okefenokee was unclear – to invest large amounts of capital based on a vague prediction of future productivity was a substantial risk. Several other legislators agreed with Cooper and accused the Okefenokee Land and Drainage Company directors of trying to cheat the state of Georgia out of revenues. They called for a minimum sale price of twenty-five cents per acre and claimed that a lower price would be unreasonable and unjust.[53]

Promoters, however, dismissed Cooper's criticisms as conservative and unpatriotic and raised their voices to shout for drainage. Frank W. Hall, a state senator from Dahlonega, Georgia, called for Okefenokee reclamation in the name of the swamp's hinterlands: "An important feature of the enterprise is that the draining of the swamp drains the country for miles around and will be of great benefit to the lands."[54] The sale would be lucrative, they argued, and the drainage and cultivation of the Okefenokee's 660 square miles would provide even more revenue for the government and the inhabitants of the Okefenokee hinterlands for years to come. This argument was persuasive to the Georgia legislators, who passed a bill to sell the Okefenokee Swamp in October 1889. However, they did not sell the acreage to the Okefenokee Land and Drainage Company. Instead, they announced that the land would be advertised for sixty days and sold to the highest bidder in a blind auction (each bidder would not know what his competitors had bid). The minimum bid was 12½ cents per acre. The highest bidder would receive the contract to drain and develop the Okefenokee and would be incorporated as "The Suwanee Canal Company."[55]

The sale was advertised in November, but problems with the dissemination of the information pushed the bid deadline to March 14, 1890. The bids already received remained, as the *Atlanta Constitution* reported, "with their seals unbroken, and the millions of dollars that lie buried under the marshy waters of the waste land remain there yet, waiting for the enterprising capitalist to drain the water and extract the dollars from the soil."[56] On the morning of March 14, the bids were opened. A company headed by Frank Coxe, P. M. B. Young, and Captain Henry Jackson was formally declared to be the highest bidder with an offer of 26½ cents per acre. The group was incorporated under the name "The Suwanee Canal Company" and conferred the right and privilege to develop the Okefenokee Swamp as its directors saw fit.[57]

The Suwanee Canal Company board members met on March 18 and accepted the charter, appointing Henry Jackson president and General P. M. B. Young vice president and secretary of the newly minted company. Jackson was a lawyer from Atlanta and Young was a businessman from Cartersville, Georgia. General Frank Coxe, Senator Frank Hall (who had pushed for the sale and whose company was awarded the drainage engineering contract), and Senator Frank C. Folks were also appointed to the board, along with a chemical manufacturing magnate from Philadelphia named Marshall A. Phillips. Phillips had already invested two million dollars in industrial enterprises in the Southeast and was rumored to have bought some of the drained Everglades land as well.[58]

The company's plan was reasonable enough. They would conduct a survey, for as Coxe pointed out to a reporter at the *Atlanta Constitution,* "We don't yet know just what we have purchased, and that must be ascertained before anything else is done." Coxe seemed to have a good idea of the Suwanee Canal Company's intentions in the Okefenokee, however, for he added, "I am a great believer in the resources under the surface of the earth." The survey set off in late May, led by the Everglades surveyor Colonel James M. Kraemer and comprised of Henry Jackson, two civil engineers, one surveyor, two chainmen (including Howell Cobb Jackson, Henry Jackson's nephew and a correspondent for the *Atlanta Journal*), a lumberman, a cook, a driver, and two guides.[59]

The survey team explored the Okefenokee for two months, moving from the southeastern side around the northeastern edge to the western border near Homerville. Although the Suwanee Canal Company board wanted to ascertain what they had purchased, Kraemer's report to the governor confirmed that the purpose of the survey was to "establish that area of the unsurveyed lands within the bounds of the Okefenokee Swamp" so that the Georgia legislature could determine the cost of the entire acreage. Henry Jackson treated the survey as an extended adventure vacation, reporting on the discomforts of camping in the swamp while surveyors and engineers measured and mapped the muck. The survey team ultimately determined that the Okefenokee contained 238,102 acres, and these were conveyed to the Suwanee Canal Company on January 1, 1891, for $63,101.80.[60]

The Suwanee Canal Company's initial goal in the Okefenokee was drainage for agricultural cultivation. The survey had not been meant to establish the feasibility of this goal, for the members of the board believed it to be possible and the civil engineers on the survey did not insist on further evaluation. Jackson and his compatriots were convinced that the machinery of drainage would easily render the Okefenokee an agricultural Eden.[61] While the Suwanee Canal Company first focused on land reclamation, the directors also turned their attention to logging as a profitable extractive industry that could finance the conversion of the Okefenokee from an entangled morass to a bucolic landscape of small farms. However, their early devotion to drainage with the long-term goal of agricultural development, based on a fundamental misjudgment of swamp ecology, ultimately proved fatal to the company's success.

The Suwanee Canal Company board members met in August 1891 and authorized Henry Jackson to hire workers; purchase land, equipment, and supplies; and secure rights-of-way for the canal between the swamp and the St. Marys River. The board also hired the Hall Brothers Engineering firm (owned by Frank Hall, a board member) to plan and carry out the drainage project.[62] The *Atlanta Constitution* raved about the company's drainage plans in an article titled "The Making of a Paradise out of the Home of the Alligator and the Swamp Fox": "If these gentlemen succeed in reclaiming these lands, they will have done greater service to Georgia than all the politicians from the revolution to the present date." Henry Jackson conceived of the project in the same light and spun his capitalist desires as a dedication to public service: "I am free to confess that my ambition is to be one of a number of gentlemen who will do this work for the state of Georgia."[63] Newspaper reporters described the company's drainage efforts as the largest public works project ever undertaken in Georgia and cheered the Okefenokee's conversion from the home of the hooting owl and the grunting alligator to a "busy scene of industry and progress."[64] The scene was indeed busy, for the drainage project began immediately and the southeastern side of the Okefenokee was converted into a meeting point for engineers, laborers, and heavy machinery. Newspaper reporters were fascinated with the image of drainage machinery trolling through "untouched" nature; an article reporting on the Suwanee Canal Company's progress in the *Atlanta Constitution* in 1893 included an illustration of a "dredge at work in the Okefenokee." In the sketch, a large dredge overwhelms the swamp vegetation, and no humans

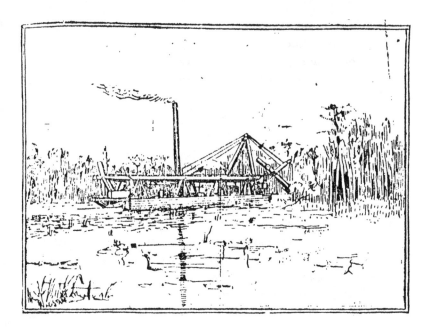

"The Dredge at Work in the Okefenokee," *Atlanta Constitution* (1893), Okefenokee File, Okefenokee Regional Library, Waycross, Georgia.

are present – this picture pits the machine against the garden, and it is abundantly clear which will emerge victorious.[65]

But the work involved in bringing about this hoped for victory was difficult and time consuming. To drain the swamp, engineers focused on the St. Marys River as the primary outlet, although only 10 percent of the Okefenokee's natural drainage moves through that waterway. Neither board members nor engineers considered the Suwannee River, which empties 90 percent of the Okefenokee waters and then meanders toward the Gulf of Mexico, as a viable route. The board of directors probably chose the St. Marys River because, while it forms the border between Georgia and Florida, it would come under Georgia jurisdiction in many cases. The Suwannee River, however, enters Florida about ten miles downriver; any infrastructure resulting from the project would be established in Florida and of no use (or profit) to the state of Georgia or any business incorporated in that state. Instead of using the Suwannee, engineers planned a drainage canal that would extend from the Okefenokee to the confluence of the St. Marys and Cornhouse Creek, where the mean elevation was twenty-five feet – a drop of one hundred feet from the swamp's surface. Board members hoped to use this confluence and the forces of gravity to release the Okefenokee's waters toward the Atlantic. This was the Suwanee Canal Company's first of many mistakes in the pursuit of a productive Okefenokee.

The project moved slowly, worked by five hundred convict laborers who began digging the canal on September 20, 1891. By April 1892 the Suwanee Canal Company executives suggested a more violent method to carve out the drainage canal: "'We are going to put tremendous loads of dynamite all under the earth the balance of the distance of the canal that is yet not cut and will each load with wires and will touch it off with electricity. It will all go off at once with a thundering explosion, tearing away the earth, and instantaneously the gigantic pumps will be throwing water into the canal at a fearful rate, thus giving a very effective washout. The work is something immense and you cannot fancy at all accurately what it is unless you could go and see it with your own eyes.'"[66] The physical violence of this plan – the "thundering explosion" and the "tearing away the earth" – and the heavy industry used to support it seemed to make good on the martial desires of earlier surveyors. The company executives clearly saw themselves, like the surveyors, as masters of a recalcitrant landscape. They also echoed the pioneering desires of Pendleton and Haines and achieved these aspirations by attempting to literally blaze a trail through the Okefenokee. But much of the Suwanee Canal Company's plans remained limited to rhetoric – there is no evidence that this method of canal digging was ever initiated. It is clear from this description, however, that the Suwanee Canal Company was dedicated to the project and invested time, energy, and capital to connect the swamp to the St. Marys River.

The convict laborers succeeded in digging a ditch sixty feet wide and thirty feet deep from the edge of the Okefenokee through the Trail Ridge (a hill of sandy soil about one hundred feet in elevation), but within a year drought followed by heavy rains in the fall eroded the sides of the ditch and they collapsed in December 1892.[67] Engineers had failed to slope the sides of the ditch to anticipate meteorological contingencies. Such miscalculations and inefficiencies continually plagued the outer canal project. Work continued, but it would take more than two more years to complete the ditch.

In the meantime engineers turned their attention to the construction of a canal into the heart of the Okefenokee from the southeastern side. The Hall Brothers' managers abandoned the dynamite plan and brought in hydraulic dredging machines and miners from northern Georgia to dredge a forty-foot-deep ditch from the edge of the Okefenokee into Grand Prairie. By the fall of 1892 the miners had dredged a canal two miles into the swamp.[68] A major accident with the dredging equipment and the collapse of the outer canal in December 1892 suspended work for several months, and during the hiatus the board met to decide what course the company should take the following year.

Some members of the board were alarmed at the rising costs of drainage infrastructure without any foreseeable signs of steady income. But dredgers had discovered a large stand of cypress trees in the swamp's interior, and several board members convinced the others that the economic potential of the Okefenokee was rooted in its cypress tree stands, not in drainage and agriculture. All board members agreed that the canal work would continue, as the loggers would need to raft the timber out of the swamp by that route. They authorized Jackson to purchase and place one sawmill and one shingle mill at Camp Cornelia on the southeastern side and to negotiate with Brooks Brothers to use their railroad for lumber shipment.[69] The Suwanee Canal Company had made its decision. In 1893 board members turned away from the dreams of a reclaimed, agricultural Okefenokee and made the harvesting of timber their priority.

The company's decision was not outlandish given the changing situation of the American lumber industry in the 1890s. Large-scale timber extraction had been underway for decades in the Upper Midwest. But between 1860 and 1880 the forests surrounding the Great Lakes were depleted, and northern timbermen began to gaze covetously at the vast pine and cypress forests of the Okefenokee hinterlands. The Tenth Census Report in 1880 reported that "the country between the Mississippi River and the Rocky mountains, now largely supplied with lumber from Michigan, Wisconsin and Minnesota, must for building materials soon depend upon the more remote pine forests of the Gulf region."[70] Developers began to buy up public lands throughout the Southeast; the Suwanee Canal Company's purchase of the Okefenokee came at the end of this buying bonanza.

Several technological developments made Okefenokee timber extraction a feasible project. The invention of heavy machinery that could enter inundated places and harvest cypress timber was crucial to the logging

of the Okefenokee hinterlands. Railroads were also integral to technological experiments and to the growth of the southeastern lumber industry. The extension of railroad lines into the Okefenokee area during these
decades provided transportation for lumber products; railroad expansion
itself also necessitated timber extraction. Millions of feet of pine ties were
needed to build the thousands of miles of tracks and trestles that traversed
the Southeast.[71] The Suwanee Canal Company's decision to focus on cypress extraction was a sound one. The exigencies of the industry and bad
timing, however, contributed to the company's failure to log the Okefenokee.

Violent storms and hurricanes plagued the Okefenokee hinterlands in
1893. The foul weather seemed a meteorological analogue to the Suwanee
Canal Company's financial woes. A combination of high tariffs, a market
crash, railroad bankruptcies, and declining silver values resulted in a
nationwide depression that year, slowing investment and rendering the
Suwanee Canal Company president Henry Jackson's fund-raising drives
useless. Moreover, while Jackson may have been an enthusiastic New
South booster and a good lawyer, he and his fellow board members knew
very little about the lumber industry. The company had never conducted
a systematic timber cruise or a complete engineering survey; no one employed by the Suwanee Canal Company had ever even explored the western side of the swamp, which contains more stands of cypress than the
eastern side, where the company had focused its efforts. Their dedication
to cypress extraction and refusal to cut and mill longleaf pines meant the
company directors had to construct their own cypress mill; the pine mills
in the area would not convert their machinery to suit the Suwanee Canal
Company's needs. Cash flow became a major problem, and Jackson was
reluctant to borrow more funds or promote further investment in the
project.[72]

Jackson's proposals for timber extraction were not all conservative and
unimaginative, however. He suggested that the company equip one of the
canal dredges with an electric generator and arc lights to enable it to work
twenty-four hours a day. He also urged the board of directors to lease turpentine and pine harvesting privileges on Black Jack and Mitchell's Islands, arguing that these funds alone "will refund to the stockholders
every dollar that has been invested thus far in this property." In addition,
Jackson suggested that the company form a club invested with exclusive
fishing and game hunting rights in the Okefenokee. All members of the

sport club would be required to hold a certain amount of Suwanee Canal Company stock. Jackson also allowed the Suwanee superintendent, S. T. Walker, to make purchases of an overhead Lidgerwood steam skidder (a machine that pulled logs from a central point in the forest to a loading dock) and a pullboat (a skidder mounted on a boat) in 1894 and 1895 in an effort to take advantage of new cypress logging technologies and increase production.[73] As he made these suggestions and investments, Jackson continued to frame the Suwanee Canal Company's projects as public works: "We are doing more for the development of this part of Georgia than is generally supposed. When we once get down to work our prosperity will affect the whole state, and especially southern Georgia."[74]

But Jackson's vision came to naught. Problems proliferated. In March 1895 Superintendent Walker reported to the stockholders that work had been suspended on the Trail Ridge canal because, once again, the soft sand banks had collapsed during an unusually rainy winter. After hearing this update, Jackson confessed, "I am very much disappointed in the time that has been consumed developing this property. . . . the canal outside of the swamp cost considerably more than the estimate of the engineers." He was determined, however, to see the project through. The "wilderness" had been opened, he wrote, and man had proven himself the master of nature: "the center of the Okefenokee swamp is illuminated night after night with electric lights." Echoing the surveyors of the 1870s, Jackson pronounced, "I am enlisted for the war, and I propose to go on to final victory."[75] The company's use of machinery was profitable for a time, but the wear and tear on the dredges and the skidders resulted in frequent breaks and time lost repairing them. As a reporter for the *Savannah Morning News* pointed out in the summer of 1895, "the machinery is all of such ponderous proportions and so unlike any machinery used elsewhere in the South that it is difficult to repair when any part is broken. Nearly all the men employed on the dredges are machinists."[76]

Machinery problems dovetailed with transportation difficulties. The Suwanee Canal Company had built a railroad line to connect the sawmill at Camp Cornelia with the main line at Folkston but then could not run it because of the high freight rates at the Folkston terminus. Efforts to build a trunk line to join the turpentine transportation system of Brooks Brothers were unsuccessful. The company ultimately built another railroad line to a dock on the Satilla River, twenty-two miles to the northeast, and floated lumber from the Satilla dock down to the coastal Georgia city of

Brunswick.[77] The burden of high transportation costs reduced any profits from timber sales the company might have earned. Sales were meager from the beginning due to a depressed market for cypress (despite newspaper boosters' predictions), a recession in the bond market, and the lack of a sales or marketing manager who could have promoted the company's products.

By 1895 the Suwanee Canal Company had experienced both technological triumph and failure in the Okefenokee, and Henry Jackson's death that year sent the company into a downward spiral. The board of directors seemed lost without Jackson's confident if misguided direction. At their annual stockholders meeting in March 1896, they wrote to their investors, "By the sudden death of the late President, the Company was confronted with the situation of laborers' and material men's claims due and falling due, with no money in the treasury, no provision for their payment, and no one familiar with the operations of the Company or with the plans of our late President." The company's debt load was assessed at $84,000 and the value of company buildings, machinery, and timber at $146,010.[78] Henry Jackson's father, General Henry Jackson, took over as president and employed a Brunswick lawyer named F. D. Aiken to handle the company's lumber marketing, but his presence created conflict and confusion among company officials. Profits for the year hovered at around $2,000. A destructive hurricane that hit the Okefenokee hinterlands in September 1896, the inability of engineers to connect the two parts of the canal, and a tendency of the board to conduct superficial studies of the property instead of promoting sales, hiring salesmen, or investigating potential markets resulted in the Suwanee Canal Company's descent into receivership in April 1897.[79]

Between April 1897 and March 1899, timber extraction in the Okefenokee slowed to a trickle and then stopped. The members of the Jackson family established the Okefenokee Trust and purchased the swamplands for $130,000 and all other Suwanee Canal Company property (machinery, mills, and cut lumber) for $130,900.[80] Several suits were brought against the company, and the Okefenokee Trust sold its remaining timber to pay off its creditors. Between March 1899 and April 1901, entrepreneurs abandoned the Okefenokee.

The environmental toll of these initial developmental projects was high. Boats and buildings rusted and sank into the swamp, and the company left several millions of feet of cypress deadened and uncut; these trees collapsed and became fire hazards. Other trees suffered great gashes made by a "sharp pointed steel plow" that cut its way through trees and stumps as it forced logs through the swamp muck.[81] Although the canal became choked with peat and vines soon after the dredges and pullboats stopped their work, the channel was so wide and so deep that it has remained a distinctive feature of the Okefenokee landscape. But most of the other marks made by the Suwanee Canal Company rapidly disappeared into the muck.

Reasons for the company's failure in the Okefenokee are multiple. The Jacksons' initial obsession with the drainage project, inexperience with industrial logging techniques, inadequate executive leadership and management, poor financing, inept marketing, and climatological bad luck were major factors. The most important reason for the Suwanee Canal Company's inability to either drain or develop the Okefenokee between 1891 and 1897, however, was the management's misjudgment of the swamp's hydrology. Ecolocal ideas about development were shaped by the overly confident assumption that the Okefenokee could and would be drained. But the company failed to map and cruise the swamp carefully, and Jackson subsequently based his plans and policy decisions on superficial surveyor observations and on conversations with inexperienced drainage engineers. Also, the company's choice to locate operations on the southeastern side of the swamp with an eye toward drainage and agricultural development was disastrous. The southeastern side of the Okefenokee is dominated by small hammocks and prairies two feet deep in water, while the western side is populated by dense cypress stands – the company was forced to tow the timber between ten and thirteen miles through the swamp canal to reach the cypress mill at Camp Cornelia. In addition, the executives employed convict labor and miners from northern Georgia, two groups of laborers with little experience working in swamp ecosystems. Jackson and the other directors of the Suwanee Canal Company board had claimed to be local producers of civic pride and prosperity. But these self-proclaimed insiders remained outsiders in the Okefenokee. Due to their lack of ecological and topographical knowledge, the Suwanee Canal Company directors failed to realize their entrepreneurial dreams in the Okefenokee Swamp.

The Suwanee Canal Company's misunderstanding of the Okefenokee's peculiar ecologies and their subsequent failures have become the stuff of legend in the Okefenokee hinterlands. Okefenokee locals refer to the company's efforts as "Jackson's Folly" and gleefully recount an apocryphal tale of the triumph of nature over capitalism. When the local historian Alexander McQueen was researching the initial drainage attempt in the Okefenokee during the 1920s, he sought out the "real" reason for the Suwanee Canal Company's inability to drain the swamp:

> I remarked one day "that I would certainly like to know the real reason for the abandonment of this drainage project," and an old negro overheard the remark and replied, "Boss, I can certainly tell you." I told him to "shoot," and he began by telling me that he was the cook on the first dredge boat and cooked for the steam shovel crew, and that he was "right there and knew." His explanation was that when the canal had been dug for about 8 miles into the swamp the "water started to run back the other way. Instead of towards the St. Marys River it wanted to run back clear through the Swamp to the Suwannee River." . . . Captain Jackson's engineer must have slipped a cog, for, quoted the old negro again, "the further we went into the Swamp the faster the water run the other way," and that is the way it runs today.[82]

This tale has become part of the local history of the Okefenokee hinterlands as told by its inhabitants. It involves the inversion of power that the Okefenokee and other swamps tend to create: the steam shovel crew knows better than Jackson's engineer, the black cook knows more than the white laborers, the Okefenokee water "wants" to run back through the swamp to the other side instead of "depositing its key" in the "bank" of the St. Marys. Most subsequent explanations of the company's failure cite this engineering mistake as the primary cause. In 1932 a reporter for the *Savannah Morning News* argued that the canal "stands as a monument to the mistake of engineers who did not know their business, or if they did, made a colossal blunder in their design of the canal."[83] The story may be a myth, but it was clear that the company engineers did make a "colossal blunder" by declining to investigate the hydraulic nature of the Okefenokee.

The Suwanee Canal Company directors thought they would unearth much in the Okefenokee: profit, social prestige, and status as civic philanthropists. They had treated the swamp, however, as if it were "useless land" that could be easily converted to productive soil. This misapprehension, borne out of entrepreneurial ecolocal ideas, was the root of the Suwanee Canal Company's failure in the Okefenokee Swamp.

The Suwanee Canal Company's mistakes benefited the developers who bought the swamp from the Okefenokee Trust for $175,000 in April

1901 – the Hebard family of Philadelphia. The Hebards had made their fortune harvesting white pine from northern forests, and in the 1890s their lumber mills in upper Michigan on Lake Superior started to slow down. The family, in search of profits, looked southward to the Okefenokee hinterlands just as the Suwanee Canal Company was placed in receivership.[84] After the establishment of the Okefenokee Trust in 1897, a local real estate developer named R. R. Hopkins acquired an option on a large part of the swamp and secured the land from the Jackson estate. In turn, he sold the option to Charles Hebard and his children. The Hebards bought the swamp from the Okefenokee Trust in 1901 and purchased additional lands in and around the Okefenokee in 1902.[85]

The Hebards' logging operations in the Okefenokee were successful for several reasons, but mostly because the management made knowledge of the Okefenokee's interior paramount in their project. They were fully invested in the ecolocal beliefs regarding swamp development, but they abandoned the agricultural dream to which so many inhabitants had clung. They thus shaped a new entrepreneurial narrative that framed the Okefenokee, not as a landscape to be tilled but as a natural resource to be tapped.

Timber operations had been underway in the Okefenokee hinterlands since the eighteenth century, but before the invention and spread of railroad technologies, extraction had been limited to acreages along southeastern rivers. Between 1732 and 1860 loggers dragged trees to the banks of the Savannah, the Altamaha, the Satilla, and the St. Marys rivers, then tied them together and rafted them to coastal cities for milling. Archibald Clark's sawmill near the mouth of Spanish Creek was a large enough operation that the British attempted to destroy it during the War of 1812; lumbermen from Maine built a steam sawmill on the Satilla River at Burnt Fort in 1838. By the 1840s Edwin R. Albertie was operating a steam mill on the St. Marys River near the southeastern margins of the Okefenokee.[86]

These antebellum operations were small scale; technologies had not yet been developed that would allow loggers to advance deep into lowland forests. Charles Lanman, a writer who traveled the Okefenokee hinterlands in the early 1850s, noted that "the shores of [the St. Johns] are as wild as they were centuries ago . . . the steam sawmills which appear in view, depart more like visions than realities." But Lanman observed at least twenty steam mills along the river, most of them run by northerners "thinking more of dollars than of nature and the picturesque."[87] Increased interest on the part of northern lumber kings, expanding railroad lines, and technological advances changed this landscape of small, individual-run sawmills and rafted logs into an industrial landscape of huge pine and cypress mills, logging railroads, and clear-cut forests. The Hebard family bought into the Okefenokee at just the right moment. The first two decades of the twentieth century were the boom years of logging in the Okefenokee hinterlands.

The first move the Hebards made after their purchase was to send a team on an extended survey and timber cruise of the Okefenokee. They chose John M. Hopkins, a young lawyer from Darien, Georgia, and the nephew of R. R. Hopkins (the real estate developer who had led the Hebards to the Okefenokee) to conduct the cruise. While he was not a trained surveyor, John Hopkins had experience measuring trees for bark thickness, taper, and lengths as part of a forestry project in the 1880s and 1890s. The Hebards persuaded him to leave his law office for a month in 1901 "to take a small crew and run a line through the swamp from East to West and make exact notes of what was found and where." After his experiences that first month, "coupled with that call of the woods," Hopkins readily agreed to another month with the survey. He ultimately spent two years in the Okefenokee in month-long stints, leaving the swamp for only a few days between forays to procure more provisions for his crew.[88]

Much like their predecessors, the Hopkins survey team encountered difficulties due to the swamp ecology. At first they attempted to measure the watery prairies on the eastern side from two small boats. They soon gave it up and slogged through the water, wearing rubber boots that in Hopkins's estimation were "worse than nothing." Sometimes, he reported, the forward chainman "showed but little above the water." The weather, particularly in the winter months, was brutal. Prosper Roberts, a French Canadian logger hired by the Hebards, told Hopkins with Twain-like wit that he "had never come so near freezing to death as during the night on a tussock in Okefenokee." The survey was the kind of trailblazing adventure that earlier surveyors had desired. The logger Liston Elkins remarked later on some of Hopkins's experiences, "well, Daniel Boone or the pioneers that went west never had any more excitement than that guy had in the Okefenokee Swamp. But he took it in stride."[89]

Over two years the team experienced many personnel changes when chainmen accepted other jobs or contracted illnesses caused by exposure. At one point, desperate for chainmen, Hopkins and Sam Mizell (a local guide) went out and recruited some Swampers – men who lived in the Okefenokee and on its immediate edges and made their living from a diverse array of modes of production. The result was less than ideal: "Sam brought in a man named Jim Drawdy who had knifed Ransom Steedley, thought he had killed him and that no one would know who did it. Ransom didn't die, and thereafter, Drawdy, fearing one of the Steedleys would 'get' him, went nowhere without his shotgun. The man I brought in was John Steedley, brother of Ransom and a powerful chap of about 190 pounds. Sam saw us coming, came out to stop us and tell me that Drawdy was in my tent with his shotgun. Steedley was unarmed. We had a 'bull by the horns'; it might be better to hold on than turn loose. We needed chainmen."[90] Hopkins disarmed Drawdy and forced the two men to work together on the survey because he needed chainmen and he did not care what kind of feuds were boiling in the Swamper community. This incident exemplifies Hopkins's management style as both the leader of the survey and as the future superintendent of the Hebard Lumber Company's operations in the Okefenokee: personal prejudices and tensions were subservient to the needs of the company, and conflicts of any kind were averted by any means necessary.

When Hopkins's survey team encountered resistance from local residents in the course of the 1901–3 timber cruises, he dealt with this threat in a manner true to his character and philosophy – he did not directly confront locals but made his point through other means. During the second year of the cruise, he noted that "an engineer running lot lines and camping [at Mixon's Ferry] shortly before I arrived had rifle bullet holes shot through the top of his tent one night." His survey was not bothered in this way, he wrote, probably due to the fact that "at that time we were somewhat proficient with rifle or revolver and when visited by some of the natives on Sunday gave some exhibitions, by request of one of my crew." Hopkins's demonstration of his and other surveyors' shooting skills signaled to any troublemakers that the team would give as good as it got. This display of prowess, in his opinion, "may have been partly responsible for being let alone."[91] Hopkins's management style and skills, in addition to his dedication to the fulfillment of the Hebards' desire for profit in the Okefenokee, contributed to the Hebard Lumber Company's success.

Beginning in 1901 and over the course of two years, the team measured out each acre, platted it, and then counted the trees within it. They compiled these acre plats and drew up a detailed map of the swamp and all of its timber reserves. The Hebards were eager to begin culling trees from the Okefenokee Swamp, but the death of the family patriarch (Charles Sr.) in 1903 put all plans for its development on hold. The Hebard sons, Charles and Daniel, knew that they had found an excellent manager in Hopkins, however, so while their father's estate was sorted out, they sent him to their Michigan mills on Lake Superior to learn more about the lumber business and to observe new technologies in industrial logging.[92]

In 1904 Charles and Daniel Hebard approved the Okefenokee project and incorporated the Hebard Lumber Company, establishing Thomasville, Georgia, as their base of operations. But the brothers took no action in the Okefenokee until a West Virginia lumber baron named Colonel J. W. Oakford suggested to them that they form a cypress-harvesting company together as a subsidiary of the Hebard Lumber Company. Cypress was in great demand as a building material due to its strength, elasticity, and resistance to water. The natural range of cypress trees – bald cypress and pond cypress – lies in the Atlantic and Gulf Coastal Plains. The conditions in these areas (deep, fine, sandy soils, with abundant quantities of water), as Robert Izlar has pointed out, "are favorable for the plant to gain a dominant position on its site." J. D. Browne, in *Sylva Americana* (1833), noted that "In the swamps of the southern states and the Floridas, on whose deep, miry soil a new layer of vegetable mould is every year deposited by floods, the cypress attains its utmost development." The Okefenokee's western side, which is dominated by large soil islands and wide waterways, is an ideal site for cypress growth, and the Hebards' timber cruise in 1901–3 revealed abundant cypress groves in this area.[93]

After running additional surveys, Oakford and the Hebards incorporated the Hebard Cypress Company in 1909, and the Hebard Lumber Company leased it 219,500 acres in the Okefenokee. Waycross and Hebardville were selected as sites for lumber mills, and the Hebard Cypress Company worked out a deal for access to two major railroad lines that connected these cities to larger markets on the Atlantic coast. Hopkins was appointed superintendent and authorized to plan and build a cypress mill, a railroad line from Waycross to the logging camps on the southwestern side of the Okefenokee, and another line to camp on the northwest side.[94]

Hopkins was also authorized to hire laborers, and he set about recruiting "some of the best cypress logging men in the business" (some from Michigan and some from Florida), local loggers, and eager young men from southern Georgia. Between 1909 and 1927 the company employed an average of three hundred men a year; half were white and half were black. At one point, twenty-five Finnish men worked two skidder crews. The pay rates, though low, were competitive with those in both northern logging outfits and other local businesses: loggers worked six days a week, twelve hours a day, and earned a daily wage of $1.75 to $2.00; skilled workers (operators, skidders, track laymen, and locomotive engineers) earned $5.00 per day before company town charges were taken out. As Monetta Hayes Hewett, the secretary of the Hebard Cypress Company, observed, "at the end of the week, they had so much taken out for doctor, so much taken out of their pay for rent, and they got the rest of it which wasn't much at the time. But enough to live on." The Hebard logger Liston Elkins considered the Hebard Lumber Company wages to be more than fair and working conditions to be far better than those of local turpentine operations: "that was the first lumber operation, probably in this country, where the common laborer got a break. Most of them were peons. . . . The Hebard Lumber Company redeemed a lot of those folks from slavery."[95]

Hopkins dealt with company laborers fairly and, in some cases, protected them from the law. During the influenza epidemic in 1919, Hopkins discovered that many Hebard workers were using whiskey as a "preventative." The camp's logging superintendent was exasperated because so many laborers had hangovers or were absent from work, particularly on Mondays. During the hunt for the whiskey source on Billy's Island (a camp town in the middle of the Okefenokee), Hopkins and the camp superintendent "found ten little stills in one day. We did not object to the distilling or securing in any other way a sufficient quantity of alcoholic beverages for medicinal purposes or a reasonable amount for social purposes, but did object to its production in abundance that would result in the conversion of a legitimate logging operation into an illicit distilling enterprise. We took steps that immediately reduced production to a quantity that, to our minds, was reasonable, and with satisfactory results."[96] Hopkins was careful to give his workers leeway but acted ultimately to protect the interests of the Hebard Lumber Company. He wanted his employees to be "reasonably happy" and to feel like they had lives and activities outside of work, but he did not want the authorities to shut down the Billy's Island operation because of illegal moonshine production. His compromise gave the workers what they needed and provided for the well-being of the company; his actions clearly satisfied both labor and management.

Both Hopkins and the company often went to great lengths to ensure that their workers were happy and protected. In one instance, the company provided lawyers for laborers arrested for gambling: "Eight of our negro laborers were playing a little five cent game of cards and a 'spotter' secured the names and they were later arrested for gambling. The only witness the State had, knew the eight names but knew no one individually, and when placed on the stand could not identify any one of them, so they went back to work without paying a fine. They were good workers and we had our lawyers look out for them." The Hebard Lumber Company was a powerful business interest in the Okefenokee hinterlands. The family threw the weight of wealth and social status behind their workers; they even arranged to make some of their loggers deputies so that they could be of service to the sheriff and keep order in the camps while providing the company with an inside track on the actions of local police forces.[97]

The company also provided living spaces for workers that were more permanent than the boomtown shacks that often proliferated adjacent to logging operations. Between 1909 and 1917 the Hebard Cypress Company housed its workers in camps located along rail lines and within an easy distance of Homerville, Waycross, and Folkston. In 1917 the Hebards told Hopkins to plan and build a permanent town on Billy's Island, at the end of the Pocket in the northwestern part of the swamp. The company had leased the island to the Twin Tree Lumber Company in 1915, and this operation logged pine timber there for two years, clearing the land for a town large enough to support six hundred inhabitants.[98] In local newspapers, the Hebards were credited with bringing "the world" to the swamp: "In the middle of the east coast's most primitive area, there sprang up a movie house, a hotel, a church, a school and other bastions of civilization." The town also boasted a sawmill, a general store, a machine shop, cafés, a blacksmith, an electric light plant, waterworks, a town garden, and a baseball diamond.[99] The streets were laid out in a grid, and company workers built forty-nine permanent private residences on the island. Billy's Island was a work site, a neighborhood, and an emblem of technology's impact on nature. It also became a tourist site, luring newspaper editors, travelers, and Boy Scouts. The island's amenities amazed visitors. "They just made [a town] in the heart of this fresh water swamp," one journalist wrote in 1924. "A more beautiful spot will be hard to find."[100]

Billy's Island was not simply an idyllic community on the edge of the wilderness, however. Workers had little control over the prices of housing, entertainment, and consumer goods. Deductions in pay to cover rent, medical bills, and company store debts left them with little extra cash. Also, the town, like many other company towns established during the early twentieth century, was segregated racially. Black workers lived on the northeast side of the garden, while white workers lived on the southeastern side. Churches and schools on the island were segregated as well. Also, the Hebards used predictably paternalistic devices such as housing, stores, schools, and social events to control their workers and create a stable and loyal workforce. However, Billy's Island workers of both races clearly acted to create their own lives within the company context. Liston Elkins, a former logger, noted that timber workers hunted and trapped during the winter, and some workers even acquired property along the edges of the Okefenokee: "even those people who worked the logging crews, that worked on the railroad that ran in there, and so forth, had their own little holdings around the fringe of the swamp."[101]

The flexibility with which the Hebards and their managers responded to these landholdings, moonshine stills, and card games reveals their desire to manage their men in the most humane and the most efficient manner possible. The loggers were usually appreciative of the company's policies and attitudes. Elkins observed that many workers had friendly feelings for management. "I give Dan Hebard a lot of credit for having established this spirit of cooperation around the swamp," he said.[102] The Hebards ultimately made a two-million-dollar investment in their Okefenokee interests and earned more than three million dollars in profits. They spent money on thorough surveys, competitive wages for labor and management, and lawyers to protect workers and their own interests. They also spent their funds on railroad infrastructure and industrial logging machinery, because they were not interested in the drainage or the agricultural prospects of the Okefenokee. They were invested only in logging.

Harvesting timber was not an easy proposition, however, even with the advanced technologies of the early twentieth century. As Jeffrey Drobney has argued, logging "is pre-eminently and fundamentally a problem of transportation." Hauling logs by animal and manpower over the sandy roads of the Okefenokee hinterlands was slow, intensive, and expensive. Rivers presented similar challenges; the unpredictability of droughts and freshets made log rafting down rivers a dangerous task. The road and river era of transportation in Georgia passed into the railroad era at the turn of the century, and the Hebard Lumber Company was one of many lumber companies to turn to railroads to solve their transportation problems. In the 1910s the Hebards developed systems of privately operated secondary railroads called "mudlines," which traversed parts of the Okefenokee and connected to the area's main lines several miles away. Mudline roadbeds, bridges, and tracks were not meant to be permanent; once the company clear-cut an area serviced by a mudline, workers would tear up the tracks, pilings, and trestles and reassemble the line abutting a swamp tract primed for cutting.[103]

Before they constructed the railroads, however, lumber companies needed to scout locations and secure rights of way. Only one Okefenokee resident resisted the Hebard Lumber Company's request – a man named Gill who operated a turpentine business on the western side of the swamp. Hopkins needed access to only one of Gill's four lots, but the landowner demanded that the company haul all of his products gratis during the life of the road in exchange for right of way. Hopkins decided to investigate Gill's deeds and soon discovered that his lease was predated by the death of the owner. The superintendent then went directly to the deceased owner's heirs (taking a notary public and blank deeds with him) and obtained the right of way. According to Hopkins, Gill "was the only party we ran into who was inclined to be nasty, and we heard no more from him."[104]

Once Hopkins secured the rights of way, construction of the Okefenokee railroad system began. During his years traveling around the United States observing logging operations, Hopkins had seen the mudlines (also called "spur lines") that cypress loggers in Louisiana and pine loggers in the marshes of Minnesota and Wisconsin had installed. But he knew from his two-year mud cruise that the Okefenokee "is different from any swamps we visited where logging by rail was being done, and we learned that some methods of road construction that were satisfactory in many swamps were not desirable for Okefenokee." Therefore, Hopkins first tried "cribbing" mudline tracks. This kind of road building necessitated "laying crosswise all the trees and brush cut in clearing the right of way and over this placed stringers, hewed two sides, then the crossties, then the rails." The cribbed road looked fine, according to Hopkins, but "the more we used it the worse it got and gave lots of troubles." Trains with full loads of logs were so heavy that they pushed the black gum or bay logs at the base of the track deep into the muck. And because much of the soil around and in the Okefenokee was sandy and other parts were mucky, some extensions of the track could sink while others seemed to float on the surface. This situation made for an undulating and perilous ride. The loggers hauled carloads of wood chips to fill in troublesome places along the track, but this tactic rarely helped: "after a few trains of logs passed over it the bottom-most chips could be seen rising to the surface of the muck twenty or more feet from the road bed."[105] Cribbed lines were meant to be temporary, but Hopkins decided that they were too dangerous – for workers and for trains.

After the Hebard Lumber Company's troublesome and time-consuming experiments with cribbed track, Hopkins decided that "the practical logging railroad in Okefenokee is one on piling." Several mudlines and the main line tracks, chartered as the Waycross and Southern Railroad in 1909–10 and first operated in 1912, were built on cypress and pine pilings, which loggers sank into the muck until the end of the piling struck solid earth. Each piling was fifteen to thirty feet long and rose up at least one to two meters above the surface of the swamp, in order to keep the train from becoming waterlogged during the rainy months.[106]

Pile roads required less maintenance than cribbed lines, but problems persisted. Occasionally, fire destroyed some pilings; they burned underground and were extremely difficult to extinguish. Also, swamp muck was a continually unpredictable force of nature. One night, while loggers were constructing a branch line, the foreman called Hopkins to say, "A 20 foot pile had gone down flush with the mud surface first time the hammer was dropped on it; that a piece of ⅝ round iron was driven part way into it and another pile placed on that, and the second pile went flush with the mud at the first blow with the hammer, that a third pile was tried with the same result, and the crew wanted to know what to do." Hopkins responded to the foreman with his usual humor and practicality. He told him, "we would not try to learn how many piles could be lost in the hole but to have the crew crib for two or three hundred feet then try the pile driver again." The avoidance tactic worked, and neither Hopkins nor his crew ever ran into another seemingly bottomless hole. Once the track was built, workers maintained it constantly; the line was always in danger of flooding during excessive rains, and piles would shift unaccountably. Resultant train accidents were not that frequent, but several loggers lost their lives when engines and cars derailed and giant logs spilled out over the tracks. Railroad work was often hazardous, but Hopkins noted that for the number of men engaged in such work, "there were comparatively few fatal accidents."[107]

The Hebards' willingness to invest in railroad logging despite structural difficulties was one of the reasons for their success in developing the Okefenokee. They did not attempt to transport logs by canal as the Suwanee Canal Company had done, and the result was an efficient, cost-effective form of transportation that helped the Hebard Lumber Company fill its mill quota of forty carloads of logs a day. The Waycross and Southern Railroad was the originating railroad for all cypress and pine shipments out of the Okefenokee, and so it was entitled, "under the law at that time, to receive fifty percent of the freight, regardless of how many roads it traveled over or where it went. This was a distinct value for the Hebard Company."[108] The Hebards were also willing to invest in the new technologies of industrial logging, technologies that the Suwanee Canal Company managers were just beginning to discover at the end of their tenure in the swamp.

In addition to using up-to-date extractive machinery, the Hebards had streamlined the harvesting process during their years in the Michigan pine forests, and as they adapted to the demands of cypress logging, they demonstrated the positive impact of good planning. The first step of the process was a cruise: an engineer or surveyor would enter the swamp looking for stands of merchantable timber. When he found a stand, the scout would survey out a "skidder set" – a basic logging unit of 185 meters square.[109] Then a guide (usually culled from the Swamper population) would blaze a trail through the swamp to the stand and a cruiser would follow, tallying the timber. Because green cypress logs would sink in the mill log pond, cruisers would then cut a four-inch line into the bark completely around the trunk, initiating a process called "girdling." This cut drained the sap and interfered with carbohydrate transfer, effectively killing the tree over the course of several months. The guide and the cruiser would then leave by the trail, throwing bushes along it to mark mucky spots or quagmires.[110]

About a year later the skidder crews (made up of twelve to eighteen men) would follow the trail and use an overhead skidder, a new form of swamp logging technology, to cut and haul the cypress. Two sawyers used crosscut saws (also called "gator tails") and axes to cut all trees more than one foot in diameter at breast height. The loggers would choose a tree at least fifty-six feet tall near the middle of the set. If the tree was taller than fifty-six feet, a logger would climb it and cut off the top at that height. The loggers then ran cables from the top of this "spar tree" to the trees at the edges of the set. A trolley ran along the cables and the men attached logs to it, by way of a device called a "choker." Through the power of an over-head skidder, which was steam operated, the trolley would pick up the logs and transport them back to the mudline. Loaders would then detach them from the trolleys, load them onto flatbed railcars, and secure them for transportation to the mill. One observer of the process was amazed at what he saw and what he heard: "You could hear them from several miles – that noise going over the trees."[111]

This extraction process was extremely complicated, highly mecha-nized, and dangerous. Cypress harvesting also caused some unique prob-lems that the Hebards had not encountered in Michigan. Girdling the cypress trees was necessary for milling, but the timing was delicate and the risk of insect infestation was always present. If the cypress trees were deadened too far in advance, the sap dried too early and the trees were vulnerable to infestations of pinworms. These worms would attack the tree through the cut and bore small holes through the dried sap, causing wood degradation and decreasing the quality of the lumber produced out of that particular tree. There was no way to fight the pinworm except through scrupulous scheduling. Hopkins noted in frustration, "from our experience and all the information I had gathered from other mills my conclusion was that each swamp had its own peculiarities, each cypress its own individuality and each pin worm its own damn pin head."[112] The size of some of the Okefenokee cypress trees also made logging more dif-ficult for the company. The vast majority of the Okefenokee's cypress stands were first growth – more than three hundred years old and im-mensely tall. Loggers were forced to dynamite some massive trees before they could lock them onto the skidder or fit them into the mill.[113]

Industrial logging was efficient, but working around falling trees and heavy machinery was dangerous for workers, and more loggers lost limbs or their lives in the cypress stands than on mudline tracks in the Oke-fenokee. The men who worked on skidder crews, according to Liston Elkins, were rugged: "In cold weather there would be a thin skim of ice on [the surface of the swamp], but that didn't bother them. . . . Those folks were hardy. I just wish we had some more like them." Some timber work-ers were more daring than others. The Hebard timber worker Will Cox knew one skidder crew member named "Geech" who would "top out the spar tree at the required sixty feet, then stand on his head at the top." But strength and daring were often no match for a falling tree or defects in equipment. One worker was injured when the rigging chain at the top of the spar tree in a cypress set broke and the block at the top of the tree fell off and hit him.[114] Despite these dangers, Hebard Company managers and foremen considered that the advantages of industrial logging far outweighed the risks.

The Hebard Lumber/Cypress Company ultimately constructed more than 250 miles of temporary logging railroads throughout the Okefenokee, and between 1909 and 1927 the company cut 425 million board feet of cypress (enough to build forty-two thousand homes) and tens of thousands of railroad cross-ties. The company's Hebardville Mill at its peak was said to have been the largest cypress mill in the world.[115] The company owners and managers succeeded in their quest for profit in the Okefenokee for several reasons. First, the Hebard family possessed years of lumbering experience, initially in the forests of Pennsylvania and then in the upper Midwest. Second, while they embraced ecolocal narratives that framed the Okefenokee as natural resource, the Hebards applied their experience and focused their attention on cypress harvesting instead of drainage and agriculture. Third, the company hired capable managers like John Hopkins, who demonstrated a flexible management style. Fourth, they cultivated a stable and loyal workforce through the establishment of permanent company towns and competitive wages.

Fifth, the company leased out the lands they were not using, in order to earn money from the parts of the Okefenokee they could not manage themselves. After the company began its operations in 1909, it leased its pine tracts to the Twin Tree Lumber Company and at least seven other large lumber companies, including the gigantic Americus Manufacturing Company, which harvested pine and naval stores out of the Okefenokee. These companies built as many miles of railroad and cut as many board feet of timber as the Hebards, but most concentrated on the pine stands within the swamp and on its edges.[116] Sixth, the Hebard Lumber Company invested in industrial logging railroads and technologies like the overhead skidder in order to make operations more efficient and productive. The Hebards made a long-term commitment to the development of the Okefenokee. Unlike Henry Jackson, they did not treat the project as a hobby but as an investment. Seventh, part of the credit for their success should also go to the surveyors who traversed the swamp from 1850 to

1880 and to Jackson and the Suwanee Canal Company. Without their experiences and mistakes to refer to, the Hebard Lumber Company would
not have been so well-informed about the nature of the Okefenokee. Nor
would they have been able to buy it. The Hebards were the beneficiaries
of, as Chris Trowell has put it, "lessons learned expensively."[117]

Last, and most important, the Hebard Lumber Company planned its
operations well and took the time to familiarize managers with Okefenokee ecology. They conducted two thorough inventories of the swamp's
timber and mapped its interior before making any location or production
decisions. The company also employed geologists and soil scientists to
survey for mineral and soil productivity levels. This preparation and thorough knowledge of the Okefenokee's geology and hydrology resulted in
the decision to place the base of operations on the western side of the
swamp, where cypress timber was most plentiful and the route into the
swamp (through the Pocket) was efficient. Familiarity with the swamp's peculiar ecology meant financial success for the Hebard Lumber Company.

But the Hebards' success in developing the Okefenokee cypress population was not long lived. In 1921 the nation experienced its first postwar
depression in the lumber market, and in 1926 the housing industry collapsed and the demand for cypress plummeted. The Hebards moved
their operations to the north side of the swamp and logged there for another year, but closed down their mills in 1927 and ceased all operations
in 1928.[118] While local families continued to cull their wood from the
Okefenokee, industrial timber corporations retreated, leaving pilings,
crib roads, and hundreds of acres of cypress stumps as reminders of their
entrepreneurial presence in the swamp.

The Hebards, working from an ecolocal conviction that the swamp was
a site of resource extraction, cut as much timber as they could in the Okefenokee. But the swamp's ecology ultimately proved too overwhelming
even for them. As the logger Liston Elkins noted, "They cut the timber
which was profitable to reach with an expensive operation. When they
reached the point where the profit on their operation reached a balancing
point and they saw it was going to cost them more to produce it (transport
it out of the swamp and process it here in Waycross) than they could sell
it for, well, they stopped."[119] The Hebard Lumber Company was not able
to clear-cut the Okefenokee; the historian Robert Izlar estimates that only
40 to 60 percent of the swamp's trees (pine and cypress) were harvested.
Due to the difficulties that the unstable peat islands, inundated soils, and

entangled underbrush (particularly on the east side of the swamp) posed, the Hebard Lumber Company was not able to continue its development of the swamp after 1927. Even if the Hebards had wanted to practice forestry management in their cutover lands, the company would not have been able to do so. Cypress trees, unlike loblolly pines, were not easily regenerated in abandoned lands. These trees, desired for their resistance to rot and most insects, are slow growers. The 450 million board feet the Hebard Lumber Company had cut in the Okefenokee between 1909 and 1927 will take hundreds of years to grow back to their early-twentieth-century heights.

Surveyors, drainage companies, and timber corporations entered "Georgia's pet swamp" between 1850 and 1927 and shaped an ecolocal narrative of development in the Okefenokee hinterlands. New South adventurers' expeditions into the swamp did bring them public acclaim, but they contributed little to an ecological understanding of the Okefenokee. This lack of knowledge hamstrung the efforts of the Suwanee Canal Company; its lack of interest in devoting funds to accurate surveys resulted in bankruptcy. The Hebard Lumber Company gained from the mistakes of its predecessor, however, and thorough timber surveys served the Hebards well in running a successful extractive operation. All of these developers saw in the Okefenokee a place that could make their hopes of an El Dorado come to pass. But their limited entrepreneurial ecolocal beliefs, in addition to the exigencies of the cypress market, the Okefenokee's difficult ecology, and the inability of cypress trees to regenerate quickly, meant that even the Hebards were unable to sustain their logging practices in the swamp.

Although Liston Elkins argued that "the swamp has changed very little as a result of that logging operation," residents of the Okefenokee and its hinterlands complained as early as the 1880s that "an invasion of a terrible army of axemen, like so many huge locusts, has swept over the whole face of the land, leaving naught of the former native grandeur but treeless stumps to mark the track of the tramp."[120] The shrapnel of industry was visible everywhere in the swamp. Charles Sperry, a wildlife biologist who visited Billy's and Floyd's Islands in 1926, was disheartened by the area's dismal aspect: "only the stumps of the big pine are left and the vegetation over most of either island now consists of former undergrowth. . . . Billy's Island presented the more desolate aspect because the lumbered area was so much greater (than on Floyd's) and because its northern end was strewn with the wreckage of a deserted lumber camp, which at one time was a flourishing village."[121] The biologist saw Billy's Island as a ruin, an environment strewn with the wreckage of industry – a rusting machine being consumed by the garden.

Sperry neglected to mention, however, the other ruin on Billy's Island: the remains of a house, cornfield, and garden that lay buried beneath the lumber camp's debris. This homestead belonged, for sixty years before the Hebards began logging the island, to the Lee family. The Lees fought the entrance of industrial logging into the swamp, and in response the Hebards initially paid them off and later evicted them. Several members of the family, however, returned to work for the Hebards and live in company housing built on ruins of their former houses. The ruins of the Lee homestead reveal yet another ecolocal culture that had developed in the Okefenokee – a Swamper culture of diverse production and flexible adaptation.

# 4 Homesite and Workplace
## Okefenokee Swampers

When Charles Pendleton arrived with his survey team on Billy's Island in the northwestern interior of the Okefenokee Swamp in September 1875, he found a well-established farmstead worked by Jim Lee, his wife, and their children. The businessman-adventurer was amazed by what he saw: "Mr. Lee is the most independent of the world. The only article that he buys besides ammunition, fishing tackle and farming and mechanical implements are coffee and salt. He raises his own bread, beans, sugar, syrup, beef, potatoes, and everything else that he consumes save fish, venison and honey, which he gets in great quantities around him. He tans his leather and makes his own shoes, and his industrious wife and daughters spin and weave and sew up every thread of clothing they wear. He lives on government land, is lord of all he surveys, and is happy in his quiet solitude."[1] The Lee homestead seemed ideal to Pendleton; it was fertile and involved the entire family in a bucolic and preindustrial domestic mode of production. The family seemed to him "the most independent of the world."

The Lees had come to the Okefenokee in the mid–nineteenth century. As Seminoles moved farther south and legislative acts made lowland purchases more affordable, the Okefenokee Swamp became a homesite and workplace for poor whites like the Lees. These migrants sought lands they could inhabit without any interference from neighbors or the law unless they looked for it. As these families began to move into the Okefenokee Swamp and its margins, they became known as "Swampers" – a socioeconomically diverse kin-based community that inhabited, cultivated, and hunted the swamp.

The nature of the Okefenokee ecosystem shaped Swamper culture – an ecolocal culture that used the swamp as site of both home and work. The unique qualities of swamp muck, flora, and fauna necessitated adjustment, and Swampers responded by diversifying their occupations. This ecolocal culture created conditions for mobility and flexibility in labor choices, and when surveyors and developers entered the Okefenokee in the late nineteenth century, Swampers had the time and ability to hire themselves out as timber scouts, skidders, sawyers, and most important, Okefenokee Swamp guides. Their complicity in these corporate pursuits, however, resulted in Swampers' eviction from the Okefenokee. An investigation of the migration of Crackers to the Okefenokee and the establishment of Swamper communities reveals the doubled irony of this community's history in the swamp: the Okefenokee's ecology made it possible and even necessary for Swampers to participate in the destruction of the ecosystem that sustained their families. Ecolocal culture, in this instance, provided the means for its own disintegration.

The poor white families who moved to the Okefenokee hinterlands in the antebellum era were most often migrating from the southeastern backcountry – an area of European secondary settlement (after initial physical and economic conquest of the Atlantic coast) that extended from Virginia to Georgia and into Tennessee. Small farms and grain-processing centers characterized the backcountry, and there was little usage of slave labor, although there was some slave ownership. This area also demonstrated a multiracial, multiethnic character; populations tended to be mobile, and various immigrant streams from Europe successively inhabited pineland communities. Also, the backcountry abutted Native American lands – in southern Georgia, Cherokees, Creeks, and Seminoles visited or inhabited the backcountry, and the presence of Native populations shaped a diversified political and economic culture.[2]

The whites who lived in the southern backcountry have often been characterized as "plain folk": landowning farmers and herdsmen whose forebears had been victims of enclosure in the British Isles and who belonged neither to the plantation economy nor to the poor white class. Plain folk, as the historian Frank Owsley has conceived of them, were members of a rural middle class who lived in open (public) lands, aspired to a comfortable subsistence, and gave up herding for farming as soon as they could acquire lands of their own. As historians have recently argued, plain folk such as Swampers were more varied and complex as a class and a community than Owsley's characterization allows.[3] In the Okefenokee hinterlands, Swampers owned slaves and many purchased land, but most could claim neither and squatted on open lands or uninhabited private property. The Swamper community was internally diverse, but it shaped a shared ecolocal culture of diverse production in the Okefenokee and its hinterlands.

The ancestors of Okefenokee Swampers were the Crackers of Georgia and Florida – poor whites who were mobile and engaged in diversified production, including crime. The etymology of the term "Cracker" reveals the complex origins and cultural practices of this community. The term was associated in the colonial period with herdsmen of Scot, Scot Irish, Irish, or Welsh descent.[4] Samuel Johnson's *Dictionary of the English Language* defined a Cracker in 1755 as a "noisy, boasting fellow," and in America he was recognized as such. Hardyng's "Chronicle to Henry VIII" related Crackers' nation of origin with their verbal style and their fractiousness: "For the Scottes will aye be bostyn and crakyng, / Euer Sekyng causes of rebellion."[5] Some scholars have claimed that the term originates in the cracking of corn at harvest frolics in the backcountry or the hunting of a specific species of long-legged crane, while others argue that the designation comes from the sound of the long whip used to urge on oxen and cattle during farm labor or trips to the local market. The etymological association of Crackers with lying and boasting, however, is the most widely accepted definition.[6]

The term's multiple connotations suggest not only the long history of this community and the diversity of its methods of production (corn growing, hunting, and herding) but also the multiple ways that Crackers were perceived to unsettle European American notions of social order. Their noisiness and their bragging (often most vividly rendered after gouging fights between men) roused passions and agitated crowds. Their mobility and engagement in herding and hunting instead of farming meant that they were strangers instead of neighbors, squatters instead of tax-paying landowners. One prominent eighteenth-century etymologist was so disturbed by the cultural practices of Cracker communities that he argued that "Cracker" and "criminal" were synonymous terms.[7]

By the 1760s and 1770s "Cracker" was a common enough identifier in the English and Spanish colonies to appear in numerous documents as a community descriptor. Colony officials on both sides of the Georgia-Florida border were concerned about Crackers' propensity for criminality and their tendency to wreak havoc through theft and property destruction. In March 1767 Governor James Wright of Georgia refused to remove fourteen men from an Augusta garrison because the backwoods town "being a frontier the Inhabitants were not only liable to the Insults of the Indians but also to those of a parcel of people commonly called Crackers, a set of Vagabonds often as bad or worse than the Indians themselves." These vagabonds were often in flight from justice, Wright asserted, and if they gathered together, they might become "formidable enough, to Oppose His Majesty's Authority . . . and throw everything into Confusion."[8] Don Vicente Zespedes, a Spanish official in St. Augustine, voiced similar worries in response to Cracker mobility and their disregard for Spanish law. In a report to a Spanish royal official, Zespedes identified several waves of Cracker inhabitation of the Okefenokee hinterlands around the St. Marys River:

> *Crackers* [are] a species of white renegade. . . . these people erect Indian-style huts in the first unpopulated space fit to grow corn that they stumble upon in order to give shelter to their wives and children. Once done, they move again, always keeping themselves beyond the reach of civilized law. In the land vacated by these *crackers,* other less antisocial groups take their place. . . . This second class of *crackers* likewise tends to abandon their homes upon the approach of a third type of settlers. Although this third wave deigns to ask and receive legal title to the land, even they give obedience to their mother republic only when they feel like it. The government's authority is always weak or held in low esteem by the population along its frontier until a fourth class of people arrive and buy at low prices the land granted to the third type. These individuals are the first to become useful to the state.[9]

Zespedes was one of the few government officials to distinguish between different types of Cracker residents in the Okefenokee hinterlands, but he was not the only one to note the Crackers' lack of deference to governmental laws and regulations. Most officials noted the prevalence of Regulator sympathies and tactics among the Crackers in the Southeast. These communities, in other words, supported grassroots efforts of local citizens to take action (outside of the law) against federal and state taxes and fees they believed to be exorbitant or illegal. Scot Irish communities were usually acknowledged as the champions of Regulator movements in backcountry areas of North and South Carolina during the colonial period – these Scot Irish were also often identified as Crackers.[10]

But the dominant observation about Crackers living in the Okefenokee hinterlands in the eighteenth and nineteenth centuries was the comparison and sometimes the conflation of Crackers and Native Americans. Wright, in his address to the Georgia House of Commons, noted that Crackers were "as bad or worse as the Indians," while Zespedes noted in his letter that they were "distinguished from savages only in their color, language and the superiority of their depraved cunning and untrustworthiness."[11] The tendency of Cracker banditti to encroach on Native lands or join forces with Cherokees, Creeks, or Seminoles in cattle and slave raids in the Okefenokee hinterlands reinforced perceptions of their similarities. Observers often conflated the two communities due to what they perceived to be their shared "savage nature" – usually meant as a condemnation of these groups' lack of respect for private property. Louis Leclerc Milfort, a French adventurer who came to America in 1775 and lived with the Creeks in Georgia for twenty years, hated southern Georgia whites, whom he characterized as "Anglo-Americans, Crackeurs, and Gougers." Descriptions of what Milfort called "les Crackeurs" dominated many of his later journal entries:

> These men are very unruly and will not submit to any government; they live for the most part by hunting. They plant some tobacco which they carry to the coast towns during the winter to exchange for whiskey, fire-arms and powder. . . . These men go almost naked. They are so given to idleness and drunkenness that the women are obliged to do everything. . . . Practically all the backwoods of America are inhabited by the same kind of people; the further one penetrates the more dangerous and vicious they are. They often assassinate travelers to rob them. Their closest neighbors are not any safer. . . . These robbers wear their hair cut very close to the head and paint their bodies and faces with different colors in the same manner as the savages; with the result that their appearance is truly terrible.[12]

Milfort was appalled by the living conditions and lifestyles of "les Crackeurs," particularly the men, who, he believed, arose from their beds only to rob, murder, or engage in vicious gouging matches. The back-woods were clearly associated with savagery in Milfort's mind – the "further one penetrates the more dangerous and vicious" the inhabitants were. This Cracker landscape was also a site of hunting and very little agriculture, which European observers deemed a waste of good land.

Milfort was careful, however, to distinguish the actions of Cracker men from those activities of Cracker women. He was a rare observer in this regard, for while women were present in almost every Cracker community in the Okefenokee hinterlands during the eighteenth and nineteenth centuries, most commentators focused on the appearance and habits of Cracker men. This absence of discussion about women could be attributable to the fact that while poor white women were not completely confined to domestic spaces, white men were more apt to congregate in single-sex groups in public and "make trouble," calling attention to themselves. Those writers like Milfort, who did write about Cracker women, tended to see them with sympathy. The men were so idle, Milfort noted, that "the women were obliged to do everything." The journalist Clare de Graffenried echoed Milfort's sentiments a century later, derisively describing a community of male Georgia Crackers: "grouped about in a single store of the village, lounging, whittling sticks, and sunning their big, lazy frames, sit a score of stalwart masculine figures, while their offspring and womankind toil in the dusty mill."[13] In these accounts, the work of the women serves only to emphasize what observers saw as the despicable laziness of Cracker men. Such condemnations of male idleness were most often misunderstandings of poor white labor practices. Cracker men, in this context, engaged in hunting as a primary labor activity, which was more sporadic work than farming; it was more flexible and created moments of leisure throughout the day, giving the impression of consistent unemployment. But observers like Graffenried continued to depict Cracker men as shiftless and included illustrations like "Around the Grocery" to prove their points. These images were part of the narrative of the primitive, in which European Americans expressed disdain for communities – Native Americans and Crackers – that did not conform to the gender and social prescriptions of "civilized" society. To writers constructing this narrative, all Crackers (the men as well as the women) were savages.

Comte de Castelnau, a French naturalist traveling in Florida in 1837 and 1838, postulated that the Crackers' savage nature was due to their environment: "Accustomed to living alone in the woods, they have adopted the habits of savages with whom they are in constant contact; at every

Edward Windsor Kemble, "Around the Grocery," from Clare de Graffenried, "The Georgia Cracker in the Cotton Mills," *Century Magazine* 41, no. 4 (February 1891): 485.

moment their conversation is interrupted with war cries. . . . They leap about and howl, and make no effort to restrain their passions." This lack of restraint (legal or moral) disturbed Milfort as well. To him, "les Crackeurs" were even more savage than the Creeks because they had been born into the legacy of the American Revolution but had taken the tenets of liberty too far. They were fallen men and therefore even more uncivilized than savages. Fanny Kemble agreed, noting in her journal in 1838, "These are the so-called pinelanders of Georgia, I suppose the most degraded race of human beings claiming an Anglo-Saxon origin that can be found on the face of the earth – filthy, lazy, ignorant, brutal, proud, penniless savages, without one of the noble attributes which have been found occasionally allied to the vices of savage nature."[14] Crackers in the Okefenokee hinterlands gave observers the chance to expound on the nature of savagery and civilization at times during which these conceptualizations informed constructs of nationhood. Although there was some truth to accounts of Crackers' cultural practices and the fear they provoked, this group of poor whites (particularly the men) often became scapegoats and victims of exaggeration and overgeneralization in attempts to bolster social order.

In reality, the life and work styles of southeastern Crackers varied widely. For example, while Fanny Kemble reported in 1838 that poor whites in the Okefenokee hinterlands "own no slaves, for they are almost without exception abjectly poor," Zespedes noted in 1790 that "the St. Marys district today, including the land around the Nassau River (which is also navigable), contains forty-four families made up of two hundred whites and seventy-one Negroes." These slaves tilled rice, indigo, hemp, flax, tobacco, and cotton on Okefenokee hinterland plantations, producing enough cotton to clothe all 271 inhabitants of the St. Marys district.[15] While many observers characterized Crackers as completely isolated in their backwoods "wigwams," others noted that Crackers had multiple and frequent ties to markets and other communities.[16] Zespedes wrote that fifteen families had settled without licenses along the St. Marys in recent months, and that they "take their goods to the stores at Cumberland, an American island located . . . at the mouth of the river." Roads and paths crisscrossed the Okefenokee hinterlands; their presence reveals the prevalence of face-to-face contact with other communities and a flow of commodities throughout the Southeast.[17]

Mobility, engagement in local and regional markets, and a preference

for squatting on public land characterized eighteenth- and early-nine-
teenth-century Cracker communities in the Okefenokee hinterlands. Thousands of migrants swept into the Georgia backwoods after the 1761 Creek
cession, and by 1780 Crackers made up 30 percent of the state population and occupied 50 percent of its land.[18] Crackers often settled in the first
place they found vacant, tilled the soil until it lost its richness or until its legal owners arrived, and moved on to another tract. These groups had various desires: access to markets of their own choosing, a life on the periphery of governmental strictures, fresh soils, and sometimes refuge from the
law. Cracker migrants began to move to the Okefenokee Swamp in the
early antebellum era and then in larger numbers after the Civil War. What
they found was an ecosystem that would enable them to live how they
chose but one that would ultimately make it impossible for them to stay.

Crackers had inhabited and traversed the Okefenokee hinterlands before
the major Creek land cessions and treaties of the early nineteenth century
and the territorial annexation of Florida to the United States in 1821. But
these major land acquisitions convinced many poor white families to
move into the area despite continued skirmishes with Seminole clans.
Florida's population, which previous to American annexation had been
made up of a confederacy of Seminole bands, fugitive slaves from north
of the border, and a few thousand military officials, swelled to 160,000 inhabitants between 1821 and 1861. By 1830, 1,139 whites (83 families) were
living in Ware County, Georgia, which at the time contained the Okefenokee and land to the north and east of the swamp. Ten years later that
number had almost doubled to 2,239 white inhabitants. In 1850 the population of Ware County increased another 50 percent; 559 families (3,600
individuals) had built homes and were living at least somewhat permanently in the area.[19]

Four towns grew up around the Okefenokee and became major trading
centers in the swamp's hinterlands during the antebellum era. Coleraine,
a former Native American village on the southeastern edge of the swamp
that became a trading post when the United States government granted
the acreage and the rights to the traders James Armstrong and James Seagrove in December 1786, throve until Seminoles and traders deserted it
for Trader's Hill (Fort Alert) and Center Village. Trader's Hill, established
in 1755, was situated in an advantageous defensive and commercial position in the Okefenokee hinterlands. Sitting at the head of navigation of the

St. Marys River, Fort Alert was meant to protect area inhabitants from Seminole raids and defend Georgia against Spanish and Seminole incursions. The principal industry in Trader's Hill was not defense, however, but trade between store and tavern keepers and the residents of Ware and Camden counties. When Charlton County was created out of the western half of Camden County in 1854, voters selected Trader's Hill as the county seat, and court sessions became another focus of social and economic life in the town.[20]

Center Village, a town downriver from Trader's Hill and established in 1800, was a border town devoted to defense and trade. Camp Pinckney housed border soldiers, and a ferry provided service across the St. Marys between Georgia and Florida and merchants. Tradesmen and other Crackers bartered, bought, and sold their wares on the town streets, settled disputes in public "fist and skull" fights, and wagered on horse racing. Waresboro, a hub for passenger, mail, and freight service on the Okefenokee's north side, was established in 1824. It was fairly isolated initially, depending on mail service from the distribution station at Camp Pinckney, but gained population and prominence as Ware County's seat during the antebellum period.[21] All four of these towns faded away as the larger cities of Folkston (Charlton County) and Waycross (Ware County) became railroad junctions in the postbellum era. But in the years before 1860, they were thriving trading centers and sites of sociability for the area's white residents.

These towns were also junctions for some of the Okefenokee hinterland's most well-traveled paths and roads. Barnard Path, blazed in the 1790s and early 1800s by a legendary mail rider named Timothy Barnard, linked Seminole and Creek villages west of Waresboro to the Spanish settlements of eastern Florida. Kennard Path, blazed by a Scot Creek "half-breed," cut across the Okefenokee hinterlands in the other direction, connecting Seminole and Creek towns with Cracker settlements along the Chattahoochee River to the west. The Blackshear Road paralleled Kennard Path, leaving the Ocmulgee and Flint rivers to the west and skirting the northern border of the Okefenokee before joining the Barnard Path toward eastern Florida.[22] These roads and paths, although rendered impassible in wet conditions or during times of war between U.S. troops, white banditti, Seminoles, and Spanish soldiers, connected Okefenokee hinterland communities and provided opportunities for commercial transactions and social interactions.

As Crackers became Swampers in and around the Okefenokee, they gathered into a community characterized by a variety of socioeconomic situations and a shared culture that used the swamp as a site of diverse methods of subsistence and market production. Some Swampers were slaveholders and accumulated property, while others squatted on public lands and drafted family members as workers. Thus Swampers were not "plain folk," small planters, or poor white trash but a community that included these and other groups of white Americans.

Gathering into communities along the edges and on interior islands of the Okefenokee, Swampers developed a distinctive ecolocal culture. They engaged in community events that strengthened their collective consciousness and identity. Many members of the Swamper community were Baptists, and most of these were Primitive (or "Hardshell") Baptists. These Baptists believed that humans were imperfect creatures in need of salvation and that their future was in God's hands. Preachers were usually laymen who earned their living as did the congregation members – "by the toil of the hands, by the sweat of the brow." The Sardis Primitive Baptist Church, built in Charlton County in the 1820s, was the first in the Okefenokee hinterlands and continued to hold services (four-hour-long affairs) until 1938. Primitive Baptists tended to dislike institutional controls of behavior (hence their use of laymen preachers), and this aversion shaped a collective conservative political stance. Most Swampers wanted both state and federal governments to stay out of their lives and their swamp, and therefore usually voted for small-government tickets. They also supported the principles of Herrenvolk democracy, a racialized egalitarian ideology that emphasized the equality of all whites despite obvious economic inequities that were rife in Okefenokee hinterland society.[23]

Swamper families came together in church and at political events, but they also took part in leisure activities that reinforced community ties. Corn shuckings, barn raisings, frolics (dances), and hollers (sings) were popular pastimes; they combined neighborly cooperation with artistic and cultural expression. One of the activities that pervaded home, work, and play in Swamper communities was storytelling. The etymology of the phrase "talking trash" reveals that oral boasting, joking, wisecracking, and narrating were traditional elements of Cracker (often depicted as "white trash") culture since the eighteenth century. Such talk covered a wide range of genres (hunting stories, tall tales, historical narratives, and rough jokes) and was predominantly a male leisure activity, although women were known to participate. Much of this talk was a staple not only at social events but also during hunting excursions. Tall tales, as Kay Cothran has pointed out, "are part of a wilderness guide's stock in trade."[24]

Swamper storytelling ability, rooted in Cracker boasting traditions, was depicted in travel narratives and in early-twentieth-century fictional literature. Cecile Hulse Matschat, a novelist and gardening expert from New York City, angered Okefenokee Swampers by transcribing their folk tales and publishing them, along with condescending descriptions of their clothes and homes, in *Suwannee River: Strange Green Land* (1938). But the appeal of these stories and Cracker verbal styles was proven in the wildly popular Okefenokee hinterland novel, *The Yearling* (1938), by Marjorie Kinnan Rawlings. Penny Baxter, the young protagonist Jody's father, is a small man but a big talker who lives in the "wild Florida scrub" southeast of Gainesville, "populous with bears and wolves and panthers." When he tells tales of a bear hunt to the taller and stronger Forrester men, he "wove a spell of mystery and magic, that held these huge hairy men eager and breathless. He made the fight an epic thing." In this instance, Penny's story so bedazzles the Forresters that they trade him a new gun for the star of the tale, a hunting dog (who in reality is a failure as a pointer).[25] As Penny's yarn in *The Yearling* reveals, Cracker and Swamper tales were forms of entertainment and community building but were also part of Swamper economic transactions.

Rawlings's depiction of Cracker talk in her Pulitzer Prize–winning novel suggests the predominance and importance of oral culture within Swamper communities but is, admittedly, a fictional description produced by outside observations. While the majority of Swamper men and women were literate, they produced little in the way of written personal records. Most information about their lives has come from novels like *The Yearling* and transcriptions of Swamper talk in local histories and texts like Matschat's *Suwannee River.* Census records, genealogies, and family biographies, however, corroborate most observers' assessments of Swamper domestic and work activity in the Okefenokee Swamp. All of these sources make it clear that between 1820 and 1937, Swampers lived according to the exigencies of swamp ecology. This ecolocal culture, ironically, provided for the Swamper community's ultimate disintegration.

The first white inhabitant of the Okefenokee Swamp itself was Israel Barber, who came to the Georgia Bend area of the swamp (the southeast side) in 1807, but most of the first wave of Cracker families migrated in the

1820s.[26] Among the families who had appeared in Ware or Clinch County by 1830 were the Crewses, the Hilliards, the Mizells, and the Lees – families who continued to inhabit the Okefenokee Swamp for more than one hundred years.[27] These early migrant families and others came from multiple places and had varying agendas. Dr. Randal McDonald of Kettle Creek, a community just north of the Okefenokee, came to the area in the 1820s from Scotland. As part of his depiction of Richard L. Hunter's survey of the Okefenokee in 1856–57, Miller B. Grant described McDonald as "a Scotch gentleman of genial disposition, high intelligence and great experience, whose refined courtesy, hospitality, and bountiful entertainment refreshed and gladdened us. More than thirty years he has been a resident of this section of the country, and has now the happiness of seeing a numerous progeny settled comfortably around him."[28] McDonald was not a "lazy Cracker" jawing at the country store but a prosperous landowner whose children purchased lands around the paternal homestead. Other large landowners emerged in the Okefenokee hinterlands: Joseph Mills moved from North Carolina to Camden County and then to the southeastern Okefenokee in 1826 and operated a large plantation, as did James Paxton, who was born in northern Georgia, moved to Charlton County in 1805, and married a local girl, Mary Ann Mizell, in 1830.[29]

Most Okefenokee Swampers, however, came to the area during a second wave of migration in the 1850s, after the Seminoles had moved into the Everglades and subsequent surveys of the swamp brought it widespread attention and fame. Some of these second-wave migrants were fairly prosperous farmers from Virginia and the Carolinas. Richard A. Baker, for example, came to the Okefenokee hinterlands from Virginia and bought up land north of Center Village. In 1855 Baker claimed three hundred acres of land valued at two dollars per acre, one thousand dollars' worth of manufacturing equipment, and twelve slaves valued at seventy-two hundred dollars. He was a mercantile agent for other farmers in the area and engaged in the turpentine business as well.[30] Another wealthy migrant, Major Philip Coleman Pendleton and his uncle, Lewis Tebeau, bought adjoining farms of nearly fifteen hundred acres each on the northeastern edge of the Okefenokee in 1858 and settled their families in a double-log cabin on Pendleton's property. Philip Pendleton had three grandchildren who were all writers and Okefenokee hinterland boosters: Constance, who wrote the war memoir *Confederate Memories;* Charles, the newspaper editor and Okefenokee explorer; and Louis, a novelist and short story writer who was one of the few Okefenokee hinterland residents to acknowledge fugitive slaves as Okefenokee denizens in his novel *King Tom and the Runaways* (1891). The Pendletons' nearest neighbor was Thomas Hilliard, who had fought with the Ware County Militia to wrest the Okefenokee from the Seminoles between 1836 and 1841.[31] The Bakers and the Pendletons were wealthier than most Swampers. Their slave-holding and property ownership reveal the socioeconomic diversity of the white population in the Okefenokee hinterlands during the antebellum period.

During the Civil War the Okefenokee again became a site of refuge. But instead of shielding fugitive slaves or Seminoles, it sheltered poor whites seeking to escape the Confederate draft. While numerous young men from Ware, Clinch, and Charlton counties went off to war (most of them comprising Company F, Twenty-sixth Regiment of Georgia Volunteers nicknamed the "Okefenokee Rifles"), many Confederate deserters began to take refuge in the Okefenokee Swamp after the tide began to turn against the South in 1863. Evidence of deserters' inhabitation of the Okefenokee is difficult to come by, but some contemporary maps show one island to be named "Old Soldier's Island" or "Soldier's Camp," and local historians trace these names to the presence of Confederate soldiers. In 1875 Charles Pendleton interviewed William Chesser, an inhabitant of an island in the southeastern corner of the Okefenokee since 1858, and Chesser remarked that, "'I get wild honey, too, occasionally, but it is not so plentiful now as it was once. You see the 'serters in the war times cleaned the bees out.'"[32] This relationship between white fugitives and the Okefenokee was alluring to American readers. Perhaps it was his brother's interview with William Chesser that led Louis Pendleton to write *In the Okefenokee: A Story of War Time and the Great Georgia Swamp* (1895), a novel about two Swamper boys who get lost in the Okefenokee in the 1860s and fall in with a band of Confederate deserters. Fictional or no, deserters' links with the Okefenokee reveal a transition in the status of the swamp. As Seminoles were pushed farther and farther into southern Florida and post–Civil War legislation emancipated slaves, the Okefenokee and other southeastern swamps were increasingly marked as white.

Local histories and genealogies reveal that Confederate deserters and many dispossessed or newly poverty-stricken southerners migrated to the Okefenokee in the years just after the Civil War. The Georgian James Cox, for example, joined a Confederate cavalry unit and was wounded near

Richmond in 1864. He returned to his farm in Tattnall County (middle Georgia) to find that nearly all of his three hundred cattle and seven hundred head hogs had disappeared. The seven hundred dollars he had accumulated before the war had been converted into Confederate currency and was therefore worthless. Cox was so disheartened that he sold his land and the rest of his belongings and moved his family southward to Ware County.[33] As Crackers like James Cox from other areas of the southeastern backcountry moved to the Okefenokee hinterlands in the 1850s and 1860s, they encountered (some for the first time) the challenges that swamp ecosystems posed. In response to these challenges, Crackers became Swampers and began to shape their lives out of the muck. To make a living and provide for their families, Swamper men and women used the Okefenokee in the way the swamp demanded: in multiple ways and in accordance with lowland geology, hydrology, flora, and fauna.

Okefenokee ecology shaped Swamper agricultural production in two ways. The mosaic character of the swamp made pockets of dry land (hammocks or islands) available for agricultural use; this same mosaic character limited Swamper agricultural activities to small acreages (usually fifty acres or less). Swampers cleared the rich, high land for cultivation over the course of several years. First, they enclosed the area, deadened the trees, and used the acreage for one or two seasons as a cow pen or grazing area. Then they felled the trees (leaving the stumps) and used the timber for houses or firewood and sold remaining logs to local sawmills. They then set fire to the underbrush. By burning vegetation, Swampers conserved time and labor; they also released nutrients in the form of ash into the soil, enriching it and providing for at least a few years of high crop yields. After the fires burned themselves out, Swampers broke up the soil, plowed it, and planted it, manuring three or four acres at a time. Swampers continued to plant this area until the yields declined, and then they abandoned this small acreage and cleared another plot in the area or moved to another part of the swamp entirely.[34]

Men, women, and their children worked the fields in every stage of clearing, tilling, planting, and harvesting. In addition, some Swampers used slave labor during the antebellum period. During his travels to the South in the 1850s, Frederick Law Olmsted observed about fifty "of the class called 'crackers'" in the Okefenokee hinterlands: "I was told that some of them owned a good many negroes, and were by no means so poor as their appearance indicated." In 1840, 132 slaves lived and labored in Ware/Clinch County – 6 percent of the total population. Ten years later that number had declined slightly to 129, and their percentage of the total population decreased as well, to 4 percent. Charlton County Swampers, who lived on the southeastern side of the Okefenokee, used more slaves than their neighbors in Ware, probably because the land along the swamp on this side was more amenable to farming larger acreages. The 1860 Census shows 557 slaves living in Charlton (46 percent of the total population), but most Swampers, if they owned slaves at all, owned fewer than ten. In 1860 the Charlton County resident Gulford Dudley owned two slaves – Tom and Violet – and was the "custodian" of seven others (Charles, Paul, Silas, Ellen, Rose, Judy, and Jake) in his capacity as administrator of another Okefenokee hinterlands inhabitant's estate. The Swamper Benjamin F. Davis owned nine slaves, as did his Okefenokee neighbor, Henry Roddenberry. By 1859 Arch Crews, a Swamper who lived in the Georgia Bend (the southeast side of the Okefenokee), had accumulated enough cash ($1,170) to buy a slave named Tom, his first such purchase.[35]

While Okefenokee Swampers were not all slaveholders and most of those who did own slaves owned only a few, it is clear that slavery was not unknown in the area and that the necessity of patch farming did not render slavery obsolete in the antebellum era. Overall, however, slavery was not a dominant form of labor in the Okefenokee hinterlands. The percentages of slaves as part of the total population of Okefenokee hinterland counties in 1850 were low (4 percent in Ware County, 31 percent average in all hinterland counties) compared to cash crop–producing areas of Georgia and Florida (67 percent).[36]

Swamper farmers produced both food and cash crops in the antebellum and postbellum years. Most patch farmers planted corn and sweet potatoes; substantial acreages devoted to cotton, rice, or tobacco were rare. Mansfield Torrance, the lead surveyor of the 1850 exploration of the Okefenokee Swamp, noted that most crops were produced for domestic purposes: "Enough corn and cotton is raised for home consumption. The black seed cotton is exclusively cultivated, and is ginned with hand roller gins fixed by uprights into a common stool. It is turned with one hand and fed with another. . . . Sugar grows well and is cultivated for domestic supply. . . . Small grain does poorly, except rice. I saw but two patches of rice and both were planted in Cyprus ponds, well ditched and drained. . . .

The gardens, like they are all over Georgia, with but few exceptions, are below mediocrity."[37] Cotton production put Swampers in contact with markets in the Okefenokee hinterlands, but this community did not get absorbed into the larger southern cotton system as did poor whites in other areas of Georgia. Those Swampers who grew cotton saved some for sale and spun and wove the rest to make clothing for family use.[38] Instead of devoting their land exclusively to cash crops like cotton, sugar, or rice, Swampers planted a diverse array of food crops. Surveyors and other visitors to Okefenokee farms were usually impressed with the well-maintained and diversified fields they observed. While Torrance was not inspired by any of the Swamper gardens, subsequent surveyors did not hide their admiration for Swampers' cultivation efforts.

Charles Pendleton, after several days of slogging through the muck along the northwestern edge of the Okefenokee in 1875, was delighted to see "a flourishing little farm, which denoted more thrift than we had seen that day. The crop looked well and . . . from appearances [the proprietor] was living well." Pendleton and his cohorts then made their way to the farm of James Inman, a friend of Pendleton's from his boyhood, "before he had secluded himself from the world to this out-of-the-way place." Inman's farm was doing well enough that he treated the entire surveying party to a "sumptuous repast" and invited them to stay as long as they liked. As noted earlier, Pendleton was similarly impressed with the Lee farm on Billy's Island, which the adventurers encountered several days later: "When we entered his field of magnificent corn, the first thing that greeted our vision was a great quantity of very fine watermelons. He gave us the liberty to pluck and eat as many as we desired. . . . Mr. Lee's farm was a small hammock before it was cleared, and it was very productive. On it I saw as fine sugar cane growing as it was ever my lot to behold. His potatoes, too, were very fine."[39] Ironically, Pendleton's delighted reaction to the Okefenokee farmers' successful cultivation and his descriptions of the verdant fields and productivity of the swampland in the *Atlanta Constitution* helped to whet the appetites of local developers. Boosters and business leaders in the Okefenokee hinterlands had dreamed of a giant swamp plantation, one that would be the South's postbellum Eden, productive and healthful. But the swamp's ecology would not sustain such visions, and the patch-farming techniques of the Swampers continued to dominate the area's agricultural production processes into the twentieth century.

While visitors continued to rave about the swamp's agricultural productivity – Howell Cobb Jackson wrote in 1890 that "for sweet potatoes this land beats the world. . . . in size and flavor they excel anything I have eaten"[40]– they also noticed that farming was not the Swampers' sole occupation. Because farm acreages were necessarily small and because the open, uncultivated lands of the Okefenokee were vast, herding became a dominant method of land use and production for Swampers in the nineteenth and twentieth centuries. While Frank Owsley has argued that the first waves of white "pioneers" engaged in hunting and trapping, the second wave in herding, and the third wave in agriculture, Okefenokee Swampers engaged in all three kinds of production at once. Herding was, as Bradley Bond has put it, "the poor man's way to pecuniary progress."[41]

Swampers accumulated cattle and hogs and then let them forage in the Okefenokee, investing very little time, labor, or capital in their upkeep. Cattle would browse on wire grass in the "burns" during spring and summer; Swamper families like the Millers, Hilliards, and McDonalds would then drive them into the Okefenokee for the winter, where they fed on herbs and grasses that were protected from frost by the dense swamp foliage. Once a year, usually in March, as Charles Pendleton noted, they would burn over the strips of woodland on the borders of the Okefenokee and "ere the tender shoots began to peek through the ashy carpet left by the forest fire, the cattle would come in great herds out of the swamp to forage on the new-born grass." Driving parties would then round up the cattle at a given point, divide them according to mark and brand, and drive them to their summer ranges near the homes of their owners.[42]

The use of the Okefenokee and its hinterlands as an open range for cattle and hogs has a long history; cattle ranches were recorded in northeastern Florida in 1657, and by 1700 ranch names, tax payments, and regulations for slaughterhouses began to appear in the Spanish colony's written records. In his 1769 map of the Okefenokee hinterlands, the British royal surveyor Samuel Savery labeled the lands around the Okefenokee as "*Low Pine Barrens and Cypress Ponds – only fit for Cattle Range*," and by the late eighteenth century, Chief Cuscowilla of the Miccosukee nation (later part of the Seminole confederacy) held such large numbers of cattle in the Alachua savanna that he earned the nickname "Cowkeeper."[43] Cattle herders found markets in Cuba and Atlantic seaboard cities in addition to sites of local consumption – houses, taverns, and in the early twentieth century, hotels. By 1850 the Okefenokee hinterlands in Georgia, which boasted one-quarter of the state's land and one-tenth of its population, produced more than 400,000 head of cattle (one-half of the state's total production), 85,000 sheep, and 356,000 swine (one-sixth of the state's total production). The Okefenokee hinterlands then, through the efforts of Swampers, contributed more than its population or land share of the total value of the livestock produced in the entire state of Georgia in 1850– $25,728,416 (a per capita value of $28.39).[44]

Visitors to the Okefenokee hinterlands noted the importance of cattle and hog herding to Swamper families. Mansfield Torrance remarked in 1850 that "the chief productive wealth of the country is beef cattle," while the Georgia-Florida boundary surveyor Alexander Allen wrote in 1854 that he met "Mr. George Johns 68 years of age healthy old man. A large stock owner & gathers his own cattle. . . . The people [here] appear very kind. Mostly hunters & stock minders & owners." Richard Hunter noticed on his expedition in 1856–57 that "some of the settlers on the head of the St. Marys are in the habit of driving their cattle into the swamp as far as [Black Jack] Island on account of the range, and I am told they thrive very well. There is a regular trail from the outside of the swamp to this island."[45]

Charles Pendleton wrote to the readers of the *Valdosta Times* in 1890 that in addition to having financial importance, herding provided opportunities for male sociability. Cattle herding was an almost exclusively male activity, and driving parties were a rite of passage for boys in the Swamper community. During these gatherings, the boys witnessed fights among the male bulls, who were "ready and anxious to dispute with all comers the right to lord it over the ridge. The fights were frequent and furious and were greatly enjoyed by the younger set in the drive." Through the driving of cattle, Swamper boys learned not only about herding tactics (firing the edges in order to draw out the cattle) and property rights and symbols (through the sorting of branded cattle), but also about the struggle for male dominance in the "herd." All of these lessons, according to Pendleton, were "valuable indeed."[46]

Young boys were also socialized into Swamper culture through the rites of hunting. In *The Yearling,* Jody Baxter comes of age during two hunts – the first an epic pursuit of the voracious bear Old Slewfoot and the second his solitary hunt for Flag, the deer he raises from a fawn and loves like a brother. After he kills Flag to save his family's crops, Jody returns "different. [He] aint a yearlin' no longer" but a man.[47] Swamper hunting was productive of manliness and, as in *The Yearling,* worked in tandem with community agricultural and herding pursuits. In the 1930s the scientist James G. Needham noted that the underbrush- and grass-burning techniques of both patch farming and livestock herding also helped Swampers manage the forest for hunting purposes. This technique, as Needham pointed out, increased visibility in the swamp with a minimum of labor. Clean-burning the ground cover at intervals of a few years served two ends: "it destroys the young trees and shrubs and lets in the light and makes opportunities for grasses and other low forage plants [food sources for wildlife] to grow and . . . it keeps the bushes down and keeps the view open so that the hunter may discover his game." Hunters and trappers maintained ground cover in portions of the Okefenokee and kept trails from interior island to island open by consistent use. They killed alligators, bears, deer, small animals, and water and land fowl in order to supplement both their domestic food supply and their cash income.[48]

Many visitors to the Okefenokee commented on the hunting prowess of the Swampers they encountered. Robert ("Allen") and Sam Chesser, who served as guides in several Okefenokee expeditions, were considered the most skillful hunters and trappers in the swamp. Charles Pendleton's 1875 survey crew made their encampment on Chesser Island and had just bedded down for the night when one of the Chesser boys

> came out and said that he had 'roosted' two coveys of partridges, and that if one of us would go with him and another with his brother to hold the lightwood torch they would kill the birds with arrows. The writer and Prof. Locke readily volunteered. The boys had collected some 'fat' splinters which made a blazing light, and when the writer and his man approached the spot where the birds had been seen to go to roost, the marksmen advanced cautiously a few steps and beckoned to the writer to stop. He saw them squatting in the grass and he drew his arrows one at a time from the quiver and in seven shots he had killed as many birds – shooting six of the number through the head. When he picked them up he said, "I shoots 'em through the head to keep from spilling the meat."[49]

Swampers were proud of their hunting abilities and, like the entrepreneurs they guided, saw their prey as symbols of their masculinity. They traversed the Okefenokee night and day in search of deer, bear, alligators, and birds. The exigencies of Okefenokee ecology that necessitated patch farming and promoted herding also provided the flexibility of time and the wealth of wildlife to make hunting profitable. The Chesser boys' prowess with both guns and arrows earned them more money than other kinds of production; it also made them legends in the area and the subjects of much local folklore. As Howell Cobb Jackson reported, the Chesser boys "attempt to cultivate small crops, but spend most of their time hunting. Their revenue is almost entirely derived from the sale of hides of alligators, deer, and bears. The quantity of these that they destroy and many of their stories of hunting adventures are incredible." Surveyors and other visitors to the Okefenokee spread the reputation of the Chesser boys throughout the Okefenokee hinterlands and the wider Southeast. Jackson seemed certain that "the dexterity with which these men use their rude bow and arrows will put to shame the average Atlanta marksman with his rifle."[50]

But most Swampers did not hunt or trap in order to gain local or regional reputations; they hunted in order to provide food for themselves and their families – to "keep from spilling the meat." This kind of work necessitated some capital outlay and usually took more time on a consistent basis than either patch farming or herding. Few Swampers, particularly the men, were without a firearm of some kind. As children in the 1890s, the Davis boys (who lived on the Trail Ridge on the southeastern edge of the Okefenokee) rode in a buggy down three path roads to the Trader's Hill ferry, crossed the St. Marys River, and walked several miles to Boulogne, Florida, where they bought boxes of ammunition at the Triggs general merchandise store.[51] In 1890 Howell Cobb Jackson listed the "armament of the Chesser family" as "one ten gauge, ten pound Remington shotgun and two Winchester rifles, one thirty-eight caliber and one thirty-two. Also a small yellow-pine bow, and a few cane arrows."[52] The guns were clearly store bought, but the Chesser boys had whittled the bows and arrows themselves from Okefenokee pine and cane.

Swamper investments in hunting – in time and money – usually paid off. At the turn of the twentieth century, hotels, restaurants, and boutiques began to proliferate in the Okefenokee hinterlands, and demand grew for skins and game, particularly venison. The profits were substantial and deer hunting increased in the Okefenokee and its hinterlands. According to John Hopkins, superintendent of the Hebard ventures, between 1917 and 1937 Okefenokee Swampers sold ten thousand raccoon skins, two hundred otter skins, twenty-five to fifty wildcat skins, twenty-five to fifty skunk skins, and two thousand alligator skins to local buyers and to purchasers as far away as St. Louis.[53]

Swamper income from hunting, however, was never stable. Markets for the skins and meat of bear, deer, and alligators fluctuated in the late eighteenth and early nineteenth centuries. Alligator skin prices, for example, rose and fell in the 1910s and 1920s in response to the mercurial nature of the fashion industry – alligator luggage, purses, and shoes for women were all the rage one moment and out of style the next. Gad Roddenberry, a hunter, trapper, farmer, and Okefenokee guide, proudly displayed his gold teeth to a tourist in 1929, and she commented that "they must have cost many a 'gator & egret's life – He is prosperous these days from his sales of gator hides because of the vogue of reptilian hides for ladies shoes. He was in bad some years ago when alligator hide luggage bags went out of style."[54] By and large, however, Swamper hunters profited monetarily from their hunting of alligators, bears, deer, fowl, and small animals. Hunting and trapping activities became a vital part of Swamper ecolocal culture.

Sometimes Swampers hunted, not for profit, but to protect their other investments. Howell Cobb Jackson noted in June 1890 that "the amount of stock that the farmers lose annually through the depredations of bears and alligators seems almost beyond belief." Dave Hiccox, for example, who lived on Cowhouse Island in the northeastern corner of the Okefenokee, told Jackson that he had lost more than one hundred hogs within the previous three months. He had also seen an alligator drag one of his cows into the muck. Okefenokee bears, as audacious and voracious as Rawlings's fictional Old Slewfoot, were also predators of Swampers' cattle and hogs. Jackson reported in 1890 that once a bear had tasted hog meat he craved it "and would hide in the neighborhood watching an opportunity to catch another." This propensity was the bruin's doom, however, "for the whole neighborhood turns out with guns, horses, and dogs, and by surrounding him in one of the innumerable cypress and gum ponds that surround the Okeefinokee like a fringe they soon cure forever his yearnings for bacon."[55] One fall the Chesser men hunted down and killed a large bear that had been responsible for killing several of their young cows. It was John Hopkins's opinion that "some of the residents near the swamp who used to go bear hunting for sport now set traps and poisoned honey and go bear hunting with an idea, not of sport, but of vengeance."[56] Hunting for vengeance helped to protect Swampers' crops, fruit trees, cattle, and hogs. They saw this form of hunting as just as vital to their livelihood as hunting for profit.

Swamper hunters clung to their hunting territories, and this adamant stand often created tensions and conflict within the Swamper community. As an accepted rule, trappers respected other trappers' rights and property – they were marked by the boundaries of common knowledge. Most Swampers were generous with their resources but expected respect in return. In 1901, while conducting a timber survey, John Hopkins and his team "found two or three little shelters in isolated parts" of the Okefenokee. Inside were a small cache of uncooked food in a box and a note on the box that read, "'Make yourself at home. Help yourself to what you need but put back what you don't need, because if I come in and everything is gone I might be in a hell of a fix.'" Despite these neighborly expectations, some Swamper trappers encroached on their neighbors' territories. Hopkins knew of one trapper "who found some of his traps had been robbed, and feeling certain as to who was guilty, went into the suspect's area the next week, took several coons from traps, hung the traps on nearby stumps and draped the stumps with guts." An ongoing dispute between Jim Lee of Billy's Island and Josiah Mixon of Mixon's Ferry had originated in contentions over hunting and trapping territory; the quarrel escalated into a series of accusations of domestic abuse, illegal whiskey distillation, and tobacco selling without a license. Both Lee and Mixon spent time in jail and considerable sums on attorney's fees as a result of these disputes.[57]

Neighbors also clashed over the hunting of livestock in the Okefenokee. Because the nature of swamp herding meant that stock owners saw their cattle and hogs only twice a year, the animals were easy prey for Okefenokee poachers. In November 1875 E. Y. Clarke wrote from the *Atlanta Constitution* expedition that the team had seen a notice posted conspicuously on a tree. It "smelt of brimstone," and read as follows: "'We the citizens of Clinch county take this method of notifying parties who are not residents of this county, that they will from this time be prohibited from hunting game of any kind. We are not disposed to be selfish, but we have been badly imposed upon by parties pretending to hunt for venison and honey, but finally make up a load of pork, etc.'" The notice was not so much a general proposition as a specific warning; Clarke noted that the bottom of the notice read, "Mush-head [John Thomas] and Dave Steedily will reap their reward if they don't stop." Several days later the survey's wagon driver encountered a group of fourteen Swamper men, "on horseback, armed with shot-guns and rifles and accompanied by dogs," riding out of the swamp. This group was returning from the "Clinch county hunt for the cattle and hog thieves," and they had been victorious: "They finally found Steedily, but as he had no contraband in his cart they permitted him to go upon the promise that he would never come back. He will be very apt not to be caught again in these parts. It would not be healthy for him."[58] Tensions over hunting and trapping territories, rights, and privileges became even more complicated when the Suwanee Canal Company and the Hebard Lumber Company bought extensive Okefenokee acreage in the 1890s and early 1900s. Swamper beliefs about the role of hunting and trapping in their communities clashed with corporate rights in the early twentieth century. These disputes over these productive practices reveal the importance of such activities to Swamper ecolocal culture.

The Okefenokee Swamp provided Swampers with small farming acreages, open range for cattle and hogs, and wildlife to hunt and trap. It also consisted of hundreds of stands of massive pine and cypress trees. By engaging in small-scale lumbering activities in the Okefenokee, Swampers participated in an industry with a long history in the swamp and its hinterlands. The first sawmills in northeastern Florida were built in the 1700s, and the naval stores industry in Georgia became an important mode of local production in the 1750s. The British government encouraged construction of sawmills in the colony by granting land to those who would build mills and promising to provide a market for lumber. These grants were often as much as one thousand acres apiece in the pine barrens of the Okefenokee hinterlands. By the early nineteenth century poor white migrants living in the Okefenokee and on its edges had begun engaging in small lumbering, sawmilling, turpentining, and the production of other naval stores (resin, rosin, potash, and tannin).[59]

Swampers removed trees to clear ground for patch farming and livestock herding. As noted earlier, those residents who lived within a mile or two of the St. Marys River or the Satilla River transported logs to the shore, tied them together into a raft, and floated the raft down the rivers to Fernandina (at the mouth of the St. Marys) or Brunswick (at the mouth of the Satilla). This kind of lumber transportation was dangerous and often destructive; freshets were unpredictable, and poorly piloted rafts often damaged bridges built across the rivers. So much timber sank to the bottom of these rivers that log reclamation became a popular pastime and income source in the Okefenokee hinterlands during the early 1900s; by law the salvager became the official owner of the sunken wood.[60]

Production of turpentine and other naval stores was less risky than log transport but was more environmentally destructive. James Baker, who moved to Charlton County from Gates County, North Carolina, in 1838, opened a naval stores operation on the edge of the swamp near Paxton Place, building a turpentine still near the present site of Uptonville (on the southeastern edge of the Okefenokee). Another early turpentine operation was located at Camp Pinckney, on the St. Marys River. When the Civil War broke out and Federal gunboats made their way up the river, the Camp Pinckney still operators burned large quantities of gum to prevent it from falling into the hands of the enemy. Similarly, when the Williams family, owners of a turpentine still on the northeastern side of the Okefenokee, heard that Sherman was marching on Savannah, they closed the still and buried the rosin so that it would not fall into Union hands.[61] Swampers living on the Okefenokee's edge often worked seasonally for these naval stores companies as boxers (those workers who cut the deep V into the tree that provoked and channeled the flow of resin into a box, in addition to exposing trees to pest infestations), still operators, or guards.

Between 1830 and 1870 local seasonal workers, contract work, and relatively small mills characterized the lumber industry in the Okefenokee hinterlands. By 1860 northern Florida had eighty-seven sawmills with twelve hundred employees and a capital investment of more than one million dollars. The industry did not expand significantly until the 1880s, when depletion of Michigan and Wisconsin forests turned the eyes of the lumber kings to southeastern forests, railroad expansion made long-distance transportation possible, and steam mills cut the costs of board production. However, even during the first years of expansion, small-scale lumbering and production of naval stores presented Okefenokee hinterland residents with opportunities to earn additional cash. Some Swampers subcontracted to cut trees on their land and raft them to a local sawmill, while others worked as seasonal laborers in nearby mills. William Lang bought property on the Satilla River north of the Okefenokee in 1865 and became a timber purchaser in addition to a farmer, while the Mizell brothers established a lumber mill on the St. Marys River at King's Ferry in the 1870s. They sawed their own trees on "large areas of fine lands near the southeastern corner of the Swamp."[62]

While most Okefenokee timber workers were male, the most successful small-scale timber purveyor in the Okefenokee hinterlands was a Swamper woman. Between 1870 and 1930 Lydia Smith Stone capitalized on local lumber practices and infrastructure and diversified her production accordingly. Stone was one of several daughters of William Smith, a Second Seminole War veteran who came to the Okefenokee area from Coffee County, Georgia, in 1838 and stayed after General Charles Floyd disbanded his troops in the spring of 1839. He bought two 490-acre lots on the northeastern side of the Okefenokee (including Cowhouse Island, an important gathering spot for open-range cattle) for ten dollars and purchased 1,000 acres more in 1849. In the 1870s, when Stone was a young girl and when timber barons began to investigate the area, her father gave her a cow and a hog and told her that she could keep whatever money she earned from them. Within two years Stone had taken the money she saved from the livestock and purchased 45 acres of land.[63]

By 1895 Stone had bought up acreages already cut for cypress by sawmill owners for less than one dollar an acre; she then let pine timber grow wild. She cut cross-ties from the remaining trees, leased some tracts to turpentine operations, and turpentined some herself. To market her cross-ties and sell her naval stores, Stone traveled by herself to Jacksonville and Brunswick, Georgia. Her idea of saving money, her obituary stated, "was to buy more land." At the time of her death in 1937, Lydia Smith Stone, known as the "Queen of the Okefenokee," had accumulated more than two thousand acres of pine barren and swampland (in addition to more than six hundred head of cattle) and had most of her land in production for lumber or naval stores. Her net worth was said to be more than one million dollars.[64] Stone was unusual in that she accumulated so much money and land, but like most Swampers, she provided for herself and her family by diversifying her modes of production.

Okefenokee Swampers spent much of their time engaged in patch farming, herding, hunting and trapping, and the timber and naval stores industries, but they also earned money and produced domestic supplies through extractive small industries in the swamp: bee-keeping, moss gathering, soap making, and moonshining. One of the surveyors on Torrance's expedition into the Okefenokee in 1850 made it clear that the swamp's reputation for good honey was long standing. However, he did not find either the quantity or the quality of Okefenokee's honey to be very impressive: "The quantities of honey so much boasted of about the Okefenoke, is not found in any of the parts herein mentioned. Two bee-trees were cut down, yielding a little trashy honey. I did not see a wild bee but once; a very few were pointed out to me going in and out of a lightwood tree, through a hole by the knot."[65] In 1858, however, the surveyor Miller B. Grant found that honey production in the Okefenokee had increased into a full-fledged swamp industry. As a member of Hunter's survey into the Okefenokee, Grant encountered Josiah Mixon, who had a "great fancy for robbing bees" and had cultivated "fifty flourishing hives." Honey production was a necessity for his family, Mixon told Grant, because "they loved sweetning."[66]

The Mixons, in addition to building and maintaining hives on their property, also went on "bee hunts" – tracking individual bees to their trees and excavating the honeycombs. In 1875 Charles Pendleton convinced one of the Lee men to accompany his survey party to Honey Island, where "we went for a regular hunt."[67] Although the journalist Clifton Johnson, during a visit to the Georgia backcountry in 1903, noted that "very little honey is marketed" and thus most of the "sweetning" was used domestically in this area, many Swamper families included jars of honey in the carts that they took to market days in Trader's Hill or Center Village. In 1875 Pendleton noted that the Swampers "get a revenue from honey and bee's wax, some of which they raise and some is found wild in the woods." It was customary that Swampers would mark any bee trees they discovered with the family brand, thereby claiming them as their own.[68] Such acts of claiming extended Swamper property beyond their acreage and into the "open" lands of the Okefenokee, just as bee-keeping expanded Swamper modes of production.

Swampers, like black slaves had before them, "got a revenue" from collecting sphagnum moss from the Okefenokee peat beds, drying it out, and selling it or using it domestically as stuffing for mattresses or as insulation for packaging. By the mid–nineteenth century, Swamper families collected the moss as it grew during the winter and sold it to purchasers who often exported it to England. The most successful extractor of moss in the Okefenokee was Robert H. Padgett, a native of northeastern Florida who, while working in an orange grove, noticed that purveyors encased the roots of orange trees with moss. As a teenager, he began to gather the moss out of local swamplands, dry it in the sun, and then sell it to plant and tree nurseries. When he first moved to the Okefenokee hinterlands in the late 1920s, Padgett visited the swamp and came out "believing that he could soon become a millionaire." He hired another man to help him, and they worked days pulling up intertwined moss ropes from the waters of Grand, Chase, and Floyd's prairies and then spent nights in the Okefenokee, sleeping in a three-sided tin shelter. As Padgett's business grew, he acquired flatbed railroad cars and hired more Swampers to help him. These workers used their rakes to extract the moss ropes, transported them to drying racks, left them for twenty days, and then loaded them into a bale press that churned out bales of four cubic feet of volume. Padgett's moss business flourished in the 1920s and 1930s, providing jobs for Swampers looking for extra work. John Hopkins noted that moss harvesting was so profitable because, unlike wildlife or trees, moss was an inexhaustible resource, "since there is a new crop each year."[69]

Swampers also used a by-product from the naval stores industry, potash, to make soap for their own use and for market. In 1858 Richard Hunter reported that on Hickory Hammock, Swampers used particular kinds of ash and oak trees to make this product: "the people resort to this place from a distance of many miles, and burn the oak and ash timber for the purpose of getting the ashes to make soap." Miller Grant noted in 1857 that the people "resorted" to Hickory Hammock at "stated seasons" to procure their ashes and that "the soap of their make we had occasion to use, and can certify to its excellence."[70] Unlike cattle herding, these "ash drives" were activities in which both men and women participated. The trips to gather ash and subsequent soap production gatherings were opportunities for Swamper women to leave the homestead and for kin groups to meet and socialize.

Another lucrative small industry that Swampers engaged in that was productive of community sociability but was also jealously guarded as a territorial right was the production of moonshine (small-batch corn whiskey). Moonshine production hit its peak in the 1920s and 1930s during Prohibition but had been part of Swamper culture for more than a century. Moonshiners, like trappers, claimed certain territories in the Okefenokee, but they were careful not to trespass on anyone else's domain. Due to its proximity to the Jacksonville market, the Georgia Bend section of Charlton County (the southeastern side of the Okefenokee) achieved a reputation in the 1920s for the quantity and quality of its liquor. But stills were all over the Okefenokee. Revenue agents went after Charlton moonshiners in the early 1930s and in one week destroyed fifteen stills. Another week they found two stills within one mile of the county courthouse in Folkston – each still had a six-hundred-gallon daily capacity. As noted earlier, John Hopkins had to destroy several stills around Billy's Island in 1919 due to the danger drunkenness and hangovers posed to timber workers operating heavy machinery. Moonshining was a widespread and lucrative industry, and most successful moonshiners, like the Swamper Ralph Davis, "though he was known for making some of the best contraband corn liquor in the Okefenokee back in the late twenties and early thirties, . . . never drank his own or anyone else's bootleg."[71] Moonshining was just one of the many productive and extractive industries in which Swampers engaged as part of their ecolocal culture. That this productive activity created controversy and clashes in the Okefenokee between 1820 and 1927 reveals the ways swamp ecolocalism both produced and emerged out of conflict between and within communities.

Swampers produced foodstuffs and products for both home consumption and market purposes, and they were able to do so because of the nature of the swamp ecosystem. Their physical and psychological adjustments to the demands of Okefenokee ecology – Swamper ecolocal culture – made it possible for them to work also as guides and timber workers when the Suwanee Canal Company and the Hebard Lumber Company developed the Okefenokee between 1890 and 1927. Their complicity in the projects of these surveyors and developers ultimately resulted in the infringement of Swamper rights in the Okefenokee Swamp.

Swampers' adjustment to the demands of Okefenokee ecology and the expertise they gained while farming, herding, hunting, trapping, and gathering in the swamp meant that they were willing and able to serve as guides for surveyors who entered the Okefenokee in the antebellum years. In 1850 Mansfield Torrance employed Robert "One-Eyed" Thrift as an additional chain carrier and guide on the first official government exploration of the Okefenokee Swamp. Thrift had been living on Cowhouse Island, in the northeastern corner of the swamp, for several decades, and Torrance felt he was qualified to lead the survey party around the Okefenokee's sinkholes and through its multitudinous and meandering waterways. The Swamper worked as the survey guide and chainman for the duration of the forty-day survey; he also acted as an instructor, conveying information about the wildlife of the swamp. After the surveyors shot and killed two alligators and inspected their mouths, Thrift explained that "a few teeth were wanting" because "they shed their teeth every year" like snakes.[72] Torrance's use of and payment for Thrift's environmental expertise during this survey set the precedent for subsequent investigations of the Okefenokee and introduced a new kind of employment opportunity for Swampers.

When Richard Hunter entered the Okefenokee seven years later, he employed multiple Swampers to aid him and his surveyors during their lengthy winter expedition. The team began its survey on the northeastern side of the swamp near Cowhouse Island and camped near the homestead of a family Miller B. Grant called "the Shorts." The "Shorts" were most likely the Thrift family, although multiple Swamper families inhabited Cowhouse Island at that time, including a man Grant identifies as "Stag Morris," his "old woman," and Lydia Smith Stone's father. Thrift told Hunter and Grant that he "knew every pig track in this range" and could guide the party if they wished. Hunter assented and Thrift led them into the prairies of the eastern Okefenokee several days later. The Swamper apparently did not accompany them to the Pocket on the western side, because at this point Hunter employed Josiah Mixon as a guide. Mixon, who had moved to the area the year before Hunter arrived, had managed to clear a few acres near a cypress pond in that time. He led them along Floyd's trail to Billy's Island, where the Lee family was already homesteading, but then, as Hunter reported, "having no further knowledge of the way . . . our guide left us, and we had to trust to our own resources to find Floyd's Island."[73] The survey party struggled on with no guide but managed to find Floyd's Island and return to Mixon's homestead in the Pocket without any incidents.

When Hunter's team later divided into two groups, one to continue the survey of the Okefenokee perimeter and the other to investigate the St. Marys River and the southeastern side, the latter group hired another Swamper, "Mr. Macklinn," to guide them in the area. They also hired "Mr. Hacket" (Obediah Barber) to lead them through the prairies of the northern Okefenokee. Barber acted as both guide and chainman on the expedition across the northern portion of the swamp, back to the Pocket on the west side, and across the Okefenokee from west to east. Hunter knew that this part of the swamp contained large marshy bays "calculated to mislead a person unacquainted with the region into the belief that they formed part of the main swamp." Barber was hired to "avoid error in relation to such matter[s]."[74] Swamper guides, therefore, would not only ensure that the surveyors survived the trip, they would also make certain that the resulting maps of the "true Okefenokee" would be accurate.

These guides also provided entertainment for adventurers in camp, telling tall tales and jokes. The surveyors initially enjoyed Barber's antics but tired of both the swamp and their Swamper guide by the end of their expedition: "Our days passed in wearying monotony; our evenings were a little enlivened by the simplicity, curiosity, and cleverness of our new employee, Mr. Hacket, though I must confess we were . . . beginning to tire of Crackerdom – their greenness and their coarseness." Barber, however, reveled in this part of his job. At the end of the Hunter survey, he performed a sentimental farewell address for the company – although Grant remarked that he had been drinking and the "muddled state of his brain did not . . . add to its brilliancy." The Swamper guide gave interviews and told stories about his adventures with the survey until the end of his days.[75]

Guiding for surveys continued to be an important monetary and psychic wage for Swampers in the postbellum years. Charles Pendleton wanted Obediah Barber to guide his first expedition in the spring of 1875, but late rains had delayed spring planting and Barber could not leave his acreage in order to lead the party.[76] Dr. W. C. Folks, a physician and railroad promoter, arranged for Pendleton to interview Ben Yarborough, an older Swamper who lived in Tebeauville, Pendleton's hometown on the northeastern side of the swamp. Yarborough claimed to know "every trail and by-path in [the Okefenokee] that was known to man," having evaded military service there during the Civil War. Pendleton secured his services at the price of fifty cents a day and announced his "intention of entering the swamp and learning all [Yarborough] knew and more." Pendleton was impressed with Yarborough's knowledge, his hunting skills, and his physical constitution:

> He was an old Okefenokee ranger and had seen as much of the Swamp as any man – killed more bear and panther than any one – in fact, it is claimed for him that he once whipped a panther, after wounding him, in a hand to hand fight with his pocket knife – and he was very familiar with some of the parts of the Swamp we expected to visit. Uncle Ben is a stout, robust man, about fifty-four years of age, and can undergo more hardship now than nine tenths of the younger men in the country – has the constitution of an ox and the digestion of a "gator" – can wade to his gills in the mud, water, alligators and mosquitoes a week without flinching, and know no words as fail.[77]

To Pendleton, "Uncle Ben" exemplified masculinity: he excelled in competition against the beasts of the forest, was an expert in swamp geography, and was physically strong. He knew "no words as fail" and was loyal – Yarborough promised that "he would be with us to the end." Pendleton aspired to this image and practice of rural masculinity and saw Yarborough as a guide not just in the swamp but also in life.

"Uncle Ben" played many roles as the survey guide. He would not let the adventurers rest on their laurels or underestimate the Okefenokee. When they complained of mosquitoes on their first night, Ben responded that "they were nothing compared to what they were a little farther in the Swamp!" He, like Barber, enlivened the camp with his storytelling. On that same first night, Pendleton and his cohorts listened, rapt, as Yarborough told his swamp stories. Pendleton noted that "it was a night for *gass* and not for sleep." Like Thrift, Yarborough also taught the adventurers about the Okefenokee's wildlife. After the party stumbled on a nest of malodorous alligators – "the stampede would have been an amusing scene to a[n] on-looker who was out of danger," Pendleton noted wryly – Yarborough explained that "alligators never emit this musk except when they are mad. This, said he, was their breeding season, and they were more dangerous than any other time of the year."[78]

"Uncle Ben" also acted as a hunting instructor. When the party discovered that they had run out of provisions and thus could not make their way to Floyd's Island, the hunter's El Dorado, "Yarborough was sad for the first time on the trip. . . . 'Boys,' said he, 'it is a glorious place. The island for game, and the lake just agin it for fishing. I am getting old, and have hunted a heap, but I never saw anything equal to it, nor have I ever been in the woods with a finer set of boys, and I longs to show 'ems to you.'"[79] This first survey of Pendleton's lasted five days, and Yarborough earned $2.50 for his services. His participation in this survey exemplifies the willingness of Swampers to engage in service work and other occupations to earn a wage income.

Yarborough again worked as a guide for Pendleton's second expedition in the fall of 1875, as did Obediah Barber and another Swamper named Hendrix. The guides immediately took Pendleton on a deer hunt and "away they went at 'full cry' into the swamp." Later in the survey Daniel Lee provided the group with provisions and joined them on an excursion to the southern point of Billy's Island and then on to Honey Island.[80] The survey party stayed in the swamp for more than two months during this trip – the guides made more than twenty dollars apiece for their services. On the next expedition, run by the *Atlanta Constitution* in the winter of

1875–76, the party again retained Ben Yarborough, who had obtained quite a reputation for his skills as a guide. Ironically, as he and other guides like the Chesser boys became better known in the locality and regionally, their exotic value as local color decreased and surveyors increasingly neglected to mention their talents and exploits in their expedition reports. Despite this literary erasure, Swampers continued to work as survey guides for the next twenty years.

During the Suwanee Canal Company's brief survey of the swamp in 1890, Captain Henry Jackson hired Allen Jr. and John Chesser as guides. Jackson, like Pendleton, was impressed with the hunting skills of Swamper "boys": "I separated from my guides fully impressed with the fact that fond as I had been of fishing and hunting during my boyhood and youth that heretofore I had had no conception of what these sports were. The Chessers are veritable nimrods, for they live by the chase."[81] During the Hebard Lumber Company's much more extended timber survey of the Okefenokee of 1901–3, John Hopkins employed the Swampers Sam and Hamp Mizell as guides, recruited chainmen from Swamper families, and employed "one Bryant Lane, whose home was near the swamp, to make occasional trips to camp with mail and supplies." Lane's son Joe often helped out with the deliveries, and one day in 1903 Joe Lane demonstrated his willingness to adjust his schedule in the name of diversifying his labor and earning income: "One day when Bryant was leaving camp I told him to have Joe meet us at Hickory Hammock with the mule and the wagon on the next Wednesday. He said we would have to name another day because Joe was to be married the next Wednesday and would use the mule and the wagon. I said: 'Tell Joe to put the wedding off till Thursday; we simply must get to the railroad next Wednesday.' When we got to the Hammock, Joe was there and apparently perfectly satisfied with the change in the nuptial arrangements. I thanked him for postponing his wedding date. He said they didn't put it off – got married Tuesday."[82] Hopkins's ability to demand such flexibility and the Swampers' compliance (with a twist) reveals the extent to which Swampers accommodated the demands of Okefenokee ecology and the desires of corporate interests. It also reveals the extent to which Swampers were engaged in large-scale entrepreneurial projects, even if these projects threatened their future in the Okefenokee. Swampers' complicity in Okefenokee surveying trips between 1850 and 1903 led them to engage in the corporate lumber industry in the first three decades of the twentieth century. These actions, although they were consistent with Swamper ecolocal culture, ultimately led to permanent infringements of Swamper property and labor rights in the Okefenokee.

Swamper experience with guiding, small lumbering, and turpentining operations in the nineteenth century enabled them to work for the Hebard Lumber Company without questioning the ecological or economic consequences. Although the Swamper Will Cox later argued that "we went after the cypress and cut down 3,000 acres of tress. I was part of that. We didn't know any better," it is clear that it was not ignorance but a cultural tradition of accepting multiple work opportunities (however they should come) that pushed Okefenokee Swampers into the corporate lumber industry.[83] The complicity of Swamper families with the large-scale projects of the Hebard Lumber Company, and the multiple companies to whom it leased timber and turpentine rights, is best understood in light of their ecolocal culture. The complexity of these relationships is explicated by the histories of three Swamper families: the Coxes, the Davises, and the Lees.

The members of the Cox family are descended either from James Cox, who moved to Ware County in 1864 after a medical furlough from the Confederate Army, or from his brother Thomas H. Cox, who moved near Black River Creek in 1861. Richard "Gid" Cox, one of the sons of Thomas and Mary Cox, cut cross-ties, worked turpentine, and farmed his land. Before he was forty years old, he had acquired more than three thousand acres around the Okefenokee; in 1903 he leased turpentine rights on a large tract of these holdings to Thrift, Tatum, and Co. for nine hundred dollars. Bud Cox, Gid's brother and Tom and Mary's oldest son, grew up in the Okefenokee and married his neighbor, Rebecca Tatum. Bud, like most Swampers, raised "piney-woods" hogs and cattle, farmed, and worked for some small lumbering enterprises.[84]

The work lives of Bud and Rebecca's three sons reveal their willingness to diversify their methods of subsistence and market production. Their oldest son, Ancil, married a Crews of Cowhouse Island, lived near his parents, and worked as a lumber checker and a convict labor guard at Oak Still, a turpentine production site. Ancil's brother Jim married another neighbor, Maggie Carter, and bought twenty-five acres on Swamp Road (on the northern side) from her father. He farmed, worked turpentine, and like his brother, earned eighteen dollars a month guarding convict laborers at the Oak Still. Another brother, Jep, also made his living farming and working turpentine. In the winters he trapped in the swamp. In 1931 Jep also worked as a scout with a Georgia state survey team sent to discover the feasibility of running a highway through the Okefenokee.[85]

One does not have to trace the Cox line very far to find family members who worked for or had dealings with the Hebard Lumber Company. Gid and Bud's brother Jasper died in 1913 and left his widow, Jane, with five children, all boys. She subsisted on the kindness of relatives until 1922, when she moved her family to Billy's Island and her sons began to work for the Hebard Cypress Company, girdling and cutting cypress trees. Her youngest son, Henry, went to school on Billy's Island until he was old enough to work; he then helped Hopkins's crews build and maintain the railroad mudlines in and out of the swamp. Ciscero Cox, the youngest son of Tom and Mary Cox (and brother of Bud), had a small farm on the northeast side of the Okefenokee. In 1908 he sold his twenty-five acres for $350 and moved to Billy's Island, where he joined his nephews and worked for the Hebard Cypress Company.[86] "Red" Cox, another family member, hunted and trapped in the Okefenokee and harvested gum from the slash pines along its borders before the Hebard Lumber Company bought the swamp. He and his family lived in Black Hammock, not far from his relatives' houses on Swamp Road, and they often burned the pines around their house to allow food to grow for their livestock. In 1909 he went to work for the Hebards, pulling cables on a logging skidder, and continued to work for the Hebards until the company ceased operations in the Okefenokee in 1927. Red "remains in awe at the size of the cypress trees he helped harvest from the Okefenokee."[87]

The Davises, like the Coxes, have a long history of lumbering in the swamp. Walter Davis and his wife, Eliza, moved to the Trail Ridge in 1896, after the Suwanee Canal Company abandoned its attempt to drain the swamp. Walter had been a blacksmith and a surveyor for the company, and he moved permanently to the area after seeing what the Okefenokee had to offer. He then spent most of his life working as a "girdling" foreman for the Hebard Lumber Company and other timber operations in the Okefenokee hinterlands. He oversaw advance operations in the interior, where crews slashed cypress trees at their bases in order to drain their sap and dry them out for cutting. Walter also sold furs and skins from the animals he and his sons trapped in the Okefenokee and raised corn, peas, sugar cane, and sweet potatoes in his fields. The family also herded cattle and hogs and raised chickens.[88]

Ralph Davis was the youngest of Walter and Eliza's four children, and he learned early how to hunt, fish, and farm. He made trips with his father to Billy's Island when he was a young boy and worked sporadically for timber operations in the Okefenokee during the 1920s and 1930s. It was a twelve-hour workday with no more than a dollar for pay, and often "we didn't get that. But if you could make it to the end of the month with 30 dollars, you were something." With his earnings from his timber work, Davis began to acquire land as a young man, and by the 1930s he owned more than 750 acres – more than half of this tract lay within the Okefenokee. During the early 1930s a timber baron named Judge Henry Johnson established a sawmill on the Davis's land between the farm and the swamp. This enterprise, called "Piddlinville," provided many much-needed jobs during the Depression, and Jack Davis, one of Ralph's brothers, became a mill hand there. Ralph Davis remembered this period of timber extraction as a difficult one: "you know, a lot of those timber people took advantage of the people around here. They came around offering what looked like a lot of money, and most 'em couldn't resist it. They took the money and moved out."[89] For some Swamper families, hard cash was irresistible. Their abandonment of their Okefenokee homes was often rooted in a need for money in addition to a conviction that they could either move to another part of the swamp or continue to exercise their hunting and herding rights within the Okefenokee.

No family encountered the complexities of conflict and complicity with the timber industry more than the Lees. In the 1850s James J. Lee was living on Billy's Island in the northwest interior of the Okefenokee, and around 1870 he sold or swapped his claim to the island to "Black Jim" Lee, so named because he sported a massive black beard. Throughout the late nineteenth century Black Jim Lee's family grew corn, wheat, beans, sugar, cane syrup, and potatoes; they also herded cattle, fished, hunted, and cultivated honey.[90] They were, as Charles Pendleton wrote, "the most independent in the world." However, they lived on government land. This fact and the community understanding that the Lees were squatters made life difficult for the family during the Hebard era. During those years the Lees' "quiet solitude" was interrupted by the railroad's screech, and the family came into conflict with the lumber company. Their diverse reactions to their situation – demands for money, lawsuits, and working for the Hebards – reveal the complexity of Swamper engagement with developers in the Okefenokee.

The Swamper community, and certainly the Lees, believed that by squatting for consecutive years, they had a right of improvement and therefore ownership of the land on Billy's Island. The Suwanee Canal Company and the Hebard Lumber Company directors understood that the Lees' residence on the island, though unlawful, would have to be rewarded monetarily if operations in the swamp were to proceed smoothly.[91] Captain Henry Jackson explained the matter to the board of the Suwanee Canal Company in 1894: "Upon Billy's Island is the only squatter of which I am aware, upon the property of the Company within the Swamp area. His name is Lee, and he has living with him a family of a wife and twelve children, and from appearances there, he shall soon have thirteen. He has lost two children by death. He has cleared and has in cultivation about fifty acres of very fine land, right on the margin of Billy's lake. He asks a thousand dollars for possessory title. There would be no difficulty in ejecting him under our grant from the state, but he is now doing no harm where he is, and at the proper time I would advise paying him what his improvements are worth, if we find it necessary to remove him."[92] That James Lee asked for a thousand-dollar remuneration for his family's removal from the swamp suggests that he understood he had some rights as a squatter. That Jackson seemed amenable to this demand reveals that the Suwanee Canal Company wanted to cooperate with Swampers in the area. The Canal Company folded before any deal could be made, however, and the Lee family dodged this initial eviction bullet.

But in 1900, when the Hebard Lumber Company purchased the Okefenokee lands from the Jackson family trust, tensions began to resurface. Pope Barrow, who was negotiating the transfer of lands, wrote to W. M. Oliff in December 1900, "I am perfectly willing to let him [Daniel Lee, Black Jim Lee's son-in-law] stay there as long as he wants to, provided he will admit that he is there by permission from me."[93] Clearly, the situation involved more than money and legal rights. Barrow's demand for Daniel Lee's public acknowledgement of his own lack of property rights seems an act borne purely out of a need to communicate the company's power. Needless to say, Daniel Lee made no such admission.

The situation remained tense until it finally came to a head in 1917. By this time the Hebard Cypress Company (under the aegis of the Hebard Lumber Company) had harvested the southwestern portion of the Okefenokee, and timber crews were advancing on Billy's Island. John Hopkins had recommended to the company that the island be used as a company town and a launching point for logging operations in the northern part of the swamp. The Hebards agreed with the plan and construction of mudlines to the island began. The Lee family again claimed possessory right, but a county court did not uphold their claim and the Lees were forced to leave the island. The Hebards wrote the family a check for one thousand dollars; the Lees took the money and moved to a tract of land on the northern side of the swamp. The company wasted no time tearing down Daniel Lee's log house and replacing it with a large frame house where the superintendent, John Hopkins, would later live.[94]

This Swamper story does not end on such a melodramatic note – in 1917, at least. After the eviction, some of the family members stayed and worked for the Hebard Lumber Company. Lonnie Lee, one of Daniel Lee's sons, left with the rest of the family when he was twelve years old and then returned to work a crosscut saw, felling cypress trees during the last years of the company's operations. After the Hebards ceased their lumber enterprise in 1927, Jackson and Harrison Lee (grandsons of Black Jim Lee) and their families returned to Billy's Island. In 1929 Walter Hill, an inspector for a credit company, visited Billy's Island and reported, "Their one venture into the great outside was when the timber crew came in, and for the time their peaceful and orderly existence was disturbed. They found it worse outside and were 'powerful glad to get back to Billys Island.'"[95]

The family lived at their former homesite, along with a pair of trouble-making brothers named Dan and Farley Steedley, for another two years after Hill's visit before the Hebards again came calling. Although he had no use in mind for Billy's Island, Daniel Hebard told the visiting scientist Francis Harper that "he was removing little Harrison Lee and his folks from Billy's Island, but was offering them all the land they would need near Hopkins." A year later Jackson Lee was dead and Mattie Lee Saunders, his widow, attempted to claim the island, again by possessory right. Again, however, the Lees were unsuccessful in their legal claims. A wildfire destroyed most of their property in April 1932, but the Lees still refused to leave. On April 13, 1932, the Hebard Lumber Company filed a dispossessory warrant against Harrison Lee, and five days later "Sheriff H. W. Mizell, with Ed Mizell, motored over to Billy's Island and made an inland trip to the old mill site, where the sheriff went to dispossess some of the Lee family." The Mizells' role in the eviction is evidence of the complexities of Swamper engagement with corporate industry in the Okefenokee. Forced to act against members of their own community, the Mizells and other company officials occupied a space between the Hebards and the Swampers. This twilight world had its advantages, but it also meant that these men had an uncertain reputation in both communities.[96]

Apparently Mizell was not successful in his initial attempt to evict the Lees, because one month later, the *Charlton County Herald* reported that "Sheriff Ed Mizell and R.L. Bunkley, district game warden, went to Billys Island Tuesday where the sheriff served warrants for trespassing on Dan Steedley and Farley Steedley and against the former for violating the game law by fishing with traps and seines. The two were brought back and jailed. Harrison Lee, also wanted, was not found. The Sheriff dispossessed his prisoners and had their belongings hauled from the island." Mizell loaded up the Lee family belongings (and the remaining family members as well) onto a flatbed truck. The going was so rough that much of the family's clothes and household goods were scattered across the swamp; one local historian depicts this act of eviction as another "Trail of Tears."[97] The Lees were ultimately evicted from their Okefenokee home because they lived on land the Hebard Lumber Company owned and wanted to use. The decision that some of the Lees made to work for the Hebards after their removal, however, is indicative of Swamper ecolocal culture of flexible and diverse production, even in the face of family dispossession. And although most Swamper families bristled at the loss of their acreage and domestic property, they were more disgruntled when logging concerns attempted to curtail their hunting and trapping rights in the Okefenokee.

Swampers often fought one another over territorial boundaries in the Okefenokee. Bee hunters marked trees and herders branded their cattle and hogs, but hunting and trapping territories were a bit harder to define as private property within the context of the open range. Swampers depended on common knowledge and belief in the possessory right of such areas to police these amorphous boundaries. When one hunter trespassed on another's domain, squabbles and often violence ensued. When the Suwanee Canal Company and the Hebard Lumber Company moved in to the swamp at the turn of the twentieth century, company officials took their property rights seriously and began to restrict Swamper movement in the prairies, hammocks, and islands of the Okefenokee. Swamper hunting rights became company-dispensed privileges.

In response, some Swampers negotiated with the Hebards. In return for his protection of Hebard property on the west side of the Okefenokee, Hamp Mizell acquired exclusive fishing and trapping privileges in that sector. True to Swamper form, Mizell used his "privilege" not only to fish and trap for himself but to establish a business. He stocked western Okefenokee waters with fish and rented boats and fishing tackle to tourists and other visitors; he also sold trapping privileges to fellow Swampers.[98]

But the Hebards angered many Swampers by refusing to let tradition or common knowledge dictate the boundaries of hunting and trapping domains. Many Swamper men reacted to these strictures by hunting and trapping according to their own schedules and territories instead of the Hebards'. While lumber company workers collected traps whenever they came across them, as John Hopkins noted, "a number of local residents have done some trapping and attempted more."[99] While he worked for the Hebard Lumber Company, "Red" Cox trapped through the winter months, disregarding company-mandated permit requirements and territories that, to Cox, existed only on meaningless pieces of paper. His traps caught "raccoon, otter, 'more possum than you wanted.' An otter pelt brought $40 to $60, Cox said, adding 'Back in those days, $40 was $40.'" His cousin Henry Cox, while working for the Hebards maintaining mudline tracks, "turned to the swamp for subsistence and lived off of the animals he found there. He, his brother, and his cousins built cabins in the swamp and often slept in the bottom of boats. They killed alligators in the summer and trapped in the winter to make money the best way they could."[100] Throughout the 1910s and 1920s the Coxes combined subsistence production, wage labor, market activities, and resistance to institutional restrictions in these acts of poaching in the Okefenokee.

Some Swampers, like J. C. Nettles, undermined the Hebards' restrictions and used company property to sustain their families. Nettles was born near the St. Marys in northern Florida and moved to the Okefenokee when he was twenty-six years old. He worked for the Hebard Lumber Company at Camp Cornelia, learning to use the overhead skidder rigs to pull logs out of the swamp. As a timber worker, he earned $1.50 a day; one winter he asked John Hopkins for permission to hunt and trap in the Okefenokee after work. Hopkins denied his request and came to regret it. Nettles waited until Hopkins had left the camp for a visit to the west side of the swamp, then stole his boat and paddled into the swamp interior. He stayed there for three months, trapping raccoons, otters, and alligators while evading Hebard patrolmen. On trapping trips, Nettles would stay in the swamp for two or three weeks at a time, return at night, submerge Hopkins's boat in the Suwanee Canal, and walk more than ten miles to sell the pelts in Folkston. He took the gator meat and the money he earned from the pelts to his family and then returned to the Okefenokee, extracted Hopkins's boat, and slipped back into the swamp. No one could ever find him, "because he stayed in the most inaccessible parts of the swamp, and few men have ever come to know their way through the swamp as well as Nettles." Through trapping, Nettles made $16 a day.[101]

The Hebards saw their system of permits and privileges as a way to monitor their employees and a strategy to make more money from their Okefenokee holdings. Swampers resisted the company's attempts to control their work schedules and territories, because hunting and trapping had been a core element of their ecolocal culture for more than half a century. Hunting and trapping without permits seemed a good way to challenge the Hebards while continuing to provide for their families.

Swampers who lived in and around the Okefenokee between 1820 and 1937 saw the swamp as a homesite and a workplace. Here, they could live a life oriented to markets of their own choosing and to the needs of their families. The irony of the ecolocal culture Swampers created in the Okefenokee between 1850 and 1937 is that the efficient and profitable system of diversified labor that Swampers practiced in order to fulfill their swamp desires led them to embrace, without contradiction or discomfort, the very entrepreneurial ideology that restricted their rights within the swamp. Swampers continually struggled with their place in the Okefenokee and those "outlanders" who would seek to define it. Increasingly in the twentieth century, they found themselves at odds with developers who sought to convert or extract resources from "their swamp." In an effort to preserve their ecolocal culture, Swampers joined forces with a group of scientists and conservationists who aimed to save the swamp as a wildlife refuge in the 1920s and 1930s. But ultimately, their complicity with these preservationists prevented Swampers from saving themselves.

# 5 A Refuge for Birds
## Okefenokee Preservation

In 1901 Roland Harper, a civil engineer who worked as a botanical collector for the state of Georgia, noted the sale of the Okefenokee Swamp to the Hebard Lumber Company with anxiety. He wrote to F. V. Coville, a botanist with the U.S. Department of Agriculture, in December 1901 that "the Great Okeefinokee Swamp of Georgia has never been explored by a botanist . . . but is being destroyed by lumbermen for its cypress timber, and I am anxious to get into it before the destruction proceeds too far." The following June, Harper wrote again to Coville to request approval and funds for a botanical reconnaissance in and around the Okefenokee. On July 8, 1902, Harper was appointed an expert within the Bureau of Plant Industry and directed to collect plants throughout southeastern Georgia, particularly in the Okefenokee Swamp.[1]

Roland Harper's expedition in 1902 initiated a new era in human interaction with the Okefenokee Swamp. Subsequent botanical, entomological, and ornithological surveys brought trained scientists into the swamp for the first time; their efforts to preserve the Okefenokee as a wildlife refuge were rooted in their collective desire to provide a professional resource for themselves. Preservationists succeeded in fulfilling their swamp desires in the long term – and were the only community that did so – because their ecolocal beliefs did not rest on misjudgments of swamp ecology or a dependence on its conversion or destruction. Like fugitive slaves, Seminoles, and Swampers, they did not seek to foist a vision or project on the Okefenokee that the swamp ecosystem could not sustain. But for preservationists, professional sustenance depended on an Okefenokee that was devoid of human habitation and use. By striving to create this "primeval wilderness," preservationists ultimately brought about the restriction of swamp access and the permanent eviction of the community that helped them the most – Swampers. Attention to narratives of preservation in the Okefenokee story uncovers the role that the search for scientific knowledge played in shaping swamp ecolocalism in the Okefenokee hinterlands between 1902 and 1940.

Scientists began to enter the Okefenokee at a historical moment in which three movements coalesced in American culture: industrial logging, conservation, and professionalization of the sciences. As noted earlier, the Hebard Lumber Company purchased the Okefenokee in 1900, and the extraction of its ancient cypress stands began in 1909. Local reactions to the Hebards' enterprise were various and complex; many Okefenokee hinterland residents, like Roland Harper, responded to the swamp's development with sadness, mourning the loss of the Southeast's "last great wilderness." This nostalgic response reveals that many Okefenokee hinterland residents, like many other twentieth-century Americans, believed that nature had to endure so that human society could continue to thrive. The conviction regarding the inextricable link between nature and culture was not new; industrialization and urbanization that accompanied the market revolution in the 1830s led to an appreciation of "wilderness," spaces that could counteract the enervating forces of civilization. These sentiments proliferated in the Gilded Age, as elite easterners began to embrace the tenets that congressman and diplomat George Perkins Marsh had put forward in *Man and Nature* (1864): the world is an integrated whole and humanity's future depended on its ability to cease destructive development, remove resources from local control, and place them in the hands of scientifically trained managers.[2]

Marsh's arguments in 1864 originated the "degradation discourse" in discussions of the natural environment. In the 1870s and 1880s the idea that imminent ecological doom awaited Americans who did nothing to safeguard natural resources seemed persuasive to a group of northeastern elites who began to espouse values they called "conservationist." This group of men gained political power in these years and exploited a national print culture – including hunting novels, wilderness poetry, and outdoor sport journalism – to disseminate their beliefs regarding the proper management of natural resources. Through the editorial and newspaper management skills of George Bird Grinnell, the political power of Theodore Roosevelt, and the forestry theories and projects of Gifford Pinchot, Progressive conservationists emphasized government ownership and efficient management of nature's bounty. These men also sought to delineate and prevent behavior they considered to be environmentally destructive and to legislate nature's future in America.[3]

The nascent conservation movement focused most of its initial efforts on the mountainous areas of the Northeast and the West. Yellowstone National Park, established by Congress in 1872, was the focal point of much early environmental activism, as were Yosemite Valley and the Adirondacks. But the southern states were not without their conservationist proponents, particularly in the context of forestry – the science of development, maintenance, and selective harvest of forested areas. In 1873, just as the timber industry turned its eyes to the South, a stand of loblolly and shortleaf pines were laid out on the Windsor Springs estate of the Civil War general W. H. T. Walker near Augusta, Georgia. Windsor Springs was thus the first forest plantation in North America. In 1892 Gifford Pinchot, the wealthy son of a prominent East Coast family, began to demonstrate the virtues of forestry within the grounds of George Washington Vanderbilt's Biltmore Estate in western North Carolina. In 1906 the University of Georgia established an academic forestry program, and both national forest managers and Okefenokee hinterland inhabitants began to call attention to the destructive practices of logging in Georgia.[4]

By 1919 knowledge and appreciation of forestry practices in the Okefenokee hinterlands were so widespread that an editor of the *Waycross (Ga.) Journal-Herald* was able to write, "The spread of forestry knowledge has made the general public familiar with the value of forest preservation. Nearly everybody knows that woods, besides providing a timber supply, serve as sponges to catch and hold moisture, thereby helping to provide a uniform water supply the year round. . . . The department of agriculture, in one of its farmers' bulletins, points out that almost any wood lot, even a small one, may be made serviceable in this way. . . . The moral is, preserve the grove around your spring or well; and if there are no trees there,

plant them. The more the better."[5] Okefenokee hinterland residents embraced both the lumber industry and forestry during the late nineteenth
century, hoping for economic health but also idealizing a perpetually re-
productive forest. The "spread of forestry knowledge" in the Okefenokee
hinterlands at this time was testament to a growing awareness that the
area's forest resources were being rapidly depleted. It also reveals that
print culture was vital to the cultivation and dissemination of a conservationist ethic. Newspaper articles and cheaply produced, specialized magazines like *The American Sportsman* (established in 1871) and *Forest and
Stream* (1873) publicized efforts to create forest preserves all over the
country. It was in this context of a conservationist-saturated print culture
and a growing concern for southeastern ecosystems that scientists began
their studies of the Okefenokee Swamp.

But nineteenth- and early-twentieth-century scientists who looked to
the Okefenokee Swamp were not so much interested in conservation,
which emphasized the efficient management of resources for economical
development, but in preservation: the protection of areas in their "natural" state for the purposes of aesthetic appreciation, spiritual renewal, and
scientific research. The scientists who entered the Okefenokee in the first
decades of the twentieth century were positioned against logging and
other destructive conversions of swamp ecosystems. As they shaped their
preservationist narrative in the Okefenokee hinterlands between 1902
and 1940, these scientists perceived of the swamp as a pristine environment that humans would enter only to observe and record in the name of
knowledge.

The Okefenokee's first scientific explorers were trained in several fields,
most prominently botany, zoology, entomology, and ornithology. During
the nineteenth century the transformation of science from literary natural
history into a set of separate specific disciplines began, and by the turn of
the twentieth century, disciplines had been diversified and as Paul Farber
has noted, "the methods of research were rigorous and narrowly presented, the topics limited to a few agreed upon significant ones, and the
audience a highly critical and specialized group of trained individuals."[6]
By the early twentieth century, however, a significant number of amateur
scientists, particularly ornithologists, still provided an audience base for
scientific journals and preservationist organizations.[7] The articles that the
Okefenokee scientists wrote about the swamp can best be described as an
amalgamation of several genres that appealed to a wide range of readers:

natural history (descriptions, lists, and drawings), field notes, and technical scientific treatises. Most of those scientists who investigated the Okefenokee dabbled in multiple disciplines, but they were fully professionalized. They had been trained in academic institutions, had published in professional journals, and were associated with and funded by universities, most notably Cornell.

By the time that a group of scientists affiliated with Cornell University embarked for the Okefenokee in May 1912, a conservationist and scientific culture had begun to take shape in the United States. And by 1900 Cornell had become a cutting-edge center of scientific study, housing the nation's first Department of Entomology (in which students studied the anatomy, habits, and habitats of insects) and a thriving Department of Zoology, in which scientists investigated the lives of animals. The Department of Zoology developed a specialty in ornithological studies and began offering curricula to undergraduate and graduate students at the turn of the twentieth century. In 1898 Bernhard Fernow organized a School of Forestry at Cornell, the first of its kind in the nation.[8] Due to these curricular developments, Cornell became a site of the production of both conservationist and preservationist ideas. The Okefenokee expedition of May–July 1912 created a movement that embraced the latter narrative in the drive to save the swamp for scientists.

In 1909 J. Chester Bradley of Cornell's Department of Entomology made his first trek to the Okefenokee area, completing brief insect counts along the Suwanee Canal and the northwestern edge. He returned alone in 1910 and again in 1911, then decided to put together a group of professors and graduate students to conduct a longer biological reconnaissance after the completion of the spring semester of 1912. On May 28 a Cornell party that included Bradley, C. R. Crosby (Department of Entomology), Albert Hazen Wright (Department of Zoology), James G. Needham (Department of Entomology), W. D. Funkhouser (then the headmaster of Ithaca High School and later a professor at the University of Kentucky), Cornell undergraduates S. C. Bishop and M. D. Leonard, and a local Georgian named Paul Battle made its way from Fargo (on the western side of the swamp) to the southwestern entrance near the Pocket. They then followed a mudline to Mixon's Ferry and hired Swamper guides secured by R. W. Bennett of the Fargo Land Company. There they met up with E. L. Worsham (the state entomologist of Georgia) and his assistant, C. S. Spooner.[9]

With their guides, they walked along old railroad beds and corduroy roads (paths made of pine logs and soil) to Billy's Island, where they established camp headquarters. From there, the expedition members explored the islands on the western side of the swamp and a heronry between Fargo and Mixon's Ferry. The scientists collected specimens and took field notes for more than a month, making forays into the swamp every day and returning at night to their Billy's Island camp. When they left the Okefenokee on July 15, they had completed the first organized, university-based scientific exploration of the swamp.[10] The publication of their studies in subsequent years brought national attention to the Okefenokee and initiated the drive for the swamp's preservation. Most of the professors, including Bradley, Wright, and Needham, also played important roles in Okefenokee preservation organizations during the 1920s and 1930s. But it was Francis Harper, a graduate student who completed his own reconnaissance several weeks before joining his Cornell compatriots, who was most responsible for shaping an ecolocal narrative of preservation in the Okefenokee hinterlands.

Francis Harper grew up in Americus, Georgia, a member of a large, creative, and achievement-oriented family – five of the seven members of the family wrote at least one book during their professional careers. Francis was particularly influenced by the career and advice of his older brother, Roland, whose article "The Okefinokee Swamp," published in *Popular Science Monthly* in June 1909, was the first scientific treatise on the swamp itself. Listening to Roland's stories and reading his article drafts, Francis realized that the Okefenokee Swamp offered a rich botanical bounty that scientists had not yet discovered. While discussing the reconnaissance with his brother, Francis also came to understand the logistics of a scientific collecting trip. Roland had received government funds, hired the Swampers Sam Mizell and J. W. Roddenberry as guides and transporters, accumulated information on the swamp from Sam's brother Hamp, photographed specimens before collecting them, taken hundreds of pages of field notes in a journal, and succeeded in publishing his findings in a popular magazine with a national readership.[11] His younger brother learned from Roland's organization and tactics and applied these skills during all of his trips to the Okefenokee between 1912 and 1937.

During his expeditions and in his subsequent publications, Francis Harper perceived the Okefenokee Swamp to be a site of unparalleled natural beauty, a "primeval wilderness" home to many ancient species (like the alligator) and birds almost lost to extinction. His assertions of the "pure" nature of some parts of the Okefenokee provided justification for his scientific incursions: an environment in such a wild state would be the perfect ecological laboratory. For Harper and his Cornell compatriots, the swamp was not refuge for humans, a battleground, a potential agricultural Eden, a forest to be culled and managed, or a homesite. It was a place in which they could study nature in order to contribute knowledge to the scientific community, the nation, and the world; it was also a place that would provide them with a perpetual source of scientific data and, through this data, a professional reputation.

Francis Harper was twenty-five years old when he first entered the Okefenokee to locate breeding colonies of egrets for the National Association of Audubon Societies on May 6, 1912. He remained in the swamp for several weeks before joining his colleagues as a junior member of the Cornell University biological survey team later that month. Harper was a graduate student in the Department of Zoology and had a more personal stake in the trip than any of the other members. He had grown up near the Okefenokee and was an impassioned admirer of the swamp's beauty, calling it "one of the great natural features of the eastern United States, with no exact counterpart in the world. . . . Its exquisitely beautiful cypress bays, vast bonnet-strewn prairies, luxuriant hammocks, and magnificent pine lands – all in their pristine glory – are infinitely . . . valuable to lovers of nature."[12]

Harper had a genuine aesthetic appreciation of the Okefenokee, and many of his earliest writings that expressly reflect on his initial interaction with the swamp contain rapturous descriptions of its ecology. In 1915 Harper described an alligator run in the northeastern side of the Okefenokee: "The run passes between lines of cypresses, from which hang long festoons of Spanish moss . . . gently swaying in the breeze and half concealing the trunks of the trees. Vistas are disclosed of glade after glade, fringed on all sides by slender files of the cypress, and of a beauty so exquisite as to appear almost supernatural." About a sunset he witnessed from Chesser's Island (on the southeastern side) in September 1922, Harper wrote, "I have seen sunsets in various lands and upon the sea, but never such a one as this evening. . . . the celestial splendor struck me fairly agape. . . . Those glorious turrets and battlements of clouds with burnished rims!"[13] Harper was a rigorously trained scientist, but he also considered himself to be a naturalist-writer; thus he often included long descriptive passages praising the swamp's beauty in his journals and published articles. In doing so, he was part of a long literary tradition that combined scientific observation with imaginative prose and imbued the swamp with aesthetic and moral significance.

But Francis Harper also believed that these "exquisite" areas were landscapes in peril. As a young boy, Harper had heard about the sale of the Okefenokee to the Suwanee Canal Company and the failed efforts of the Jackson family to wrest agricultural land out of the swamp. He was witness to the sale of the swamp to the Hebard Lumber Company, a corporation that seemed a much more serious threat to the Okefenokee's forests. By the time he entered the swamp in the spring of 1912, the Hebards had been harvesting cypress trees for three years, and the impact on the swamp was already obvious. Harper echoed his brother's concern for the Okefenokee's deforestation in his first article about the 1912 expedition, lamenting, "During the past several years an ever-widening gash has been cut in the stand of cypress on the northwestern side of the swamp, to feed one of the largest lumber-mills in the South. The cypress is not expected to replace itself to any extent, and at the contemplated rate of destruction the next generation will never look upon the real Okefenoke." Here Harper mobilizes the degradation discourse to attack the lumber industry's incursions into the swamp and to mourn the future loss of the "real" Okefenokee. Primeval conditions were not only valuable in the sense that they represented real nature in opposition to false commercialism, but they were also vital, in Harper's view, to the work of scientists. Harper was cheered that primeval areas still existed in the Okefenokee, enough to "delight the heart of the ecologist. . . . The loss to science, therefore, in the destruction of the Okefenoke would be incalculable and irreparable."[14]

What Harper saw as the Okefenokee's "undisturbed wilderness" areas were sites of refuge for "rare and interesting animal life," particularly birds – it was the perfect ground on which to establish the reputation and scholarly oeuvre of a young ornithologist. In his first Okefenokee article, Harper notes that the Okefenokee is "virtually a *terra incognita* to the scientific world. Many an ornithologist, while en route to some more southerly Mecca, has doubtless passed almost within sight of its borders without turning aside to explore the enchanting Okefenoke wilderness." Because natural historians like William Bartram and John Muir bypassed the Okefenokee on their way to more southern climes, "only the scantiest reference to the swamp exists in the literature of ornithology, and exceedingly little definite information concerning its bird-life has been available."[15] The lack of ornithological information simultaneously disappointed and thrilled Harper; every scholar hopes for an original discovery, and the Okefenokee offered Harper a professional boon, a *terra incognita* ignored by prior scientists. Harper trained during his undergraduate years to be an ornithologist, and he decided to study the lives of egrets and other rare birds in the Okefenokee Swamp as part of his graduate research.[16]

With funding from the National Association of Audubon Societies, Harper set out to make an ornithological reconnaissance for several weeks in the summer of 1912. He was particularly interested in the ivory-billed woodpecker, a species that was nearly extinct in the early twentieth century and whose ghosts still haunt the prairies of the Okefenokee. This bird appealed to Harper's imagination – he never actually saw one – and to his degradation theories. Although he was unable to find any of the rumored nesting sites, Harper wrote with confidence, "There is no doubt that the Ivory-bill still exists, though in very small numbers, in the Okefenoke." For Harper, this particular woodpecker was the tragic avian of the swamp, the ultimate emblem of rapidly depleting primeval conditions: "A true bird of the wilderness, peculiarly incapable of withstanding the swift advances of civilization, it seems inevitably doomed to the fate of the Great Auk and the Passenger Pigeon."[17] Bird life, an index to environmental health, was a major area of study in the Okefenokee and one that would ultimately justify the swamp's preservation as a wildlife refuge.

Harper viewed the remaining "primeval" areas of the Okefenokee as ideal sites of ornithological and more general zoological study. The environmental mosaic of the swamp – its bays, prairies, islands, peat bogs, and waterways – was to Harper a distinct map of wildlife habitats. That so many different kinds of habitats existed within the swamp interior and that the transitions between them (though mucky) were obvious meant that scientists could easily study life histories and habitat use in this ecosystem. To Harper and other scientists, clear habitat demarcation and primeval conditions meant that "opportunities abound, not only for learning the original habitats of many species that have become accustomed elsewhere to frequenting habitats that have been greatly modified by civilization, but also for studying the life histories of these species in a perfectly natural environment."[18] Harper believed in the duality of the swamp; the Okefenokee could be a vanishing wilderness and a "perfectly natural environment" simultaneously.

Throughout the 1910s and 1920s scientists shared Okefenokee islands and prairies with timber cruisers, log cutters, and mudline tracks, constant reminders of the possibility that their ecological laboratory would disappear from under their feet and over their heads. It was with a sense of urgency – out of concern for wildlife but also for his own career – that Harper pleaded to the readers of *Natural History* in 1920 that "the Okefenokee would be an ideal location for a field biological station for the universities, museums, and other scientific institutions of the country. And its whole tremendous value for this purpose – the study of life histories and ecological relations – depends on the preservation of natural conditions."[19] To achieve the "preservation of natural conditions" and to create a continual source of specimens for their studies, Francis Harper and other scientists interested in the Okefenokee relied on conservationist print culture, clubs and associations, and professional connections to shape an ecolocal narrative of preservation in the first half of the twentieth century.

Between 1912 and 1951 Francis Harper produced thirty-eight volumes of notebooks on Okefenokee birds, frogs, alligators, and mammals. Most of these notes he converted into articles that he published in a variety of scientific journals, magazines, and newspapers. His studies of Okefenokee wildlife appeared in *Scientific Monthly, American Midland Naturalist, Natural History, Bird-Lore, Oriole,* and *National Geographic,* among others. Most of these publications were tied to local organizations with a readership of both professional scientists and amateur naturalists, but publications like *National Geographic* boasted a national reading audience made up of Americans of diverse professions with an abiding interest in adventure and world geography. These publications were the apparatus through which scientists disseminated their knowledge and preservationist narratives; they also provided professionals with a record of productivity and an imagined community of scientific colleagues. By spreading their call for Okefenokee preservation within a variety of magazines and journals, Harper and other scientists studying the swamp recruited both academics and amateurs to their cause.[20]

Through such publicity, they also courted the attention of national and regional clubs and associations that could contribute members, funds, or other forms of support. By 1918 a critical mass of scholarly scientific articles on the Okefenokee had appeared in print, and Congress had passed the Migratory Bird Treaty Act, which outlawed the killing and transportation of migratory birds across state and national borders. Publications and legislation thrust specific migratory bird species – many of which used the Okefenokee as a wintering ground – into the preservationist limelight. The time seemed right to organize a society for the preservation of the Okefenokee Swamp. J. F. Wilson, the editor of the agricultural journal *Nut-Grower* and a resident of Waycross, Georgia, gathered a group of Cornell scientists, including Francis Harper, James G. Needham, and Albert Hazen Wright, in addition to S. W. McCallie (the state geologist of Georgia), to form the core of what he called the Okefinokee Society (preservationists preferred the use of "i" in "Okefinokee," fancying that it was more primeval). Wilson contacted these men through letters and then began to print a bulletin of information to be distributed to members and to other preservationist organizations. Such print distribution would, he asserted to James Needham, "begin building a selected membership." The society received financing from the Progress Club of Waycross, and Wilson courted the Waycross Chamber of Commerce by promising publicity in exchange for funding.[21]

By 1919 the Board of Directors of the Okefinokee Society included Wilson, Needham, Francis and Roland Harper, W. D. Funkhouser, J. C. Bradley, Robert Cushman Murphy of the Brooklyn Art Museum (whose quarterly journal had published Francis Harper's "A Sojourn in the Primeval Okefinokee" in its April 1915 issue), Forest Shrive (the aptly named secretary of the Ecological Society of America), and T. Gilbert Pearson (the secretary of the National Association of Audubon Societies).[22] The Okefinokee Society members, feeling that their purpose lay in giving "authentic publicity regarding the Okefenokee Swamp; to secure its reservation and preservation for public, educational, scientific, and recreational uses," wrote letters to local and regional newspapers and sent their board members to national conservation organization meetings.[23] J. F. Wilson believed that the Okefinokee Society influenced the introduction of a joint resolution in the Georgia legislature in 1919 that urged Congress to enact legislation to preserve the Okefenokee:

*Whereas,* In the northwest and southwest sections of United States great areas have been purchased and set apart so that people there might have a place in which to go and see the life that has disappeared forever from the plains and forests and mountains of the far West, the National government having purchased seven great parks to carry out this work, and, *Whereas,* Here in the Southeast no friendly hand has been held out to help us in preserving for future generations the wild life that once existed in this section of the United States; nature has worked hard and furnished here a natural sanctuary; commerce has come in now, and the axe of the lumberman is heard throughout the Swamp and the coverts for game; the dense jungles in which birds and animals hide themselves from danger will disappear forever unless protected, and the great forests, jungle and Swamp which form the headwaters for two great rivers will disappear unless steps are taken to preserve the same.[24]

J. L. Sweat, a state congressman from Ware County, engages here in a narrative that depicts American wilderness areas as constantly under siege: the Okefenokee is a sanctuary deliberately created by Nature and threatened by the "axe of the lumberman." He also displays a conception of the world as interrelated, as Marsh did in *Man and Nature;* he notes that the swamp forms the headwaters of the Suwannee and the St. Marys, "two great rivers" vital to agriculture and other forms of commerce underway in the Okefenokee hinterlands. The Okefinokee Society lauded this resolution.[25] Although no state or federal legislative action resulted from it, Sweat's words were printed and reprinted in Georgia's newspapers and appealed to inhabitants' regional pride and growing appreciation of local natural environments.

Through their use of print culture and the cultivation of professional and legislative contacts, the Okefinokee Society received endorsements from the National Parks Association, the U.S. Biological Survey, the American Museum of Natural History, the National Association of Audubon Societies, the Ecological Society of America, the American Game Protective Association, the State Geological Survey of Georgia, and the Cornell University Departments of Zoology and Entomology.[26] The society members proudly reproduced a list of these endorsements in many of their publicity bulletins, establishing their links to a wider preservationist culture and, in so doing, legitimizing their efforts.

The Okefinokee Society's original plan was to identify certain portions of the swamp – those in primeval condition – as the nucleus of a preservation landscape and to raise private funds for its purchase. As the funds increased, members could buy up lands around the nucleus. After securing the area, the society planned to "present it to the United States Government, in order that it may be administered and perpetuated as a national wildlife refuge." Although these funds never materialized and the society's membership dwindled after the death of J. F. Wilson in 1921, the Okefinokee Society was the first preservationist association in the Okefenokee hinterlands and the first in the United States to focus solely on the preservation of a swampland. The society's members briefly reunited with local inhabitants to create the Okefenokee National Association in 1922, and while this organization did not achieve much legislatively or economically in the drive for Okefenokee preservation, it did manage to keep "the primeval Swamp" in the public eye throughout the 1920s.[27]

Organized campaigns to preserve the Okefenokee resurged in the late 1920s, most notably with the formation of the Georgia Society of Naturalists in 1929. This association was much more stable than previous organizations due to its broad membership base, influential leadership, and production of print culture. Francis Harper was an active member of this society, as were several other Cornell scientists, but most members were Georgians. Taking advantage of both the wider American culture of preservation and the appeal of grassroots initiatives, the Georgia Society of Naturalists was successful in cultivating membership. Half of the members were professors at Emory and other Georgia colleges and universities, but the other half were Georgia residents with no science degrees. Some of them were, however, quite influential within the state. The society's most famous member was Lucien Harris Jr., the grandson of Joel Chandler Harris and the president of the society for most of its years. Harris was interested in entomology, and the society published his "List of the Butterflies in Georgia" as its first *Bulletin* in the 1930s. Members of the organization deemed him "The Grand Caterpillar," a title that recognized his interests and linked the society to the Masons, another important social and economic organization in Georgia.[28]

Under Harris's leadership, society members lobbied state and federal legislators, wrote articles for newspapers, and enlisted support from a variety of wealthy individuals in Atlanta, local preservationist societies, and national conservation groups. Its members distributed their *Bulletins* to libraries and conservation organizations, funded scientific studies of the swamp, and made field trips to the Okefenokee – always joined by several reporters for the *Atlanta Constitution* and the *Atlanta Journal* – to popularize it "as a unique natural area."[29] Their trips to the swamp were facilitated by another society member who lived in both Philadelphia and Folkston and was even more influential than Lucien Harris in bringing about the Okefenokee's preservation: Frederick V. Hebard. Frederick was the son

of Daniel Hebard, the manager of the Hebard Lumber Company's Okefenokee lands, and he made the Hebards' hunting lodge on Floyd's Island
available to all Georgia Society of Naturalists members. In 1925 he
started making notes on the birds he observed while hunting on Floyd's
Island and continued to make lists from his own and his family's sight-
ings in addition to the hunting records at the lodge. His father, according
to Frederick, "co-operated with my amateur ornithological endeavors
throughout and gave me permission before his death to publish the shooting records in the Okefinokee from 1926 to 1936." In 1941 the Georgia
Society of Naturalists published Hebard's list of winter birds in the Okefenokee as its third *Bulletin,* and he considered it an endeavor to redress
"the paucity of published work on the birds of southern Georgia."[30]

Frederick Hebard also used his contacts within the state legislature to
bring the U.S. Senate Special Committee on Conservation of Wildlife Resources to the Okefenokee hinterlands to evaluate the swamp as a potential wildlife refuge in 1931. Senators Frederick C. Walcott, Harry B. Hawes,
Key Pittman, and Peter Norbek traveled to Waycross in early March and
were met at the train station by Paul Reddington, chief of the U.S. Biological Survey; former Okefinokee Society member and Audubon secretary T. Gilbert Pearson; Georgia Society of Naturalists president Lucien
Harris Jr.; and two reporters for the *Atlanta Journal.* The party took a train
to Folkston, and then half of the group took a plane ride over the swamp
while the others proceeded to the Swamper Hamp Mizell's fishing camp
on Suwannee Lake. Later that day they returned to Waycross and the
Woman's Club fed them an "old-fashioned Okefenokee dinner." The next
day the committee explored the Okefenokee in boats, camped and hunted
with Frederick Hebard and seven Swamper guides on Floyd's Island, and
then returned to Waycross for a banquet in honor of "The Conservationists."[31] These kinds of junkets entailed the cooperation of scientists, amateur naturalists, local boosters, and Swampers; they reveal the growing
enthusiasm for Okefenokee preservation and the realization that this goal
could be achieved only through legislative action.

The members of the committee were impressed enough to dispatch a
group from the U.S. Biological Survey to make their own inspection trip
and appraisals. The survey members did so in late March 1932 and subsequently concluded, "The area has only a very limited value for water-
fowl sanctuary purposes and does not appear to come within the scope of
the migratory bird conservation act. It would, however, make an ad-

mirable wild life refuge offering sanctuary for all time to all forms of wild life indigenous to this region." The economic exigencies of the Great Depression, however, stalled this effort. The committee ultimately determined that "at this time there is no money available with which to acquire these lands and such acquisition would have to be authorized by special legislation."[32] Despite this setback, the Georgia Society of Naturalists continued its publicity and lobbying campaigns throughout the 1930s.

Ultimately, however, it was not the support of universities, museums, national magazines, conservation organizations, or the influence of well-known Georgians that gave Francis Harper and other scientists the legitimacy they sought in the heart of the Okefenokee. Swampers helped these scientist-conservationists find their way through the swamp's labyrinthine waterways, provided them with wildlife specimens, and told tales of birds and animals that Harper and others used as scientific data. By cooperating with professional scientists, Swampers themselves gained access to a regional and national print culture and became experts in their own right. They also provided economically for their families and supported preservation as a way to maintain their ecolocal culture. But preservationist narratives dictated that humans were only to be observers of the primeval wilderness. As the swamp became a refuge, the "feathered tribes" that Harper sought to save replaced Okefenokee Swampers in the depths of Georgia's pet swamp.[33]

When Roland Harper began his first biological reconnaissance of the Okefenokee in 1902, he engaged local men as guides and sources of information. He turned to Hamp Mizell, "who had recently helped John M. Hopkins on his timber survey for the Hebard Lumber Company," for botanical information; Hamp's brother Sam, who had also worked on the Hebard survey, helped Harper avoid sinkholes and alligators for $1.50 a day. J. W. Roddenberry, who supplied two buggies and a driver for Harper, also provided "considerable information about common names and economic plants."[34]

Ten years after his brother engaged the Mizells and Roddenberry as guides, Francis Harper hired nineteen-year-old David Lee to take him through the Okefenokee in search of avian breeding grounds. Lee was an exemplary guide, Harper noted, who safely led "us over the tortuous water trail, through unblazed cypress 'bays' and wide expanses of 'prairie,' to Billy's Island." Lee was familiar with landmarks that Harper could not spot; individual trees, birds' nests, and gator runs were markers that only Swampers could recognize as navigation points. Harper marveled at Lee's eyesight and his familiarity with the Okefenokee. He noted that the Swampers' environmental expertise allowed these communities to claim the swamp as their own: "The absence of blazes deters outsiders from attempting to follow the trail far into the interior, and gives the Billy's Island folk a sort of unique proprietorship over these solitary wastes." As night fell during their first day of travel, Harper worried that the party would have to camp in the muck. But even in the pitch black of an Okefenokee night, Lee had an almost instinctive knowledge of the swamp's interior: "For any one except a native, who knew every rod of the way, it would have been folly to attempt a nocturnal trip over the three remaining miles to Billy's Lake. But Dave was the master of the situation."[35]

Harper depicts David Lee not as an awe-inspiring example of rural masculinity (as Charles Pendleton had seen Ben Yarborough) but as a trained expert. Lee had been born and raised in the Okefenokee, and his resourcefulness, expertise, and thoughtful answers to Harper's questions revealed to the scientist "the thoroughness of nature's schooling." The Swamper had more knowledge and ability in the Okefenokee than the university-trained scientist; Harper both recognized and admired this fact. Other naturalists and scientists also commented on Swampers' rare abilities to navigate and observe wildlife in the Okefenokee. Frederick Hebard acknowledged the aid of the Swamper John W. Burch, "a very accurate observer, who has the best eyes and ears of any man I have known," in compiling his list of the migratory birds of the swamp. He also noted that Thomas and James Roddenberry (two of Gad Roddenberry's sons), "like many another resident, could tell a mallard from a black duck with their naked eye before I could with a 7×50 Zeiss glass." Alexander McQueen, a local lawyer and Charlton County historian, noted in 1926 that some "old-timers in the Swamp can even tell the directions by the growth of bark on the trees, etc., but it requires an expert to do this." Guiding and observational skills of Swampers were invaluable to scientists and naturalists between 1902 and 1940. Guides like David Lee and the Roddenberrys made it possible for scientists to complete their biological surveys safely and called attention to specific species of wildlife or particular habitats that their "Northern eyes," even with the aid of binoculars, would have missed.[36]

Swampers were also valuable to scientists as collectors of specimens.

While Francis Harper did not shy away from shooting wildlife for the purposes of taxidermic examinations, he increasingly turned to Swampers as suppliers of birds and amphibians. Harper and his colleagues used their research time (which lasted only through the summer months and perhaps a week in the spring) to make field notes and gather specimens, then returned to their universities. Therefore, these scientists depended on the year-round collecting capabilities of Swampers to provide them with specimens that formed an empirical base for their studies. In 1927 Harper acknowledged that "to the efforts of either the Lees or the Chessers we owe most of the game animals, as well as a considerable number of the smaller species, that have been added to the collection of specimens."[37]

Some specimens that Swampers provided for Harper were rare and thus valuable. Joe Saunders, a Swamper who had explored Billy's Island and Honey Island in 1927, "collected and prepared the first Okefinokee specimen of the Golden Mouse that I have examined." Harper could not believe his luck when Sam and Allen Chesser brought him another golden mouse after capturing it alive in "the hammock beside which they have spent their lives." The golden mouse was extremely rare, and Harper's acquisition of these two specimens was a coup for both him and the museum collection at Cornell. The Swamper E. L. Griffis of Mixon's Ferry contributed a similarly rare rodent, supplying "the only specimen of the Star-nosed mole that has been taken in the region." Most Swamper residents knew where to find Harper, particularly after the scientist bought some land and built his family a cabin on Chesser Island in 1922; they brought him samples of Okefenokee fauna almost daily. That summer he noted in his journal, "Specimens are fast accumulating, some of a particularly desirable sort. The Chessers come and sit around camp, giving us their own local names of plants and animals, and imparting various highly interesting bits of swamp lore."[38] Children and their parents brought Harper plants, amphibians, birds, and fish, but these Swampers and others in the Okefenokee community brought him something even more important than specimens: they supplied him with ecological knowledge.

During his first trip to the Okefenokee in 1912, Francis Harper realized that Swampers, in addition to having keen eyesight and a working knowledge of the swamp's geography, had information that could be used as scientific evidence. In his 1912 "Report" of his expedition into the Okefenokee, Harper noted, "I was informed by inhabitants of the swamp, some of whom possess a surprising knowledge of its bird, animal, and plant life . . . that considerable numbers of wading birds, including Egrets and Ibises, were found there regularly, and nested in small clumps of cypresses, known locally as 'heads' or 'houses,' that dot the prairies."[39] This comment reveals several components of scientists' use of Swamper knowledge in their Okefenokee studies. Swamper information brought Harper and his colleagues to places where they could observe wildlife and make field notes. Such counsel also indicated the existence and habits of certain species and provided a timeline for scientists. For example, the inhabitants of the Okefenokee Swamp in Harper's description were clearly familiar with the nesting habits of egrets and ibises. Their information reveals that such habits were seasonal and that these birds had been nesting in the Okefenokee for quite some time. Swamper information also provided a new nomenclature for wildlife species. After 1912 Harper and other swamp scientists began to include Swamper vernacular names for species and for topographical elements – heads and houses – present in the swamp interior.

Francis Harper freely acknowledged the major role that Swamper expertise played in his scientific studies. In 1968 he reflected, "Some of the finest days in my whole life have been spent in the pleasant company of such friends as the Lees, the Chessers, the Mizells, and the Thrifts. They were such keen observers of nature that I have felt privileged to fill many pages of my biological writings with verbatim comments of theirs on the wildlife of the swamp. Some of their observations have exceeded those of professional naturalists. I have often remarked that they contributed more to my biological knowledge than I have to theirs. . . . All told, I should say that both Georgia and the nation owe a debt of real gratitude to the wonderful Okefinokee people." Harper clearly viewed Swampers as scientific experts who had become adept through direct experience. He found Swamper knowledge to be specific and, when compared with other studies, accurate. Harper noted that Swampers had such a penchant for accuracy that they distinguished between first-hand and second-hand information when answering the scientist's questions. Most Swampers used phrases like "folks *say* that is" instead of "that is" in order to relay information gleaned from others and not directly; that they did so helped Harper and other scientists distinguish between field observations and anecdotes as distinctive forms of evidence.[40]

Only when Swampers claimed ignorance of a particular species was Harper surprised. When the scientist began to investigate the life and habitat of a pygmy oak toad in 1931, for example, he discovered that Swampers had not heard of or seen it. But Harper considered this lack of knowledge to be a form of scientific evidence as well. The fact that Swampers had not encountered this amphibian was evidence of the pygmy oak toad's possible extinction in the area.[41] Swamper specimens and information made up the bulk of scientists' empirical base for ecological study in the Okefenokee Swamp. It is unclear whether the locals accepted payment for the samples they collected for scientists or for the knowledge they shared.

Swampers cooperated in this way with Okefenokee scientists for several reasons. Some Swampers may have seen it as an element of their guiding duties. Many guides included storytelling around the campfire as a major element of their Okefenokee tours, and most of these stories, like southwestern humor tales, involved the wily ways of the hunter and the hunted. These tales thus relayed information about wildlife in the guise of entertainment. Other Swamper guides saw their cooperation with scientists as a chance to gain some notoriety in the region and publicize themselves as guides to any other scientists, sportsmen, or tourists who wished to visit the Okefenokee. Scientific articles often acted as advertisements for Swamper guides, giving their names, locations, and areas of expertise. Such publicity was part of a successful economic strategy. Some Swamper guides also achieved a sense of pride through sharing their knowledge; it was a chance for them to engage in their own expertise and gain satisfaction from acting as specialists. Other Swampers, like Hamp Mizell, had more specific goals in mind.

Mizell was involved in both the timber and sport industries in the swamp. He had helped John Hopkins complete a timber survey from 1901 to 1903 and worked as a timber scout throughout the duration of the Hebards' extraction of Okefenokee cypress and pine trees. In so doing, he acted in a way consistent with Swamper ecolocal cultural practices. Taking advantage of his status as a timber cruiser, Mizell negotiated with the Hebards to obtain a fishing license and established a sport camp in the Pocket, where Suwannee Lake empties into the Suwannee River. Mizell's interests in the Okefenokee were rooted in his financial situation; both development and preservation suited his plans. By sharing his knowledge of the swamp's wildlife, he could help to preserve the Okefenokee, and swamp preservation would support his burgeoning tourist-driven business. But Mizell also engaged in the ecolocal narrative of preservation for another reason: to defend the Swamper community.

When Hamp Mizell agreed to coauthor a book on the history of the Okefenokee Swamp with the local historian Alexander S. McQueen in the 1920s, he saw it as a chance to aid in Okefenokee preservation efforts, court inhabitants and visitors to the area, and redeem the reputation of Swampers. McQueen and Mizell's *History of Okefenokee Swamp* (1926) was an attempt to claim the Okefenokee as a refuge for birds but also as a community of healthy Swamper families.

*History of Okefenokee Swamp* is, in part, a protest against scientists who depicted Swampers as unhealthy, degenerate, illiterate criminals in the context of the early-twentieth-century American eugenics movement. In 1910 social scientists had established the Eugenics Record Office in Cold Spring Harbor, Long Island, and it became a major center for the study of "cacogenic" families – purportedly degenerate clans who were believed to be illiterate, feebleminded, sexually deviant, lazy, and violent. Many eugenics programs focused on eliminating "inferior" racial groups from the American population, but sterilization programs and eugenic family studies centered on rural, poor whites. And while several of these family studies "tested" poor white families in the Northeast and Midwest, the southern Cracker was the movement's central, confirmational image.[42] Eugenic beliefs infiltrated many scientific disciplines during this time, and Okefenokee Swampers became subjects of eugenicist inquiry and discussion after the first Cornell expedition of 1912.

One of the members of the expedition, W. D. Funkhouser, stopped at the University of Kentucky on his way back from the Okefenokee and gave a talk about the Swampers he had met. Most of his speech focused on the expedition members' interactions with the Lee family on Billy's Island, "a family of persons who in many ways can be compared only to animals. It consisted of an old, old woman, her three sons and two daughters, who had intermarried, and their eleven children. All of them were degenerate weaklings, undernourished, and had hookworm and bad blood, as the tests we made showed." Eugenicist rhetoric frames rural whites as diseased, although there is no evidence to confirm that members of the Cornell party would have had the training or the equipment to test the Lee family for hookworm (an intestinal disease caused by malnutrition and filth) or "bad blood" (syphilis). By referring to these particular ailments, Funkhouser suggested that the Lees led lives of moral and physical degeneracy. The scientist also noted the Lees' refined senses of sight and smell but described these abilities not in terms of admirable expertise but in reference to their savage natures: "The development of their senses and their acute powers of observation can be compared only to animals. They could smell a rattlesnake in the Swamp, and could trail by smell like dogs."[43] Funkhouser aligned Swampers with Okefenokee fauna yet clearly disassociated them from those species to be preserved. They were kin to dangerous rattlesnakes and simpleminded dogs, two species that did not make anyone's conservation lists.

Funkhouser went on to link the Swampers to hillbillies of Appalachia through their use of ancient languages: "While they spoke English, we had much difficulty understanding them, as their vocabulary was Chaucerian, Spenserian and Shakespearian." The Lees, according to Funkhouser, lived in isolation and therefore retained centuries-old linguistic patterns, as had, he believed, the folk of Appalachia. Swampers were so sheltered that "they had never heard of reading, writing, or any of the things we take for granted, and on learning that we were from New York inquired if it were another island or a turpentine still."[44] As one would expect, Funkhouser did not note that the Lees' awareness of turpentine stills indicated their links to other communities in the area and market networks in the Okefenokee hinterlands. Clearly, Funkhouser's lecture on the Lees was informed by eugenics discourses and by a burgeoning American print culture that depicted poor whites as objects of disgusted fascination. Articles like "Cracker Dialect in South Carolina" (1884), "The Georgia Cracker in the Cotton Mills" (1891), and "Among the Georgia Crackers" (1903–4) appeared in popular national magazines like the *Atlantic Monthly, Century Magazine,* and *Outing: The Gentleman's Magazine of Sport, Travel, and Outdoor Life* between 1880 and 1910. Enough of these articles were published in national magazines to shape a "white trash" genre within turn-of-the-century literary culture.[45]

One of Hamp Mizell's goals in coauthoring *History of Okefenokee Swamp* in 1926 was to defend his community from these eugenic depictions. His theory was that Funkhouser was not just an irresponsible cad, but that he had been deliberately led astray by a Swamper who was "'stringing' the learned doctor," because everyone knows that "the Georgia Cracker dearly delights in telling fairy tales to Yankee scientists." Mizell and McQueen turn the tables on Funkhouser in their book, noting that "These so-called scientists are a simple-minded lot, despite their great learning, and they are more credulous than a fourteen-year old Georgia Cracker boy" due to their eagerness to find the swamp as they expected – full of "uncivilized savages." In the authors' depiction, then, it is Funkhouser who is the misinformed, slack-jawed yokel. By contrast, argued Mizell and McQueen, the Lees are "all well developed, healthy, normal children, who are now big, strong men and women." The family is literate, God fearing, law abiding, and most important, not incestuous: "There were no intermarriages between brothers and sisters. . . . They are married to men and women none of whom were any relationship to them whatever. . . . Not a thing has ever been said against one of the Lee girls, who always conducted themselves, whether in their primeval home on Billy's Island, or upon the mainland, as perfect ladies, and they are now married and the mothers of healthy children NOT INBRED."[46] To illustrate the healthy nature of the Lee family, Mizell and McQueen included a photograph of James Henry Lee, one of the grandsons of Dan Lee. The obviously healthy boy stands in the Okefenokee, holding a turtle and grinning at someone off camera. This tactic also undermined eugenics proponents, whose use of photographs to illustrate degeneracy was a strategy to promote their "scientific" theories.

*History of Okefenokee Swamp* was only a modest seller, however, and the image of Swampers as incestuous and degenerate endured. In 1941 the New York travel writer and novelist Cecile Hulse Matschat published *Murder in Okefenokee*, the story of a woman who works at the Fair Harbor Home for Nervous and Mental Disorders in New York, an allusion to the Eugenics Record Office in Cold Springs Harbor. The novel opens as Andrea Reid accepts an invitation to visit her boyfriend Peter's ancestral home in the Okefenokee. A series of murders ensue, and Luke Corn, the Swamper overseer of Mosshaven, is the first victim. Luke's wife, Epistle, is a "huge Amazon-like woman" whose two children bear the marks of bad genes: "Their pitiful heritage was stamped on their faces: vacant, staring eyes, open, drooling mouths, and from the younger a continuous twittering sound that set my teeth on edge." Ultimately, Andrea discovers that it is Peter who has murdered most of his guests and employees in order to prevent them from knowing that he is by birth a Ravenel, a Swamper whose children "might just be idiots." He throws himself into the flames of his burning house and Andrea concludes, "I did love Peter in a way. But I'm not the only woman who has mistaken shadow for substance."[47]

Literary images that associated poor whites with disease and degeneracy were compelling to readers – it was more comfortable to submit Swampers to the literary and scientific gaze than to grapple honestly with

Francis Harper, "James Henry Lee with a Hard-Backed Cooter on Billy's Island" (May 1921), from Delma Presley and Francis Harper, *Okefinokee Album* (Athens: University of Georgia Press, 1981), 112, and the Francis Harper Papers in the Delma Eugene Presley Collection of South Georgia History and Culture, Special Collections, Zach S. Henderson Library, Georgia Southern University.

their ecolocal culture. In *Murder in Okefenokee,* Swampers become shadows. In preservationist scientific literature produced between 1912 and 1937, Swampers become biological specimens and objects of field observations themselves – not only through the writings and lectures of Funkhouser but even those penned by their greatest advocate and admirer, Francis Harper.

In Francis Harper's scientific writings, Swamper habits and habitats became as much the focus of his attention as Okefenokee ecology. In "A Sojourn in the Primeval Okefinokee" (1915), Harper includes long passages describing David Lee and his family. Swamp foliage becomes an object of scientific description and definition, but Harper also depicts it as an integral element of Swamper culture: "Presently, after passing on our right a group of particularly tall slash pines, we pointed our boat's prow toward another pine that towered above the far southern horizon. These 'saplin's' (for in the native speech every pine in the swamp, be it ever so tall, is a 'saplin') serve as familiar landmarks for Dave and his brothers in their journeys between Billy's Island and the northern border of the swamp." Swamper nomenclature (saplin') claims a dominant place in all of Harper's writing on swamp wildlife and botany. It became an indicator not only of Swampers' unique relationship with their environment but also a way for Harper to separate himself (through the use of quotation marks and his verbatim spelling of their words) from them as an observer. Swampers were initially uncomfortable with Harper's characterizations of them and their dialect in his publications, but Harper assuaged them with arguments that he, just a boy from Americus, Georgia, was as Cracker as they came. As a local, he could be trusted with depicting Swampers accurately (and with admiration) in national publications.[48] Just as the Lee brothers used saplin's to guide them through the Okefenokee, Harper used Swamper vernacular to map out this community's cultural territory within a scientific context. In doing so, he had to both claim kinship with Swampers and distance himself from them; it was a double identity he was not often able to reconcile.

Despite his admiration of their ecolocal culture, some of Harper's descriptions of Swampers verged on the eugenic in nature. In August 1922 Harper met a Swamper from Moniac who piloted Harper and Hamp Mizell to Ellicott's Mound on the southeastern side of the Okefenokee. "Hardy Johns," he wrote, "is a swamp character. . . . He bore with him his trusty gun, inseparable companion of your true swamper. Gun on shoulder, he bothers little with other equipment. A voluble talker, it took a little time to catch on to his curious lingo. And some of the uncommonest-looking eyes I have ever gazed at – I can hardly say *into*. For when facing you directly, he seems to be looking and talking off to one side, somewhat out of the corners of eyes and mouth. Also a sort of set, glassy expression to those pale blue orbs, as if they might also be sightless."[49] Hardy Johns is here a "character," not quite a man, almost a parody of a Swamper. Harper can barely understand his "curious lingo"; the scientist's comment on this point falls in line with Funkhouser's and other eugenicists' claims that cacogenic families were communicatively regressive. Also, Harper's long description of Johns's eyes engages with a major element of eugenics "data." The Swamper's "pale blue eyes," like those of the Corn children in *Murder in Okefenokee,* drift to the corners of his sockets, "as if they might also be sightless." Crossed or roving eyes were, in a eugenics context, evidence of hereditary degeneracy. Harper does not ever say as much, and he describes Johns as a "true swamper" who is the inveterate hunter and knowledgeable swamp traveler. Still, Harper often felt the urge to separate himself from Swampers and to exoticize their characters and culture.

Some of Harper's photos and the captions he placed with them were directly critical of some elements of Swamper ecolocalism. His first article on the 1912 expedition included only one photograph, although Harper captured many of the swamp's flora and fauna on film. The photograph, labeled "A Georgia Family Which Destroys Many Birds and Animals," is linked to a caption that reads, "The fawn had just been killed by the dogs in the foreground." The photo depicts ten members of a family (the Lees) on the porch of a log dog-trot cabin with seven pelts and a doeskin stretched over the entranceway. Harper disapproved of what he saw as local overhunting of deer, otter, egrets, and other Okefenokee wildlife. He lamented that "here, as in most other remote regions, game laws are accorded the scantiest sort of respect," and wholesale slaughter of herons and egrets for the feather trade was unrestricted. Before a bird protection law was enforced in Georgia, Swamper plume hunters killed as many as two hundred egrets a day in the Okefenokee.[50] At Cornell, Harper had been imbued with conservationist ideologies that demonized local hunting as aggressive and wasteful. His inclusion of this photograph as the only image in his first article concerning the Okefenokee (and only the third ever published) is indicative of the strength of this class-based

Francis Harper, "Lee Family and Connections, Billy's Island, Okefenokee, Georgia" (May 1912), by courtesy of Department of Special Collections, Spencer Research Library, University of Kansas Libraries.

element of the conservationist discourse.[51] It is also representative of Harper's complicated and often contradictory perception of Okefenokee Swampers. He found some of their cultural practices to be distasteful, but overall he admired them and considered them, like the Okefenokee itself, worthy of preservation.

Harper argued in several articles that his photographs and transcriptions of the Swampers' language were not only vivid and faithful representations of the "intimate relations between the human inhabitants and the wonderful animal and plant life of the swamp" but were also efforts at preservation. Swamper language and customs, like the swamp itself, were in danger of extinction: "An urgent reason for recording without delay the speech and folk-ways of this region is the rapidity with which they are being modified by the encroachment of outsiders engaged in industrial enterprises."[52] Swamper tales of wildlife within the Okefenokee, then, acted as both scientific evidence to be used in the campaign for swamp preservation and an archive of "archaic" linguistic customs to be preserved from the ravages of industrialization.

By depicting Swampers in opposition to "industrial enterprises," Harper effectively erased the long history of Swamper engagement with those very enterprises. Choosing to ignore his subjects' participation in the timber and naval stores industries, in addition to their production of agricultural and animal products for barter or cash sale in local markets, Harper focused instead on Swampers' community customs and subsistence activities – evidence of their "primeval" natures. The scientist saw a link between environment and human culture in the swamp:

> The piney woods appear to give a distinctive flavor to the manners, customs, and speech of their human inhabitants. There is a sturdy and independent quality about these settlers that is doubtless fostered by their rather isolated and primitive existence – a quality that has produced some intrepid Indian-fighters and mighty bear-hunters, and that is further expressed in a general and strong belief in the doctrine of individual rights and liberties. It is also in the wide expanses of these piney woods that there has grown up a genuine American musical art – a wonderfully melodious and thrilling yodeling, which the inhabitants themselves refer to simply as "hollerin'." Widespread as this art is (extending westward as far as Arkansas), it may be doubted whether it reaches as high a development anywhere else as in the fastnesses of the Okefinokee.[53]

Here, Harper offers his field observations of Swampers, rather than wildlife, within the swamp. He argues that the piney woods habitat has developed a unique culture that inculcates bravery, hunting prowess, and independence – a culture that is to be appreciated and preserved.

Harper was particularly interested in Swampers' "hollerin'." He heard this sound first from David Lee, whose "weird, prolonged halloo – a sort of yodel, with measured cadences – broke the stillness of the night and resounded afar over the swamp" in 1912. This musical art form indicated to the scientist that "in very truth, the mysteries of the Okefinokee had not all vanished."[54] In the 1920s Harper took a picture of Hamp Mizell standing in his swamp canoe, mouth wide open and fingers in his ears, in midholler. This image bears a striking resemblance to another of Harper's photographs – "*Hyla Femoralis* calling on fine tune" – that depicts a frog with its vocal sac extended in midcall.[55] To Harper, Swamper calls were not at all unlike the calls of birds or other swamp animals; he observed their communities as he would an egret rookery and took notes on their actions because he saw them as a unique swamp species.

To Harper, Swampers were, like the Okefenokee, rare and valuable natural resources to be preserved, yet they had no place in the primeval swamp, a pristine ecological wonderland devoid of human inhabitation or use. His treatment of Swampers as both experts and specimens, ironically, relegated them to the past and erased their very complex relationships with the Okefenokee environment. Swampers' ecolocal culture had made it possible for this community to aid scientists in the fight for Okefenokee preservation, but ecolocal narratives of preservation restricted Swamper access to their homesites and workplaces after 1937.

Due to the publicity scientists had generated and the formation of regional and national conservation associations supportive of Okefenokee preservation, public and government awareness of the Okefenokee Swamp as an endangered ecosystem began to build in the years after the Cornell expedition. The Okefenokee preservation movement was also aided by several concurrent developments in the late 1920s and early 1930s. The Hebards, who had halted operations in the Okefenokee in 1927, increasingly made it clear that they were willing to sell their cutover lands and that the family was strongly in favor of preservation. Natural forces (that in many ways were not all that natural) also provoked discussion of the Okefenokee's fortunes. In the spring of 1932 wildfires destroyed thousands of acres of Okefenokee pines and cypress. Conservationists argued that the fire had been a result of years of drought exacerbated by development schemes and debris left by logging operations that had

Francis Harper, "Hamp Mizell Demonstrates His Two-Mile Swamp Holler" (1920), from Delma Presley and Francis Harper, *Okefinokee Album* (Athens: University of Georgia Press, 1981), 27, by courtesy of Department of Special Collections, Spencer Research Library, University of Kansas Libraries.

Francis Harper, "*Hyla Femoralis*
Calling on Fine Tune,
Suwannee Lake, Ware County,
Georgia" (June 1929), by
courtesy of Department of
Special Collections, Spencer
Research Library, University
of Kansas Libraries.

become flammable tinder over the years. Numerous houses and barns in
the area were destroyed, and the Okefenokee received national publicity.[56]

At the same time, competing projects for Okefenokee development
began to make the papers. A push for an Atlantic-Gulf canal across the
Okefenokee was taken up again in 1933. President Roosevelt authorized
funds for a preliminary survey, and canal planning and lobbying continued in 1934 because "the prospect of hundreds, maybe thousands of jobs
in the midst of the Great Depression made the proposal especially attractive." A plan with similar goals gained favor in 1934 and 1935, as local
businessmen lobbied for an Okefenokee Scenic Highway that would connect major roadways in Georgia to Florida's thoroughfares, creating a
seamless conduit to tourist sites along the southeastern Atlantic coast.
Planners estimated that although the highway would cost around two million dollars, it would benefit at least seventy-four hundred residents of the
Okefenokee hinterlands.[57]

In response to these developments, Okefenokee preservation organizations began to increase their lobbying efforts. But the most decisive
force in bringing the Okefenokee to federal attention was Jean Harper, a
folklorist and photographer who had joined her husband, Francis, on his
Okefenokee forays between 1929 and 1937. After she had graduated
from Vassar College, Jean Sherwood Harper had worked for Franklin and
Eleanor Roosevelt as a tutor for their children, Anne and Elliott, at their

Hyde Park estate in New York. After hearing of the Okefenokee ship canal proposal, Jean Harper wrote to her former employer (whom she considered a close friend) in November 1933:

> There is a matter that needs your immediate attention – the preservation of the Okefinokee Swamp. Perhaps you may recall that a few years ago, Francis sent you some of his reprints of the Swamp. . . . For twenty odd years naturalists and nature-lovers have been working for the preservation of this marvelous wilderness; unique in its nature not only in this country but in the world. The character of its fauna, its flora, and its human life is unsurpassed. . . . We now learn of the project to put a ship canal through the swamp. You well know what this would mean to the beauty of the area and to the wild life. The destruction that would thus be brought on is unthinkable. Our hope lies in you to stop the project before it goes farther, and spend the money in the purchase of the swamp for a reservation, where beauty and scientific interest may be preserved for all time.[58]

Jean Harper's appeal to the president is a concise expression of the ecolocal narrative of preservation. The swamp is a "marvelous wilderness," "unique in its nature," and unsurpassed in the quality of its fauna and flora, as evidenced by Francis Harper's photographic reprints. Intriguingly, Jean Harper also makes a case for the "character" of the human life in the swamp – the ecolocal culture of the Swampers. She makes no argument here, however, for the swamp as a reservation to be given over to the Swamper community in order to save it. Instead, preservation would replace Swampers with birds and provide experiences of "beauty and scientific interest" for those who visited there "for all time."

Roosevelt responded to Jean Harper several weeks later, promising to talk to congressional members about it and noting that he "should hate to see the Okefinokee Swamp destroyed."[59] Roosevelt had collected bird specimens and initiated a forestry project on several acres of his family's Hyde Park estate when he was a young boy; while recuperating from polio, he sought the waters of several "healing springs" in Georgia and Florida in the 1920s.[60] These experiences shaped his conservationist sensibilities and familiarized him with Okefenokee hinterland ecologies. Roosevelt reassured Jean Harper that he was a proponent of federal purchase of the Okefenokee – if it was economically feasible. An opportunity arose when a bill authorizing the appropriation of six million dollars for the purchase of a series of tracts for retention in their "natural state as a wildlife preserve" was introduced in Congress in June 1935. Senator Walter F. George of Georgia asked that the Okefenokee Swamp purchase be incorporated into the measure and argued that the South was a desirable region for wildlife preservation.[61]

In response, Roosevelt dispatched a team from the U.S. Biological Survey to survey the Okefenokee lands owned by the Hebard Lumber Company in March 1936. The team determined that the Hebards' Okefenokee property was worth $1.50 an acre, and they offered this price as a bid for a core tract of 292,979 acres. The Hebards accepted a total bid of $400,000 for all of their Okefenokee lands, and the Biological Survey announced on March 15 that it would assume responsibility for the management of the property at midnight on November 30, 1936. Survey officials then appointed the former Hebard superintendent John M. Hopkins to be the game manager.[62] The Biological Survey continued to inspect the area and add parcels to the prospective refuge until it had accumulated almost 480,000 acres. The purchase of the Okefenokee Swamp and its legal shift from swamp to refuge occurred on March 30, 1937, when Roosevelt signed Executive Order No. 7593, stating that "in order to effectuate further the purposes of the Migratory Bird Conservation Act (45 Stat. 1232), it is ordered that all lands, including lands under water, acquired or to be acquired by the United States, lying within the following described area, and comprising approximately 479,450 acres in Charlton, Clinch, and Ware Counties, Georgia, be and they are hereby, reserved and set apart for the use of the Department of Agriculture, subject to valid existing rights, as a refuge and breeding ground for migratory birds and other wildlife."[63] In contrast to the review of the Biological Survey in 1931, the federal government did deem the Okefenokee to be a viable breeding ground for migratory birds, and thus it became federal property in 1937.

The immediate effects of this designation of the swamp as a refuge were multiple. Wildlife populations that had previously been declining began to recover. Frederick Hebard noted in 1941 that as regards the wood duck, "unquestionably government ownership has increased the numbers within the swamp."[64] Tony Carter, a local scientist appointed as the refuge biologist, claimed to have seen "the magnificent ivory-billed woodpecker, once feared to be extinct." Newspaper columnists wrote approvingly, "The fearful and wonderful place is reverting to the wild again." Game wardens reported that the fur-bearing animals, particularly raccoons and otters, showed remarkable increases in population, while the Florida crane (which had almost been decimated) numbered at least five hundred by the 1940s. Alligators, hunted almost to extinction in the name of women's fashions in belts and purses in the 1920s and 1930s, rebounded so rapidly that in the late 1940s, "it is not unusual to see thirty or forty in a single trip up the canal."[65]

Offsetting wildlife population gains were some environmental depredations resulting from the construction of refuge facilities. The creation of Civilian Conservation Corps barracks, access roads, recreation buildings, and new entrances to the swamp resulted in clear-cutting of some Okefenokee tree stands, particularly on the southeastern side. When Francis and Jean Harper traveled to their cabin on Chesser's Island to begin their summer stay in 1938, they saw "a huge, long pile of pine logs, partly sawed up. We learned, to our amazement and dismay, that the logs had come from the south end of Chessers Island and were being used for cooking the rations at the adjacent camp." Jean Harper wrote immediately to Roosevelt, and "the vandalism was forthwith stopped, after irreparable damage had been done to some twenty acres of nearly primeval pine timber." Francis Harper noted the irony of this situation – that the refuge personnel were destroying what they had succeeded in saving. He also recognized, in later years, the effects of the refuge designation on the Swampers: "I get increasingly depressed on the island in recent visits [due to] my own increasingly general pessimism about the passing of the picturesque old-timers."[66] Harper never acknowledged, however, that the "passing" of the Swampers from the Okefenokee in the 1930s and 1940s had much to do with his literary construction of them as "picturesque."

When the U.S. Biological Survey team completed negotiations with the Hebards to purchase the Okefenokee Swamp lands, they took possession of the tract at midnight on November 30, 1936. From this moment, and particularly after Roosevelt's signing of Executive Order 7593 the next spring, the swamp ceased to be a local space and became the public property of the nation. This shift entailed monetary exchanges and legislative action, but it also involved the delineation of boundaries and restriction of access. Ironically, the ecolocal narrative of preservation had shaped a vision of the swamp as an unchanging wilderness, but it also provoked the greatest change in the Okefenokee's history. As a swamp, it had been a contact zone of Okefenokee hinterland communities, a place in which individuals were mobile. As a refuge, the Okefenokee became a restricted space, marked by prohibitions and exclusions.

On March 19, 1937, the *Charlton County (Ga.) Herald* reported that decisions had been made regarding the development of the Okefenokee Swamp Refuge: "Official announcements to this effect are reassuring to those who lament the havoc with which a miscalled 'progress' often has played with our country's few remaining haunts of uncommercialized and unchallenged nature. . . . There is nothing inhospitable about this program. It is intended simply to shelter and save the plants, trees, birds, and animals, including many rare species that make their home in the Okefenokee Refuge, and keep this incomparable piece of wilderness unspoiled. Scientists, nature-lovers and discriminating tourists will be welcome; but the taint of exploitation and the peril of uncontrolled crowds will be rigorously excluded."[67] Despite this report's claims to hospitality within the borders of the swamp, it is clear that federal plans for the refuge involved the depiction of the Okefenokee as a wilderness rescued at the last minute from the prospective perils of commercial enterprise. Twenty years of clear-cutting on the part of the Hebard Lumber Company fall out of the picture here as the author conceives of the swamp as "uncommercialized and unchallenged nature" unspoiled by the "taint of exploitation." The refuge is framed as a counterpoint to national obsessions with progress, a wilderness untouched by the soiled hands of humans. This depiction erases Swamper presence and notes their future absence from the refuge as well – only "scientists, nature-lovers and discriminating tourists will be welcome." And although the author of the article goes on to note with relief that the supervision of the project is in the hands of two locals (John Hopkins and Earle E. Greene, both residents of the Okefenokee hinterlands), it is clear that the refuge would from that day forward play host only to scientists trolling the waters in pursuit of scientific data or tourists contemplating beautiful vistas.

Much of the initial refuge rhetoric was restrictive. Once Roosevelt officially signed his executive order, the Okefenokee was "under the terms of the order, now closed to the public." John Hopkins, appointed game manager and agent in charge of the area, announced the following in April:

Hunting is strictly forbidden, with the provision that fire-arms may not be carried into the refuge area, and fishing and sight-seeing will not be allowed except under permit. . . . Lines will be posted, . . . but that doesn't mean that visitors will not be welcomed. . . . Permits for fishing, during open seasons, and for sight-seeing, are already available. They may be secured from Mr. Hopkins' office in Waycross, at Folkston, at Camp Cornelia, or at Fargo, the latter two places being points of entrance to the natural wonderland. Fishing will be allowed in restricted areas only, and the Georgia state fishing law will prohibit fishing from April 15 to June 1. All persons entering the Okefenokee must be accompanied by registered guides.[68]

The language of the refuge is full of prohibitive words and phrases: forbidden, may not, will not be allowed. Hopkins's statement reveals the federal government's legal restriction of the Okefenokee; it also discloses the management's plans to shape human interaction with the swamp administratively and spatially.

The permit system, administered by the refuge officials under the authority of the federal government and in reference to Georgia's game laws, strictly regulated both locals' and visitors' contact with the Okefenokee for the first time in its history. The Hebards had established a license and permit system and employed patrollers in 1901, but they did not establish a permits office, keep records, or fence off their Okefenokee property. However, after March 1937, anyone who desired to fish in the "natural wonderland" had to apply for a permit from Hopkins, purchase it, and then reapply during the next "open season." This system allowed the refuge staff to keep track of visits, visitors, and use of the property. It also allowed them to deny access to anyone they believed might encourage "uncontrolled crowds." The permit system was aimed not at visitors so much as locals. In October 1937 Hopkins announced that since April, a total of 1,541 permits had been issued at his office; 277 of them were issued to "visitors interested in the study of wild life," and 1,264 were issued to fishermen. Ninety-eight percent (1,505) of the permit holders were Georgians.[69]

Administrative control of the refuge also included the regulation of guiding. All visitors to the swamp, as Hopkins had announced, had to be accompanied by a guide or a refuge official, and all guides had to register with the refuge and receive permission to engage in this activity. This rule was also obviously aimed at locals, for whom guiding had been an important source of wages throughout the nineteenth and early twentieth centuries. Scientists and tourists could no longer engage Swampers as guides through local contacts and for a negotiated price. They had to notify the refuge of their intentions, and an officially registered guide would be appointed to their group. And because guns and hunting were prohibited in the refuge, Swamper guides lost their most important and highest-paying customers: wealthy sportsmen who wanted to relive Charles Pendleton's experience of a heroic bear hunt. They also lost their previously unrestricted access to the wildlife of the swamp, a major source of Swamper sustenance and a dominant product through which they entered the market economy. Refuge prohibitions and administrative structures thus changed the ways that Swampers engaged with the Okefenokee economically, fundamentally altering their ecolocal culture.

Swamper access to the Okefenokee was also restricted spatially. As part of refuge development plans, federal managers in the swamp immediately posted boundary signs and controlled entrances to the refuge itself. In April 1937 a Civilian Conservation Corps camp moved to Camp Cornelia and began to build roads and buildings, creating the primary official access route to the swamp. The town of Fargo on the west side of the swamp was deemed the second official point of entrance. CCC workers erected fences along the boundary lines on the east side of the swamp, building a 8¾-mile "stock proof fence, woven and barbed wire," and an eighteen-mile "single strand boundary marker." Refuge personnel roamed the swamp day and night, patrolling the new boundaries and the interior, looking for trespassers. Any locals or visitors caught entering the swamp anywhere else (from backyard docks or former timber roads) would be arrested. These trespassers might also have had trouble obtaining refuge permits to fish or travel within the swamp due to such infractions. Refuge officials made it clear that visitors were welcome but would be allowed to observe only "restricted parts of the refuge." Travel would be confined to "boat runs and foot trails which are now being improved."[70] The Swamper landscape of gator runs, cattle paths, and hunting trails faded with disuse as refuge managers confined travel to major arteries (the Suwanee Canal and Billy's Lake) and groomed these areas to keep them free of choking vegetation or peat islands. The federal government carved out trails that suited its own purposes in the Okefenokee and erased the local landscape that had previously existed within it.

Mapping out boundaries in an attempt to control access to this presumably public space was not unusual in the national context of conservation. As Karl Jacoby and Louis Warren have recently shown, the delineation of boundaries within the preserved environment was part of the federal government's exertion of control over coveted wild areas and potentially destructive human populations.[71] And as these two scholars also point out, the restriction of access through both administrative and spatial control provoked action on the part of locals whose vision of these spaces as their own "commons" conflicted with the federal government's definition of these environments as national places. As a result of the Okefenokee Swamp's preservation, Swampers no longer had the freedom to herd, hunt, log, and guide in these lands as they pleased. Instead, they were forced to interact with the Okefenokee through the administrative system of the refuge. They became visitors in the landscape that had previously been their homesite and workplace.

Once the Okefenokee became federal property, the Swamper community began to disintegrate. The Lees had no more recourse in their attempts to regain their Billy's Island property and moved away permanently. Many Swampers found that huge parcels of land they had previously assumed to be theirs were condemned by the federal government and absorbed into the refuge. John Hopkins's first job as refuge manager was to secure disclaimers from some Swamper families or to "satisfy the court of the absence of any title, right, or claim."[72] The scientific literature that had depicted Swampers as primeval inhabitants of a wilderness landscape did not help them in their fight to keep their lands. If they resisted, this opposition was seen as a betrayal of their ancestral home and their community. They had been part of the swamp's past and were expected to make way for tourists, who were the refuge's future.

Some Swampers moved to larger towns in the Okefenokee hinterlands like Folkston, Fargo, Homerville, or Waycross, while others gave up their strategies of diversified production and took wage-paying jobs in Savannah, Macon, or Atlanta. Many families stayed on their homesteads just outside the refuge boundaries for several years after federal officials took over, but most found it hard to maintain and range their cattle herds without the use of guns and in light of the almost nine miles of "stock proof fence" extending down the eastern side of the swamp. The Chessers, who stayed on their island lands until the 1950s, were forced to sell their remaining cattle and hogs in the early 1940s because they were not able to protect them from burgeoning populations of predatory animals in the refuge. As the teenager Wade Chesser wrote to Francis Harper's daughter Robin in August 1941, "the first thing I want to tell you about is the bears.

They ate up nearly all my grandfather's hogs! He and some men killed one of the bears, and said there were three more. . . . Bears [go] for the grown hogs and cows, and wild cats for the pigs. So the future looks pretty dark for stock." Refuge officials had warned the Chessers and other Swamper families remaining in the area that the prohibition on guns in the swamp extended to their defense of their cattle and hogs. Ultimately, the Chessers found it impossible to keep their livestock because "the government forbade the use of firearms"; they moved to Folkston in the 1940s.[73]

Other Swampers were not so law abiding. As in other federally mandated and bounded environments in the northern and western United States, many locals demonstrated their anger at their dispossession through poaching and other violent activities.[74] Some Swampers had poached before in defiance of the Hebards' attempts to regulate their land rights through the permit system, but hunting and trapping in the refuge took on a greater significance. John Hopkins initially scoffed at the notion that poaching was a constant problem, noting that "Hunters have been guilty of but few violations because the report of a gun can be heard at too great a distance." But soon after the president's executive order went into effect, the refuge officials did see fit to appoint the Swampers Jesse B. Gray and Sam Mizell as refuge patrollers. They anticipated infractions of their administrative and spatial rules, and patrol groups grew in size throughout the 1930s. Trapping was still a common activity in the Okefenokee, and by 1945 refuge patrolmen had collected "quite a stock of traps" that they impounded at Camp Cornelia. Refuge rules provoked some locals to engage in "fire-hunting" of deer and alligators. Hopkins noted, "Alligator hunters make at least one raid on the gators each summer if prices are up." Most fire-hunters took their prey at night, using a light to blind them and then a twenty-two-caliber rifle – which Hopkins called "almost noiseless" – to "dispatch the unsuspecting possessor of seven or eight dollars' worth of crude leather."[75]

Hopkins, despite his earlier nonchalance regarding trespassing, increasingly felt that poaching was a dangerous problem in the refuge. In the early 1940s he suggested that the federal government approve the building of "two dwellings and other buildings and structures necessary for a field headquarters at Jones Island." The construction of these headquarters should be given a high priority, Hopkins argued, because "the mere presence of protectors at Jones Island would go a long way toward preventing alligator hunting in Billy's and Minnie Lakes – the most provoking violations with which we have had to contend." Hopkins wanted to build permanent structures because poachers, in addition to killing wildlife within the boundaries of the refuge, often destroyed federal property in their attempt to foil patrolmen. An overnight cabin at Big Water, he argued, "would be extremely acceptable to a patrolman on some occasions," and "a poacher would hardly yield to the temptation to make use of [it]." Sometimes, though, as Hopkins admitted, just a clearing and a wood foundation would do the trick. At McNeil Island, such a space could "accommodate a small tent where a patrolman could, with little trouble, erect a tent and spend a night or two." Big Water and McNeil Island were two sites of concern for Hopkins, for "they are favorite operating localities for poachers."[76]

Hopkins saw patrolmen's action against poachers as protection of the swamp itself, but Swampers read their presence and the restrictions they faced within the refuge as a direct usurpation of their rights and destruction of their ecolocal culture. Illegal hunting and trapping excursions in the refuge were more than just acts of meat procurement and became gestures of defiance. As Karl Jacoby has noted, poaching touched on many issues and ideologies at the heart of early-twentieth-century rural life: the desire for self-sufficiency in opposition to workplace dependency, the idea that one was responsible to the community only and that all Americans had the right to the hunt, and the need to prove one's manliness and daring. Some Swampers took particular delight in the excitement of such illegal activity. One family from Baker County, Florida, got a thrill from the danger of poaching alligators in the refuge. The patriarch of the family enjoyed "slicking" the refuge patrolmen and often led them in deliberate chases in order to prove both his ability to outwit authority figures and his right to hunt in a place he believed belonged to him and other locals.[77]

Some Swampers walked a fine line and hunted along refuge boundaries but not in the refuge itself. Ralph Davis, who hunted alligators in the Okefenokee before and after 1937, made it his business to know the lines and thus redefined his actions according to refuge rules and regulations: "'At first there were big parts of the swamp the government didn't own. I could go hunting out there without ever getting into government land. People would come up to me and say, 'Ralph, you been poaching again?' but I never needed to poach. I knew where to hunt without poaching.'" Other Swampers went to great lengths to secure alligators and other animals despite refuge rules. Henry Cox had subtle answers for refuge patrolmen who came calling. When one official asked him if he had been poaching alligators on federal property, Cox adamantly denied it; he later confided to an interviewer, "I was doing the watching." Cox and his sons were cautious when they poached, using walkie-talkies to communicate with one another and leaving behind one member of the party with the skins while others patrolled the swamp for wardens. They skinned the alligators and then submerged the carcasses in gator caves, leaving little evidence of their activities.[78]

Poachers were difficult to catch, and the fact that many refuge patrolmen (like Ralph Davis's son Steve) were local men made the conflicts created by Okefenokee poaching even more complex. But today, illegal hunting within refuge boundaries remains a way for Swamper men and women to assert control over federal spaces. Many local residents still report carcasses of deer and alligators on the refuge margins, tangible reminders that the swamp continues to be a contested landscape.

Ecolocal narratives of preservation emerged in the Okefenokee hinterlands between 1902 and 1940, within a larger context of conservation and as part of an increasingly specialized system of scientific inquiry. Scientists like Francis Harper saw the Okefenokee as a biological laboratory, a source of their own professional prestige and longevity. They succeeded in fulfilling their ecolocalist desires because they did not seek to destroy or convert the Okefenokee. Through the imaginative construction of the Okefenokee as a primeval wilderness, scientists and preservationists had hoped to erase the human past of the Okefenokee. But Swampers refused to be erased and have continued to use parts of the Okefenokee as they see fit. Some locals still see the swamp as their property and the refuge as another space entirely, one that symbolizes their victimization by the federal government, and outside control. As a refuge for wildlife, the Okefenokee became in 1937 what it had not ever been in its history: a restricted place, with administrative and spatial boundaries, mediated by boardwalks and viewing towers.

In the years following 1937 the ways that communities interacted with the Okefenokee became more and more tied to the structures of fictional literature, visual culture, and tourism. In all of these contexts, the Okefenokee's human past has been depicted as harmful to the swamp or erased entirely. Swampers have been relegated to the pages of pulp novels like Cecile Matschat's *Murder in Okefenokee* and Virginia Lanier's more recent Bloodhound detective series and have been constructed as murderous degenerates. Swampers find no place at all in Walt Kelly's cartoon series *Pogo,* which presented the Okefenokee to the nation as a site of rambunctious animal life, threatened by the outside world. Humans exist for Kelly only on the periphery of the swamp in the 1950s, as "wisps of smoke" that "denote harvesters at work" and threaten Pogo the Possum and his friends' ecosystem. In his preface to *The Pogo Papers* (1952–53), a series that depicts Pogo's return to an Okefenokee that is defiled by human activity, he writes that "we shall meet the enemy, and not only may he be ours, he may be us."[79] Kelly engages here with the centuries-old rhetoric of wilderness and thus frames the Okefenokee as the proper home of animals and not of men.

But men and women did flock to the Okefenokee after 1937, as visitors. The tourist-driven Okefenokee has given rise to a different kind of swamp ecolocalism, one shaped through brief encounters by boat, along a wooden boardwalk, or through a camera lens. The swamp, as a wildlife refuge, has shifted from a site of refuge, of battle, of industry, of home, and of work to a site of visitation and a landscape of memory. The tourist takes a boat ride, snaps some photographs, and experiences the swamp in subsequent years within the boundaries of the photo album, perused only sporadically since.

# Tourist Attraction
## *The Most Photogenic Spot in America!*

In late June 1941 a French director, several American actors, and a film crew from Twentieth-Century Fox traveled to Waycross, Georgia, to film scenes for the movie version of Vereen Bell's best-selling novel, *Swamp Water.* The novel, which tells the tale of a young boy alienated from his family who finds solace in hunting trips and friendship with a fugitive in the Okefenokee Swamp, was just the type of fast-paced adventure story that would translate well on screen. Jean Renoir, son of Auguste Renoir and an already well-established director in France, chose *Swamp Water* for his American debut. He insisted, against Twentieth-Century Fox's wishes, that he film some scenes in the Okefenokee itself. Renoir, the actors, and the crew stayed in Waycross for two weeks and fraternized with many of the inhabitants, including John Hopkins, who introduced the French director to the delights of Okefenokee moonshine.[1]

As a result of the brief shoot, the citizens of Waycross and Ware County thought of *Swamp Water* as their film and began a campaign to host the premiere. They besieged Twentieth-Century Fox with requests and went so far as to send Darryl Zanuck and other executives live baby alligators with tags affixed to their necks announcing, "Even the gators in Okefenokee went to the premiere in Waycross." Zanuck ultimately capitulated and notified Lamar Swift, the proprietor of the town's two movie theaters – the Ritz and the Lyric – that he could host the premiere, slated for October 23, 1941. The Georgia governor Eugene Talmadge declared the day of the premiere "*Swamp Water* Day" in the state, the merchants of the town decorated the streets and their stores, and Waycross residents put on a parade, special dinner, and wagon ride on the day of the premiere. Vereen Bell was the guest of honor. The premiere extravaganza was a roaring success in Waycross, and moviegoers flocked to theaters all over the South when the movie opened in limited release one week later. While film critics were not so enthusiastic about the film – one called the script insipid, "sentimental bosh" tricked out with "pretentious hokum" – by November, *Swamp Water* was well on its way to becoming one of Fox's biggest moneymakers for the year.[2]

*Swamp Water*'s release brought images of the Okefenokee Swamp to a national audience and promoted tourism in the area, just four years after the swamp became a refuge. Both the movie and its on-location filming became a source of pride for Waycross and Okefenokee hinterland businessmen; they referenced the film and its stars in their marketing materials. The Okefenokee Swamp Park, a privately run tourist attraction established on the northeastern side of the swamp in 1947, published a promotional pamphlet in the early 1960s that frames back-to-back photographs of wildlife, tourists, and film crews with black, perforated edges – the Okefenokee gone celluloid. The pamphlet proclaims that Hollywood had already discovered the swamp's "unmatched charm" and argues that the Okefenokee is "the most photogenic spot in America!"[3]

The Swamp Park brochure's claim for the Okefenokee's peculiarly photogenic character is not merely a naive assertion symbolic of the tourist Okefenokee's postmodern nature. The photograph, as Roland Barthes has written, "is literally an emanation of the referent," an image revealed and extracted through the action of light. The way that light encounters the Okefenokee Swamp – reflected sharply off of the black surfaces of tannin-infused water and refracted through tangled vines and leaves – means that film crews and camera-wielding tourists alike often return home with strikingly sharp images of Okefenokee prairies, hammocks, and cypress stands. The swamp, when converted to an image through the process of photography, is more vivid than photographs of other landscapes might be; it is, in truth, photogenic. But what one sees in a photograph of the Okefenokee is not something "real" but, as Barthes has noted, "reality in a past state: at once the past and the real."[4] The existence of the swamp it-self (at the time of the photograph) and the photographer's presence there are confirmed by the existence of the image. But the photographer is al-ways shaping the Okefenokee "scene." She raises the camera at certain moments, adjusts the focus and the zoom lens, and decides when to de-press the button. And despite the powers of modern telephoto technology, she cannot possibly fit the entire ecosystem into one frame. The Okefe-nokee photograph, then, is indicative not only of the past, of some mea-sure of reality, and of human manipulation but is also revelatory of the swamp's resistance to being fully captured. The swamp is just too large, too unruly to be caught on film.

It was these characteristics – the size and disorderliness of the Okefeno-kee Swamp – that provoked human desires between 1732 and 1940. Dif-ferent communities desired divergent things within the Okefenokee over time and often came into conflict with the swamp itself and with other communities when they acted to fulfill these desires. As a result of these collisions, communities changed and the Okefenokee transformed as well. Some groups failed to fulfill their swamp desires completely, while others faced the ironic implications of their success. This pattern of desire, then conflict, and ultimately, failure, and the ideas and beliefs that both informed and emerged from human action within the Okefenokee and its hinterlands, shaped swamp ecolocalism in the American Southeast be-tween 1732 and 1940.

Swamp ecolocalism is a process through which Okefenokee hinterland residents – rice planters, slaves, fugitive slaves, antebellum fiction writers, Seminoles, U.S. military personnel, surveyors, adventurers, developers, Swampers, and preservationists – identified themselves as part of com-munities delineated by interaction with the Okefenokee and with other communities in the area over time. These people did not conceive of themselves as united by accents, foodways, place of birth, political agen-das, religious affiliations, or in defense against "outsiders." Instead, they shaped cultural identities through conflict in, over, and through the Oke-fenokee Swamp. Swamps like the Okefenokee have always been marginal places, sites of heavy traffic and contact, spaces that seemed to promise change. The Okefenokee Swamp allowed ambitious colonial adventurers to become rice planters and empowered slaves to become free men and women. It provided a space in which Seminoles could resist American imperialism. The swamp also gave postbellum men a way to prove their manhood and a chance for civic boosters and industrialists to realize their dreams of economic success. It supplied an opportunity for Swampers to be independent producers and offered a site in which scientists could acquire a national reputation. Swamps like the Okefenokee are places of transition, and although humans have historically been uncomfortable there, Okefenokee hinterland inhabitants sought these spaces out between 1732 and 1940. They were drawn to the Okefenokee because this ecosystem seemed to offer a blank space in which they could invent new selves.

For more than two hundred years, southeastern communities attempted to inscribe their identities into the Okefenokee Swamp. Just as writing in the margins of a book is both destructive of and an act of dialogue with the text, the actions of communities in the Okefenokee Swamp have been both deleterious and productive. The kinds of clashes that occurred in, over, and through the Okefenokee Swamp have often been violent. They have involved the collisions of ideas, of images, of bodies, and of machinery. Through these violent encounters, Okefenokee hinterland inhabitants created a cultural identity rooted in disagreement rather than unity, emergent from a desire for change rather than protection of the status quo. Attention to processes of cultural formation through encounters with local ecosystems provides a new way to think about the relationship between nature and culture.

Ecolocalism imagines a role for environments in cultural identity formation that is not deterministic, passive, or constantly in danger of being destroyed. As such, it is a dynamic replacement for regionalism, whose critics have decried its tendency to give environments the power to determine human action. They have also framed regionalist identities as provincial: unsophisticated, suspicious of those perceived to be outsiders, and self-centered. A shift to an ecolocalist schema emphasizes, instead, nature and culture as catalysts for one another. One does not overly determine the other; they are mutually constitutive. Swamp ecolocalism reveals that Okefenokee hinterland communities, far from being isolated or inward looking, have been aggressively expansive in their production of ideas, beliefs, and actions within the swamp and have thus clashed with other communities within its depths. They have not perceived of these "others" as outsiders, however. In the miry muck of the Okefenokee, all of these communities were outsiders. They traveled through this space of marginality, of ambiguity, of blurring. Their presence there was real, but fleeting, because the Okefenokee has resisted constant inhabitation.

The Okefenokee Swamp, like its image, cannot be fully captured. It is a landscape of desire, conflict, and failure. And as such, it is a space that conjures visions of both the future and the past. One first-time visitor to the Okefenokee, on boating out into Mizell Prairie, exclaimed to John Hopkins, "O, Mr. Hopkins! It is wonderful! It reminds me so much of something I have – never seen!" Roland Barthes has said of such landscapes of predilection that "it is as if *I were certain* of having been there or of going there."[5] Because it is a place in which land and water, desire and disgust, image and reality, and past and future mingle, the Okefenokee Swamp is an environment with both a tangible and an imaginative history. Those who lived in and around it were able to imagine themselves as, alternatively, wealthy, free, independent, or successful within the Okefenokee because there is freedom on the margins, and flexibility. It is out of such places of intermingling, of ambiguity, that cultures are forged.

NOTES

*Abbreviations*

CRG        *Colonial Records of the State of Georgia*
CCPL       Charlton County Public Library, Folkston, Georgia
Countway   Rare Books and Special Collections, Francis A. Countway Library
           of Medicine, Harvard University, Boston, Massachusetts
EAN        *Early American Newspapers*
EFP        *East Florida Papers*
GHS        Georgia Historical Society, Savannah, Georgia
Hargrett   Hargrett Rare Book and Manuscript Library, University of
           Georgia, Athens, Georgia
ORL        Okefenokee Regional Library, Waycross, Georgia

*Introduction. Twilight Ground: The Okefenokee Swamp and Ecolocalism*

1. Hurd, *Stirring the Mud,* 4, 7.

2. New Regionalists have argued that "the history of American regional identities cannot be extricated from the development of American nationalism." Ayers et al., introduction to *All Over the Map,* 10.

3. Ghosh, "Mythic Swamps."

4. Gael Sweeney, "The King of White Trash Culture: Elvis Presley and the Aesthetics of Excess," in *White Trash,* edited by Newitz and Wray, 252–53.

5. The primary role of the West in shaping American culture can be seen in Limerick, *Legacy of Conquest;* Limerick et al., eds., *Trails;* Worster, *Dust Bowl, Rivers of Empire,* and *River Running West;* Cronon, *Nature's Metropolis;* Cronon, Gitlin, and Miles, eds., *Under an Open Sky;* Richard White, *Middle Ground* and *"It's Your Misfortune and None of My Own."*

6. Stowe, *Palmetto-Leaves,* 138.

7. David C. Miller, *Dark Eden;* Vileisis, *Discovering the Unknown Landscape;* Hugh Prince, *Wetlands of the American Midwest;* Kirby, *Poquosin;* and Stewart, *"What Nature Suffers to Groe."*

8. Matschat, *Suwannee River,* 55.

*One. A Path to Freedom: Slavery and Resistance*

1. Kemble, *Journal,* 18.

2. Ibid., 200, 241.

3. Stewart, "*What Nature Suffers to Groe*," 22–23, 28–29.

4. Ibid., 30–31.

5. Ibid., 54–59.

6. Coleman, *Colonial Georgia;* Coleman, *Georgia History in Outline;* Phinizy Spalding, "Colonial Period," in *History of Georgia,* edited by Coleman; Betty Wood, *Slavery in Colonial Georgia.*

7. Ghachem, "Sovereignty and Slavery."

8. Tailfer, Anderson, and Douglas, *True and Historical Narrative,* 51, 58–59.

9. LaRoche, *Yellow Fever,* 2:18.

10. Dennis Smelt, "An Account of the EPIDEMIC DISEASE Which Prevailed at Augusta, and Its Neighborhood, in the State of Georgia," in *Medical Repository,* edited by Mitchell and Miller, 3:126–27.

11. Peter H. Wood, *Black Majority,* 84.

12. Todd L. Savitt, "Black Health on the Plantation: Masters, Slaves, and Physicians," in *Sickness and Health in America,* edited by Leavitt and Numbers, 314–16; LaRoche, *Yellow Fever,* 2:66; Kiple and Kiple, "Black Yellow Fever Immunities," 420–21, 422, 424–25; Peter H. Wood, *Black Majority,* 76–85; Haller, "Negro and the Southern Physician," 238–53.

13. Savitt, "Black Health on the Plantation," 314–16.

14. Ibid.

15. Tailfer, Anderson, and Douglas, *True and Historical Narrative,* 94, 139.

16. "Account Showing the Progress of the Colony of Georgia" (1738) in *CRG,* edited by Candler, 3:394–95.

17. Coleman, *Colonial Georgia;* Coleman, *Georgia History in Outline;* Spalding, "Colonial Period"; Betty Wood, *Slavery in Colonial Georgia.*

18. The Georgia census of 1750 reported a colonial population of 4,200 whites and 1,000 slaves. By 1760, 6,000 whites and 3,578 blacks lived in Georgia; in 1770, 12,750 whites and 10,625 blacks resided in the colony. At the commencement of the American Revolution, 17,000 whites barely outnumbered the slave population (16,000). Julia Floyd Smith, *Slavery and Rice Culture,* 22.

19. Peter H. Wood, *Black Majority,* 59–62; Littlefield, *Rice and Slaves;* Carney, *Black Rice.*

20. Gray, *History of Agriculture,* 277–78.

21. Stewart, "*What Nature Suffers to Groe*," 93.

22. Chaplin, *Anxious Pursuit,* 227–28.

23. Albert Virgil House, introduction to Grant, *Planter Management,* 23–24.

24. Bartram, *Travels,* 6.

25. Kemble, *Journal,* 56, 118.

26. Ibid., 159.

27. Grant, journal, September 18, 1841, October 9, 1841, and September 7–8, 1854, *Planter Management,* 91, 92, 120.

28. Kemble, *Journal,* 203.

29. Julia Floyd Smith, *Slavery and Rice Culture,* 9.

30. Philip D. Morgan, "Black Society in the Lowcountry, 1760–1810," in *Slavery and Freedom*, edited by Berlin and Hoffman; Blassingame, *Slave Community;* Joyner, *Down by the Riverside.*

31. Carney, *Black Rice*, 11, 13, 16–18, 29.

32. Ibid., 31, 81; Littlefield, *Rice and Slaves.*

33. Carney, *Black Rice*, 100.

34. Ira Berlin, introduction to *Slavery and Freedom*, edited by Berlin and Hoffman, xix, 105; Morgan, "Black Society in the Lowcountry."

35. Dusinberre, *Them Dark Days;* Young, "Ideology and Death"; Julia Floyd Smith, *Slavery and Rice Culture*, 49–50; John Brown, *Slave Life in Georgia*, 154–55.

36. Kemble, *Journal*, 208.

37. Olmsted, *Journey in the Seaboard Slave States*, 484–85.

38. Stewart, "*What Nature Suffers to Groe*," 135–36; Carney, *Black Rice*, 23.

39. Kemble, *Journal*, 276.

40. Vlach, *Back of the Big House*, 14.

41. Ibid., 183, 228.

42. Marvin L. Michael Kay and Lorin Lee Cary, "'They Are Indeed the Constant Plague of Their Tyrants': Slave Defence of a Moral Economy in Colonial North Carolina, 1748–1772," in *Out of the House of Bondage*, edited by Heuman, 39.

43. Richard Price, ed., *Maroon Societies;* Genovese, *From Rebellion to Revolution.*

44. Morgan, "Black Society in the Lowcountry," 138–39.

45. Herbert Aptheker, "Maroons within the Present Limits of the United States," *Journal of Negro History* 24 (April 1939): 170–71; Kay and Cary, "'They Are Indeed,'" 40–41; Turner, *Confessions of Nat Turner;* Oates, *Fires of Jubilee.*

46. "Runaway Slave," *Georgia Gazette*, September 1, 1763, *EAN.*

47. Paine was caught aiding Sampson and spent six years in one of Georgia's prisons for helping a fugitive slave. Paine, *Six Years in a Georgia Prison*, 28.

48. John Brown, *Slave Life in Georgia*, 61–62.

49. "Petition against the Introduction of Slaves" (1739), *CRG*, edited by Candler, 3:427.

50. Jane L. Landers, "Traditions of African American Freedom in Spanish Colonial Florida," in *African American Heritage of Florida*, edited by Colburn and Landers, 22–23.

51. Oglethorpe to the trustees, June 29, 1741, *CRG*, edited by Candler, 23:51–52.

52. The Stono uprising of September 1739, which took sixty lives (thirty-five black and twenty-five white), as Peter Wood has argued, was a turning point for South Carolina's black population and "a brief but serious groundswell of resistance to slavery, which had diverse and lasting repercussions." Peter H. Wood, *Black Majority*, 308–20.

53. Landers, *Black Society in Spanish Florida*, 1–2, 86.

54. Landers, "Traditions of African American Freedom," 29.

55. The *Georgia Gazette*, Georgia's first newspaper, was founded in Savannah and provides runaway slave documentation for the years 1763 through 1770. The

*Milledgeville (Ga.) Reflector* provides information on runaways between 1817 and 1818, when Seminole towns and the presence of the Spanish in Florida lured fugitive slaves. The *Milledgeville (Ga.) Federal Union* provides information on postannexation southbound runaways between 1830 and 1845. All of these newspapers were published weekly and offered advertising space for a fee. To determine the direction the slave was running, I kept the following in mind: for runaway slave advertisements, I considered the owner's guess as to where the slave was headed and the location of the owner's plantation in relation to the location of the newspaper in which he was advertising; for brought to jail notices, I analyzed the location of the jail and the information provided about the owner's residence, assuming that the runaway was apprehended in flight away from the plantation. Runaways may have lied to jailers about their owners' names and whereabouts, using intentionally vague names to prolong their stay in jail and improve their chance for escape. However, I have gone forward on the assumption that those brought to jail did not lie (as a result of whipping or other violent methods jailers used to wrest information out of their captives). But if fugitives did lie, they had the wherewithal to mislead their jailers with very specific and correct county names, which indicates an intimate knowledge of the Okefenokee hinterlands.

56. Morgan, "Colonial South Carolina Runaways," in *Out of the House of Bondage,* edited by Heuman, 57.

57. Ibid., 66.

58. Alexander Temple to Captain McTernan, December 16, 1786, bundle 108D9, *EFP;* Jane L. Landers, "Acquisition and Loss on a Spanish Frontier: The Free Black Homesteaders of Florida, 1784–1821," in *Against the Odds,* edited by Landers, 91; Landers, *Black Society in Spanish Florida.*

59. John Blackwood to Captain Howard, August 15, 1792, and Spanish official (name unknown) to John Blackwood, August 20, 1792, both in bundle 108D9, *EFP.*

60. "List of 43 slaves," May 4, 1797, bundle 109E9, *EFP.*

61. James Seagrove to Henry White, July 4, 1797, bundle 109E9, *EFP.*

62. James Seagrove to Governor Henry White, July 26, 1803, bundle 109E9, *EFP.*

63. "Articles entered into by the Honorable Henry White . . . and James Seagrove," May 19, 1797, bundle 109E9, *EFP.*

64. James Spalding to the governor of St. Augustine, May 20, 1794, bundle 108D9, *EFP.*

65. Kennedy, *Swallow Barn,* 253, 261.

66. Simms, *Helen Halsey,* 20, 25.

67. Simms, *Scout,* 14.

68. Henry Clay Lewis, *Odd Leaves,* 192, 198–99, 202.

69. See Stowe, *Dred;* Longfellow, "The Slave in the Dismal Swamp;" Houston, *The Fugitive Slave* (oil, 1853), Strother, "Osman," and Moran, *Slaves Escaping through a Swamp* (oil, 1862, 1865), all in David C. Miller, *Dark Eden* (Figures 3.2, 3.3, 3.4): 91, 93, 94.

70. Douglass, *Heroic Slave,* 158.

71. Delany, *Blake,* 110, 112–14.

72. Pendleton, *King Tom and the Runaways.*

## *Two. Battleground: The Seminole Swamp*

1. Porter, *Black Seminoles,* 9; Mulroy, *Freedom on the Border,* 4.

2. The Seminole chief Micanopy, incensed that slave hunters were invading his lands to recover fugitives, claimed Seminole rights of slave ownership in 1828: "these negroes are ours, and the whites have no rights to them." Seminoles owned slaves, but as most historians of Seminole slavery have argued, they did not establish a clear-cut master-slave relationship, often allowing their slaves to live in separate towns, to own property and guns, and to move around at will. William Duval to Gad Humphreys, March 20, 1827, and "Micanopy's Speech," April 17, 1828, quoted in Sprague, *Origin, Progress, and Conclusion,* 42, 50; Mulroy, *Freedom on the Border,* 17, 19; Porter, *Black Seminoles,* 5–6; Simmons, *Notices of East Florida,* 50, 45, 76.

3. Joel Martin uses the phrase "gaze of development" to describe an Anglo-American practice of viewing and evaluating landscapes that "trained Europeans and their descendents to view land as an assemblage of resources open to human manipulation and commercial exploitation." Joel W. Martin, *Sacred Revolt,* 92.

4. James J. Miller, *Environmental History of Northeast Florida,* 39–40.

5. Ibid., 79, 86.

6. Ibid., 93, 104, 113.

7. Covington, *Seminoles of Florida,* 10–11.

8. J. Leitch Wright Jr., *Creeks and Seminoles,* 2–3; Weisman, *Like Beads on a String,* 7.

9. Mulroy, *Freedom on the Border,* 7.

10. J. Leitch Wright Jr., *Creeks and Seminoles,* 4; M. M. Cohen, *Notices of Florida,* 31; Covington, *Seminoles of Florida,* 13.

11. Joel W. Martin, *Sacred Revolt,* 6–12.

12. J. Leitch Wright Jr., *Creeks and Seminoles,* 4.

13. Joel W. Martin, *Sacred Revolt,* 50.

14. It is unclear whether census takers included maroon men, women, and children in their assessment of the Seminole population. Mulroy, *Freedom on the Border,* 1–2, 7, 12; J. Leitch Wright Jr., *Creeks and Seminoles,* 173, 175, 177; Porter, *Black Seminoles,* 11, 66; Landers, "Separate Nation," 11.

15. "Map" (1766), reprinted in William Stork, *A Description of East-Florida,* and in Albert Hazen Wright, *Our Georgia-Florida Frontier,* 1; Samuel Savery, "Map, 1769," reprinted in Albert Hazen Wright, *Our Georgia-Florida Frontier,* 1–3.

16. Benjamin Hawkins to an unknown recipient, February 18, 1797, quoted in Albert Hazen Wright, *Our Georgia-Florida Frontier,* 41–42.

17. Hawkins, 1799, quoted in Albert Hazen Wright, *Our Georgia-Florida Frontier*, 3.

18. Bartram, *Travels*, 17–18.

19. Ibid., 18.

20. Captain B. Romans, "A General Map of the Southern British Colonies in America" (1776), reprinted in Albert Hazen Wright, *Our Georgia-Florida Frontier*, 37.

21. Greenblatt, *Marvelous Possessions*, 2, 14, 23–24; Pratt, *Imperial Eyes*, 4–6, 7.

22. M. M. Cohen, *Notices of Florida*, 40; Heidler and Heidler, *Old Hickory's War*, 77.

23. John Twiggs to Governor George Walton, May 31, 1789, Letters Describing Indian Depredations, C. Mildred Thompson Papers, Hargrett.

24. Deposition of Henry Carvel, September 6, 1793, Thompson Papers, Hargrett.

25. Milfort, "Memoir," GHS.

26. James Seagrove, September 8, 1792, quoted in Albert Hazen Wright, *Our Georgia-Florida Frontier*, 16.

27. Benjamin Hawkins to unknown recipient, 1797, quoted in Albert Hazen Wright, *Our Georgia-Florida Frontier*, 36.

28. Archibald Clarke to General Gaines, February 26, 1817, quoted in Albert Hazen Wright, *Our Georgia-Florida Frontier*, 38.

29. Alvar Nunez Cabeza de Vaca, *Relation of Alvar Nunez Cabeza de Vaca*, 31–40, quoted in Albert Hazen Wright, *Our Georgia-Florida Frontier*, 12–13, 15. Vaca's original narrative was published in Zamora, Spain, in 1542.

30. Garcilaso de la Vega, *Conquest of Florida, by Hernando de Soto*, quoted in Albert Hazen Wright, *Our Georgia-Florida Frontier*, 30–31. Vega's original narrative was published in Lisbon in 1605.

31. Beckett, *Encyclopedia of Guerrilla Warfare*, ix–xi.

32. See Donaldson, *Sergeant Atkins;* Whitman, *Rape of Florida;* Victor Perard, "A Great Sheet of Flame Leaped from the Roadside" (frontispiece), in Munroe, *Through Swamp and Glade;* Munn, *Seminole Song;* and Jerome Tiger, "Osceola" (1966), "Through the Everglades" (1967), "Everglades Sunset" (1967), and "Observing the Enemy" (1967), reprinted in Tiger and Babcock, *Life and Art*, 71, 72, 81.

33. Beckett, *Encyclopedia of Guerrilla Warfare*, ix.

34. Bass, *Swamp Fox*, 40, 111, 155; Simms, *Life of Francis Marion*, 152.

35. Beckett, *Encyclopedia of Guerrilla Warfare*, 13.

36. Hawkins, 1807, quoted in Albert Hazen Wright, *Our Georgia-Florida Frontier*, 36.

37. Porter, *Black Seminoles*, 4–12.

38. Ibid., 11; Covington, *Seminoles of Florida*, 32.

39. Porter, *Black Seminoles*, 19.

40. Letter to *Savannah Museum*, March 17, 1818, *EAN*.

41. General Andrew Jackson to Secretary of War John C. Calhoun, April 8, 1818, Antonio J. Waring Jr., Papers, GHS.

42. Covington, *Seminoles of Florida,* 45.

43. General Andrew Jackson to Secretary of War John C. Calhoun, April 20, 1818, Antonio J. Waring Jr. Papers, GHS.

44. Joseph Vallence Bevan, 1814, and John H. Bell to the United States Congress, February 1821, both quoted in Albert Hazen Wright, *Our Georgia-Florida Frontier,* 8, 37.

45. Sprague, *Origin, Progress, and Conclusion,* 100–101, 111.

46. Gad Humphreys to Joseph L. Smith, July 8, 1825, quoted in Sprague, *Origin, Progress, and Conclusion,* 31.

47. Covington, *Seminoles of Florida,* 79.

48. Porter, *Black Seminoles,* 41–43.

49. "Alligator's Report," quoted in Sprague, *Origin, Progress, and Conclusion,* 90.

50. Sprague, *Origin, Progress, and Conclusion,* 98.

51. "Statement of Rawson Clarke," quoted in M. M. Cohen, *Notices of Florida,* 71.

52. Wiley Thompson to Lewis Cass, December 11, 1835, quoted in Sprague, *Origin, Progress, and Conclusion,* 88.

53. Porter, *Black Seminoles,* 44.

54. Covington, *Seminoles of Florida,* 81.

55. Ibid., 82.

56. Beckett, *Encyclopedia of Guerrilla Warfare,* xii.

57. Frank Laumer, introduction to Henry Prince, *Amidst a Storm of Bullets,* 1–4.

58. Prince's journal, February 27, 1836, quoted in Henry Prince, *Amidst a Storm of Bullets,* 18.

59. Ibid., March 10, 1836; March 31, 1836; and April 4, 1836, pp. 30, 36–37, 38.

60. Ibid., October 7, 1836, pp. 59–60.

61. Ibid., June 14, 1836, and September 31, 1836, pp. 53, 59–60.

62. Ibid., March 14, 1837, and February 14, 1837, p. 83.

63. Cohen's journal, April 25, 1836, quoted in M. M. Cohen, *Notices of Florida,* 219.

64. Sprague, *Origin, Progress, and Conclusion,* 166.

65. Joel R. Poinsett to General Thomas Jesup, May 17, 1837, quoted in Sprague, *Origin, Progress, and Conclusion,* 179.

66. Cohen's journal, February 28, 1836, quoted in M. M. Cohen, *Notices of Florida,* 148.

67. Prince's journal, May 31, 1838, pp. 121–22.

68. Sprague, *Origin, Progress, and Conclusion,* 97.

69. "The Court of Inquiry's Response to General Scott," March 21, 1837, quoted in Sprague, *Origin, Progress, and Conclusion,* 158.

70. J. Leitch Wright Jr., *Creeks and Seminoles,* 271.

71. Sprague, *Origin, Progress, and Conclusion,* 505.

72. Albert Hazen Wright, *Our Georgia-Florida Frontier,* 35.

73. Sprague, *Origin, Progress, and Conclusion,* 261.

74. Thomas Hilliard to Governor William Schley, July 28, 1836, quoted in Laura Singleton Walker, *History of Ware County, Georgia,* 217–18.

75. Hilliard to Schley, August 26, 1836, quoted in Laura Singleton Walker, *History of Ware County, Georgia,* 219.

76. Hilliard to Schley, October 5, 1836, quoted in Laura Singleton Walker, *History of Ware County, Georgia,* 221–22.

77. Hilliard to Governor George Gilmer, June 4, 1838, quoted in Laura Singleton Walker, *History of Ware County, Georgia,* 200–201.

78. Hilliard to Gilmer, July 3, 1838, quoted in Laura Singleton Walker, *History of Ware County, Georgia,* 202–3.

79. General Zachary Taylor to Gilmer, July 13, 1838, quoted in Laura Singleton Walker, *History of Ware County, Georgia,* 204.

80. Robert Brown to Governor McCall, November 1838, quoted in Albert Hazen Wright, *Our Georgia-Florida Frontier,* 41.

81. "Governor's Message to the Georgia House of Representatives," November 5, 1838, *Savannah Daily Republican,* November 8, 1838, p. 2.

82. Vocelle, *History of Camden County, Georgia,* 73–74.

83. "Obituary, General Charles Rinaldo Floyd," *Savannah Daily Republican,* March 28, 1845, p. 2.

84. Charles Rinaldo Floyd Diary, October 27, 1838; November 2, 1838; November 3, 1838; November 10, 1838, pp. 254–58.

85. Ibid., November 11, 1838, and November 11, 1838, pp. 258–59.

86. Ibid., November 13, 1838, p. 259.

87. Floyd's troops were rumored to have also left their marks on bee trees in order to secure honey extraction rights. Floyd Diary, November 14, 1838, p. 260.

88. Floyd Diary, November 15, 1838, pp. 260–61.

89. Floyd to *Savannah Georgian,* November 17, 1838, reprinted in *Savannah Daily Republican,* November 27, 1838, p. 2.

90. Ibid.

91. "Letter from General Charles Floyd to the *Savannah Georgian,*" written December 5, 1838," *Savannah Daily Republican,* December 11, 1838, p. 2.

92. Ibid.

93. "Order, by the Commander in Chief, January 17, 1839," *Savannah Daily Republican,* January 24, 1839, p. 2; Floyd Diary, February 2, 1839, p. 283.

94. Sprague, *Origin, Progress, and Conclusion,* 256, 262, 411.

95. "Oral Account of Alexander Eunice" (1934), quoted in Laura Singleton Walker, *History of Ware County, Georgia,* 17.

96. Sprague, *Origin, Progress, and Conclusion,* 284.

97. Ibid., 471.

98. President John Tyler, "Speech before Congress," May 10, 1842, quoted in Sprague, *Origin, Progress, and Conclusion,* 476–77.

99. "Conversation between Colonel Worth and Halleck Tustenuggee," April 29, 1842, quoted in Sprague, *Origin, Progress, and Conclusion,* 464.

*Three. El Dorado: The Okefenokee and Dreams of Development*

1. Starke, *W. W. Starke's 'Amusing Sketch' Resketched,* 5, 8–9, GHS.
2. Andrew Ellicott, *Journal of Andrew Ellicott,* 276, 300.
3. Cadle, *Georgia Land Surveying History,* 213, 217.
4. Neill, "Surveyors' Field Notes," 331.
5. Physicians had long believed swamps to be the origin of miasmatic disease and therefore promoted drainage as a way to bring about public health. They suggested dry culture (the removal of standing water from rice fields and the dry cultivation of that cereal) and swamp drainage to prevent epidemics. These public health strategies did improve living conditions in Okefenokee hinterland cities but proved deleterious to smaller swamps and lowlands that, unlike the Okefenokee, were easily drained and converted. See Nelson, "Landscape of Disease," 555–67.
6. The First Swamp Land Act, approved March 2, 1849, was enacted to aid Louisiana in constructing levees and drains to "reclaim the swamp and overflowed lands therein" that are "unfit for cultivation." After state surveys, the surveyor general would apply to the secretary of the Treasury for fee simple, which would be granted on any lands proven to be overflowed. The state could then sell the land and use the proceeds "exclusively, as far as necessary, to the construction of levees and drains." Subsequent Swamp Land Acts passed in 1850, 1855, 1857, 1860, 1866, and 1917 codified swamp reclamation throughout the nation. *Swamp Land Act of 1849,* 30th Cong., 2nd sess., *U.S. Statutes,* 352; *Swamp Land Act of 1850,* 31st Cong., 1st sess., *U.S. Statutes,* 520–21; *Swamp Land Act of 1855,* 33rd Cong., 2nd sess., *U.S. Statutes,* 634–35; *Swamp Land Act of 1857,* 34th Cong., 3rd sess., *U.S. Statutes,* 251; *Swamp Land Act of 1860,* 36th Cong., 1st sess., *U.S. Statutes,* 3; *Swamp Land Act of 1866,* 39th Cong., 1st sess., *U.S. Statutes,* 218; *Swamp Land Act of 1917,* 64th Cong., 2nd sess., *U.S. Statutes,* 995.
7. Trowell, *Mansfield Torrance Survey,* 1, 4–5.
8. Charles Rinaldo Floyd to *Savannah Georgian,* November 17, 1838, in *Savannah Daily Republican,* November 27, 1838, p. 2.
9. Trowell, *Mansfield Torrance Survey,* 5–6.
10. Ibid., 8.
11. *State of Georgia Executive Minutes,* 1843–49, 1849–55, quoted in Trowell, *Mansfield Torrance Survey,* 20.
12. One of the surveyors, "The Okefenokee," *Milledgeville (Ga.) Southern Recorder,* July 1850, quoted in Trowell, *Mansfield Torrance Survey,* 24.
13. Trowell, *Mansfield Torrance Survey,* 25.
14. Mansfield Torrance to *Columbus (Ga.) Southern Sentinel,* in *Southern Cultivator,* August 1850, quoted in Trowell, "Another Description," 1.
15. One of the surveyors, "The Okefenokee" and Governor George W. Towns to Georgia Legislature, November 3, 1851, both quoted in Trowell, *Mansfield Torrance Survey,* 25, 26, 29, 30, 33; Trowell, *Mansfield Torrance Survey,* 32, 33–37.

16. Trowell, *Richard L. Hunter Survey,* viii; Cadle, *Georgia Land Surveying History,* 227n67; *Savannah Republican,* January 11, 1854, quoted in Trowell, *Richard L. Hunter Survey,* 11–12, 13.

17. As an article in the *New Orleans Bulletin* suggested in 1852, "Railroads are the grand secret of Georgia's prosperity; they are permeating every section of the State, uniting with their iron bands of the most distant counties, and establishing a perfect work of intercommunication." *Savannah Republican,* January 9, 1852, quoted in Trowell and Fussell, *Railroads of the Okefenokee Realm,* 1.

18. Trowell and Fussell, *Railroads of the Okefenokee Realm,* 4.

19. Trowell, *Richard L. Hunter Survey,* 5; Scott C. Martin, "Don Quixote and Leatherstocking," 72.

20. Miller B. Grant, "The Okefenokee," *Savannah Morning News,* November 22, 1875, quoted in Trowell, *Richard L. Hunter Survey,* 7.

21. Ibid.

22. Trowell, *Richard L. Hunter Survey,* 9–10, 12, 14.

23. *Columbus (Ga.) Times-Sentinel,* November 24, 1857, and December 17, 1857, both quoted in Trowell, *Richard L. Hunter Survey,* 59.

24. *Columbus (Ga.) Daily Sun,* March 31, 1857, quoted in Trowell, *Richard L. Hunter Survey,* 58.

25. Ayers, *Promise of the New South,* viii.

26. Ibid., 9.

27. Trowell, *Letters from the Expeditions,* 2.

28. W. C. Folks, "Cuyler's Desert," *Savannah Morning News,* April 19, 1875, quoted in Trowell, *Letters from the Expeditions,* 7–8.

29. Ayers, *Promise of the New South,* 20–21, 87.

30. Wyatt-Brown, *Shaping of Southern Culture,* 257; Mayfield, "'Soul of a Man!'" 477.

31. Kimmel, *Manhood in America,* 59; Kriegel, *On Men and Manhood,* 69, 73; Wyatt-Brown, *Southern Honor;* Greenberg, *Honor and Slavery;* Gorn, "'Gouge and Bite'"; Ayers, *Promise of the New South,* 64–65.

32. *Valdosta (Ga.) Times,* May 8, 1875, and *Savannah Morning News,* May 12, 1875, both quoted in Trowell, *Letters from the Expeditions,* 11–12.

33. *Valdosta (Ga.) Times,* May 8, 1875, quoted in Trowell, *Letters from the Expeditions,* 9.

34. Charles R. Pendleton to *Savannah Morning News,* May 25, 1875, quoted in Trowell, *Letters from the Expeditions,* 21–22.

35. W. C. Folks to *Valdosta (Ga.) Times,* August 7, 1875, quoted in Trowell, *Letters from the Expeditions,* 25.

36. *Valdosta (Ga.) Times,* August 21, 1875, quoted in Trowell, *Letters from the Expeditions,* 27.

37. Scott C. Martin, "Don Quixote and Leatherstocking," 62; Ownby, *Subduing Satan,* 26–28; Mayfield, "'Soul of a Man!'" 481; Kimmel, *Manhood in America,* 100.

38. Charles R. Pendleton to *Atlanta Constitution*, October 5, 1875, quoted in Trowell, *Letters from the Expeditions*, 50.

39. Bederman, *Manliness and Civilization*, 176.

40. Charles R. Pendleton to *Atlanta Constitution*, September 15, 1875, quoted in Trowell, *Letters from the Expeditions*, 38.

41. Kimmel, *Manhood in America*, 44.

42. *Atlanta Constitution*, September 5, 1875, and E. Y. Clarke, editorial, *Atlanta Constitution*, September 14, 1875, both quoted in Trowell, *Letters from the Expeditions*, 70, 69.

43. *Atlanta Constitution*, September 5, 1875, quoted in Trowell, *Letters from the Expeditions*, 69.

44. E. Y. Clarke to *Atlanta Constitution*, November 6, 1875, and November 15, 1875, both quoted in Trowell, *Letters from the Expeditions*, 80, 82, 85.

45. E. Y. Clarke to *Atlanta Constitution*, November 14, 1875, quoted in Trowell, *Letters from the Expeditions*, 92, 102.

46. C. A. Locke, "Abstract," December 1875, quoted in Trowell, *Letters from the Expeditions*, 117, 119–21.

47. *Savannah Morning News*, November 4, 1878, and *Brunswick (Ga.) Weekly Advertiser and Appeal*, May 28, 1881, both quoted in Trowell, *Letters from the Expeditions*, 144, 142–43; Trowell, *Letters from the Expeditions*, 141–43.

48. Luther C. Bryan, "Okefenokee" (1883), quoted in Trowell, *Suwanee Canal Company*, 73–75.

49. Trowell, *Suwanee Canal Company*, xii, 4.

50. "Drainage of the Everglades," 598, 601; Trowell, *Suwanee Canal Company*, 73.

51. Lott et al., *Okefenokee Swamp*, August 12, 1889, pp. 7–8, CCPL.

52. W. G. Cooper, *Atlanta Constitution*, July 14 and 29, 1889, quoted in Trowell, *Suwanee Canal Company*, 75–77, 86–87.

53. Senator Boyd, *Valdosta (Ga.) Times*, September 28, 1889, quoted in Trowell, *Suwanee Canal Company*, 95.

54. Frank W. Hall, *Atlanta Constitution*, July 25, 1889, quoted in Trowell, *Suwanee Canal Company*, 77, 79.

55. *Savannah Morning News*, November 11, 1889, and *Waycross (Ga.) Reporter*, November 23, 1889, ORL, microfilm.

56. *Atlanta Constitution*, January 8, 1890, quoted in Trowell, *Suwanee Canal Company*, 100.

57. *Waycross (Ga.) Reporter*, March 22, 1890, ORL, microfilm.

58. *Atlanta Constitution*, July 25, 1889, quoted in Trowell, *Suwanee Canal Company*, 16, 81.

59. *Atlanta Constitution*, March 20, 1890, quoted in Trowell, *Suwanee Canal Company*, 111, 113.

60. *Waycross (Ga.) Reporter*, May 24, 1890, ORL, microfilm; James M. Kraemer, *Report to the Governor of Georgia*, October 9, 1890, and Henry Jackson, *Atlanta Journal*, May 24, June 4, June 9, June 21, July 4, and July 19, 1890, all quoted in

Trowell, *Suwanee Canal Company,* 115–31, 132–33; Trowell and Izlar, *Jackson's Folly,* 188; Trowell, *Suwanee Canal Company,* 134.

61. During the 1890s drainage projects were in progress throughout the Oke-fenokee hinterlands and particularly on the outskirts of cities and towns, where suburban expansion provoked swampland reclamation. Blandford, *Reports,* 9, 25, 27, 31, GHS; "Drainage Needed Near City Limits," *Savannah Morning News,* September 8, 1897, J. F. Waring Papers, GHS.

62. Trowell and Izlar, *Jackson's Folly,* 188; Trowell, *Suwanee Canal Company,* 140, 155.

63. *Atlanta Constitution,* August 12, 1891, quoted in Trowell, *Suwanee Canal Company,* 141–42; *Waycross (Ga.) Reporter,* May 24, 1890, ORL, microfilm.

64. *Atlanta Constitution,* April 28, 1892, quoted in Trowell, *Suwanee Canal Company,* 144.

65. "Dredge at Work in the Okefenokee," *Atlanta Constitution,* 1893.

66. Trowell and Izlar, *Jackson's Folly,* 188–89; Trowell, *Suwanee Canal Company,* 144; *Atlanta Constitution,* April 28, 1892, quoted in Trowell, *Suwanee Canal Company,* 145.

67. Trowell and Izlar, *Jackson's Folly,* 189; Trowell, *Suwanee Canal Company,* 151.

68. Trowell and Izlar, *Jackson's Folly,* 189.

69. *Savannah Morning News,* February 14, 1893, quoted in Trowell, *Suwanee Canal Company,* 11; Trowell and Izlar, *Jackson's Folly,* 11, 153.

70. Drobney, *Lumbermen and Log Sawyers,* 32–38.

71. Laurence C. Walker, *Southern Forest,* 43, 99, 103–5.

72. Trowell and Izlar, *Jackson's Folly,* 189–90; Trowell, *Suwanee Canal Company,* 151.

73. Trowell and Izlar, *Jackson's Folly,* 190–92; Henry Jackson, "Report to the Stockholders," March 19, 1894, quoted in Trowell, *Suwanee Canal Company,* 159–60.

74. *Savannah Morning News,* April 25, 1895, CCPL.

75. S. T. Walker, "Report to the Stockholders," and Henry Jackson, "Report to the Stockholders," March 18, 1895, quoted in Trowell, *Suwanee Canal Company,* 163, 166–67.

76. *Savannah Morning News,* August 6, 1895, CCPL.

77. Trowell and Izlar, *Jackson's Folly,* 192.

78. "The Directors' Report to the Stockholders," March 17, 1896, quoted in Trowell, *Suwanee Canal Company,* 177, 179, 176.

79. Trowell and Izlar, *Jackson's Folly,* 193; Trowell, *Suwanee Canal Company,* 183, 186, 187.

80. Trowell, *Suwanee Canal Company,* 193; Trowell and Izlar, *Jackson's Folly,* 194.

81. Hopkins, "Forty-five Years"; *Savannah Morning News,* August 6, 1895, CCPL.

82. McQueen and Mizell, *History of Okefenokee Swamp,* 69–70.

83. F. M. Oliver, *Savannah Morning News,* January 1, 1932, quoted in Trowell, *Suwanee Canal Company,* 205.

84. Trowell and Izlar, *Jackson's Folly,* 194; Trowell, *Suwanee Canal Company,* 204; Purdom, "Logging Lowdown," ORL.

85. Robert L. Izlar, "A History of Okefenokee Logging Operations: A Bourbon and Branch Water Success Story," in *Okefenokee Swamp,* edited by A. D. Cohen et al., 8; Trowell, *Hebard Lumber Company,* 1; Izlar, "Hebard Lumber Company," 71, 85–86.

86. Trowell, *Mansfield Torrance Survey,* 5–6.

87. Drobney, *Lumbermen and Log Sawyers,* 19.

88. Hopkins, "Forty-five Years," n.p.

89. Ibid., 16–17, 18; Izlar, "Hebard Lumber Company," 79.

90. Hopkins, "Forty-five Years," 22–23.

91. Ibid., 22.

92. Ibid., 29; Izlar, "Hebard Lumber Company," 91.

93. Izlar, "History of Okefenokee," 8; Trowell, *Hebard Lumber Company,* 1; Izlar, "Hebard Lumber Company," 40–44.

94. Trowell, *Hebard Lumber Company,* 1; Hopkins, "Forty-five Years," 31.

95. Hopkins, "Forty-five Years," 35; Trowell, *Hebard Lumber Company,* 5; Izlar, "Okefenokee Logging Operations," 9, 125, 126.

96. Hopkins, "Forty-five Years," 39; Izlar, "Hebard Lumber Company," 87.

97. Hopkins, "Forty-five Years," 37.

98. Trowell, *Hebard Lumber Company,* 3–4.

99. Leon Brown, "Logging of the Okefenokee," 13; Gibson, "Billy's Island," ORL; Trowell, *Hebard Lumber Company,* 5; Hopkins, "Forty-five Years," 38–39; Trowell, *Billy's Island,* 19, 21.

100. Trowell, *Billy's Island,* 21; Izlar, "Hebard Lumber Company," 129–30.

101. Drobney, *Lumbermen and Log Sawyers,* 179; Izlar, "Okefenokee Logging Operations," 9.

102. Izlar, "Okefenokee Logging Operations," 15.

103. Ibid., 62–65; Clark, *Greening of the South,* 18–19; Trowell, *Hebard Lumber Company,* 3.

104. Hopkins, "Forty-five Years," 32.

105. Ibid., 33.

106. Izlar, "Okefenokee Logging Operations," 10–11; Hopkins, "Forty-five Years," 33; Izlar, "Hebard Lumber Company," 94.

107. Hopkins, "Forty-five Years," 38, 41; Izlar, "Okefenokee Logging Operations," 13.

108. Izlar, "Okefenokee Logging Operations," 14; Izlar, "Hebard Lumber Company," 73.

109. Izlar, "Hebard Lumber Company," 101.

110. Izlar, "Okefenokee Logging Operations," 11.

111. Ibid., 12; Izlar, "Hebard Lumber Company," 102.

112. Hopkins, "Forty-five Years," 35.

113. Purdom, "Logging Lowdown," ORL.

114. Izlar, "Okefenokee Logging Operations," 9; Izlar, "Hebard Lumber Company," 101; Hopkins, "Forty-five Years," 41.

115. Trowell, *Hebard Lumber Company*, 4–5; Trowell, *Suwanee Canal Company*, xii–xiii; Clary, "Research Paper"; Izlar, "Hebard Lumber Company," 117.

116. Trowell, *Hebard Lumber Company*, 5–6.

117. Trowell and Izlar, *Jackson's Folly*, 195; Izlar, "Okefenokee Logging Operations," 15–16; Trowell, *Suwanee Canal Company*, 206–7; Izlar, "Hebard Lumber Company," 82.

118. Trowell, *Suwanee Canal Company*, 206; Purdom, "Logging Lowdown," ORL.

119. Izlar, "Hebard Lumber Company," 139.

120. Ibid., 152; Trowell and Fussell, *Railroads of the Okefenokee Realm*, 19–20.

121. Charles Sperry, August 2, 1926, quoted in Trowell, *Billy's Island*, 3–4.

*Four. Homesite and Workplace: Okefenokee Swampers*

1. Charles Pendleton to *Atlanta Constitution*, September 15, 1875, quoted in Trowell, *Letters from the Expeditions*, 41; Trowell, *Life on the Okefenokee Frontier*, 13.

2. David Colin Crass et al., introduction to *Southern Colonial Backcountry*, edited by Crass et al., xvii.

3. Owsley, *Plain Folk of the Old South*, v–vi, 3, 8, 16, 24, 133–34; John B. Boles, foreword to *Plain Folk of the South Revisited*, edited by Hyde, ix.

4. Grady McWhiney, "Crackers and Cavaliers: Shared Courage," in *Plain Folk of the South Revisited*, edited by Hyde, 190.

5. Presley, "Crackers of Georgia," 113.

6. Andrews, "Cracker English," 87; Rummel, "Crackers and Cattle Kings," 41.

7. Gorn, "'Gouge and Bite,'" 18–43; Milfort, "Memoir," GHS; James A. Lewis, "*Cracker*–Spanish Florida Style," 185.

8. "Journal of the Commons House of Assembly," 1763–68, and Governor James Wright to unknown recipient, 1771, both in *CRG*, edited by Candler, 14:475–76, 28:840–44.

9. Don Vicente Zespedes, "Report to His Excellency Senor Conde del Camp de Alange," June 20, 1790, quoted in James A. Lewis, "*Cracker*–Spanish Florida Style," 190–91.

10. Presley, "Crackers of Georgia," 112.

11. Zespedes, "Report," quoted in James A. Lewis, "*Cracker*–Spanish Florida Style," 190.

12. Milfort, "Memoir," GHS.

13. Graffenried, "Georgia Cracker," 484.

14. Denham, "Florida Cracker," 462, Milfort, "Memoir," GHS; Kemble, *Journal*, 181–82.

15. Kemble, *Journal*, 181; Zespedes, "Report," quoted in James A. Lewis, "*Cracker* – Spanish Florida Style," 194.

16. There has been some debate about the extent of yeoman farmer and poor white contact with capitalism. According to most New Rural historians, rural stag-

nation did not necessarily follow the capitalist transformation of the countryside in the late nineteenth century. Instead, rural residents devised creative strategies to preserve their farmsteads and engage in the market without succumbing to its fluctuations. My findings in regard to Swampers support the contention that rural residents were semisubsistence producers who had connections to both local, barter-dominated markets and larger metropolitan capitalist complexes involving surplus commodity production. Swierenga, "New Rural History," 211–23; Swierenga, "Theoretical Perspectives," 495–502; Hahn, *Roots of Southern Populism;* Hahn and Prude, eds., *Countryside in the Age of Capitalist Transformation;* Barron, "Rediscovering the Majority," 141–52; Kulikoff, *Tobacco and Slaves;* Kulikoff, "Households and Markets," 342–55; Merchant, *Ecological Revolutions;* Vaught, "State of the Art," 759–74.

17. Zespedes, "Report," quoted in James A. Lewis, "*Cracker*–Spanish Florida Style," 197; David C. Hsiung, "'Seeing' Early Appalachian Communities through the Lenses of History, Geography, and Sociology," in Crass et al., eds., *Southern Colonial Backcountry,* 166, 169–76.

18. Presley, "Crackers of Georgia," 104; Robert D. Mitchell, "The Southern Backcountry: A Geographical House Divided," in Crass et al., eds., *Southern Colonial Backcountry,* 21.

19. Denham, "Florida Cracker," 454; *Ware County Census,* 1830, 1840, 1850.

20. McQueen, *History of Charlton County,* 19, 21, 22.

21. Ibid., 25–29, 23–24, 47; Hurst, *This Magic Wilderness,* 8, 85.

22. Hurst, *This Magic Wilderness,* 43–44.

23. Delma E. Presley, "Life and Lore of the Swampers," in Cohen et al., eds, *Okefenokee Swamp,* 20; *Charlton County, Georgia,* 137; Wyatt-Brown, "Antimission Movement," 503, 514; Lacy Ford, "Popular Ideology of the Old South's Plain Folk: The Limits of Egalitarianism in a Slaveholding Society," in Hyde, ed., *Plain Folk of the South Revisited,* 206–7; Fredrickson, *Black Image in the White Mind,* 61; Ellis, "Legitimating Slavery," 340–51.

24. Cothran, "Talking Trash," 342, 346.

25. Matschat, *Suwannee River;* Rawlings, *Yearling,* 33, 76.

26. Trowell, *Life on the Okefenokee Frontier,* 15.

27. *Ware/Clinch County Census,* 1830, CCPL.

28. Miller B. Grant, "The Okefenokee" (1858), quoted in Trowell, *Richard L. Hunter Survey,* 80.

29. *Charlton County, Georgia,* 131–32.

30. Ibid., 131.

31. Hurst, *This Magic Wilderness,* 92–93.

32. Trowell, *Life on the Okefenokee Frontier,* 11–12.

33. Thrift, *Coxes of Okefenokee,* 10–11.

34. Otto, "Plain Folk," 5–6; Otto, "Oral Traditional History," 25; one of the surveyors, 1850, quoted in Trowell, *Mansfield Torrance Survey,* 30.

35. Olmsted, *Cotton Kingdom,* 206; Owsley, *Plain Folk of the Old South,* 157; *Ware*

*County Census,* 1840, 1850, CCPL; *Charlton County Census,* 1860, CCPL; *Charlton County, Georgia,* 243–44.

36. Julia Floyd Smith, *Slavery and Plantation Growth,* 25; Julia Floyd Smith, *Slavery and Rice Culture,* 217; *Ware County Census,* 1850, CCPL.

37. Mansfield Torrance, 1850, quoted in Trowell, *Life on the Okefenokee Frontier,* 5.

38. Hahn, *Roots of Southern Populism,* 4, 9–10; Steven Hahn, "The 'Unmaking' of the Southern Yeomanry," in Hahn and Prude, eds., *Countryside in the Age of Capitalist Transformation,* 179–203; Charles Pendleton to *Atlanta Constitution,* September 15, 1875, quoted in Trowell, *Letters from the Expeditions,* 38–41.

39. Charles Pendleton to *Atlanta Constitution,* September 9/12 and 15, 1875, quoted in Trowell, *Letters from the Expeditions,* 30, 38–41.

40. Howell Cobb Jackson to *Atlanta Journal,* June 25, 1890, quoted in Trowell, *Suwanee Canal Company,* 126.

41. Owsley, *Plain Folk of the Old South,* 30–34; Bradley Bond, "Herders, Farmers, and Markets on the Inner Frontier: The Mississippi Piney Woods, 1850–1860," in Hyde, ed., *Plain Folk of the South Revisited,* 93.

42. Charles Pendleton to *Valdosta Times,* March 6, 1900, quoted in Trowell, *Life on the Okefenokee Frontier,* 7–8.

43. Rummel, "Crackers and Cattle Kings," 36; Trowell, *Life on the Okefenokee Frontier,* 3; Bartram, *Travels,* 163.

44. Owsley, *Plain Folk of the Old South,* 44–45, 51.

45. Mansfield Torrance, 1850, and Allen, *Allen's Journal,* 1854, both quoted in Trowell, *Life on the Okefenokee Frontier,* 5; Hunter, *Report,* 5.

46. Charles Pendleton to *Valdosta (Ga.) Times,* 1890, quoted in Trowell, *Life on the Okefenokee Frontier,* 7–8.

47. Rawlings, *Yearling,* 366–88, 469.

48. James G. Needham, "Okefenokee Notes," quoted in Trowell, *Billy's Island,* 3; Hopkins, "Forty-five Years," 21.

49. Charles Pendleton to *Atlanta Constitution,* quoted in Trowell, *Life on the Okefenokee Frontier,* 12.

50. Howell Cobb Jackson to *Atlanta Journal,* May 1890, quoted in Trowell, *Suwanee Canal Company,* 116–17.

51. Mays, *Settlers of the Okefenokee,* 7.

52. Howell Cobb Jackson to *Atlanta Journal,* May 1890, quoted in Trowell, *Suwanee Canal Company,* 117.

53. Elliott, *Carolina Sports,* 253–54; Hopkins, "Forty-five Years," 43.

54. Dolores Floyd, "Notes Made during a Trip into Okefenokee Swamp" (1929), folder 51, box 5, Marmaduke Hamilton and Dolores Boisfeuillet Floyd Papers, GHS.

55. Howell Cobb Jackson to *Atlanta Journal,* June 14, 1890, quoted in Trowell, *Suwanee Canal Company,* 123.

56. Mays, *Settlers of the Okefenokee,* 55; Hopkins, "Forty-five Years," 44.

57. Hopkins, "Forty-five Years," 44; Trowell, *Suwanee Canal Company*, 8; Trowell, *Billy's Island*, 8.

58. E. Y. Clarke to *Atlanta Constitution*, November 12, 18, and 19, 1875, quoted in Trowell, *Letters from the Expeditions*, 81, 85, 89.

59. Drobney, *Lumbermen and Log Sawyers*, 15; Herndon, "Forest Products of Colonial Georgia," 130–35; Laura Singleton Walker, *History of Ware County, Georgia*, 34, 75, 77–81.

60. Drobney, *Lumbermen and Log Sawyers;* Hurst, *This Magic Wilderness*, 43.

61. *Charlton County, Georgia*, 16–17; Hurst, *This Magic Wilderness*, 41–43.

62. Drobney, *Lumbermen and Log Sawyers*, 13, 23; Trowell, *Suwanee Canal Company*, xii; McQueen, *History of Charlton County*, 55; Henry Jackson, "Report to the Stockholders, March 19, 1894," 1894, quoted in Trowell, *Suwanee Canal Company*, 159.

63. Marie Wylie Jones, "Okefenokee Queen Marries," *Savannah Morning News*, October 28, 1928, p. 7.

64. Ibid., 7; "Obituary of Lydia Smith Stone Crews," *Savannah Morning News*, 1937, Marmaduke and Dolores Floyd Papers, GHS; Dodson, "Old Man and the Swamp"; Hurst, *This Magic Wilderness*, 24–26.

65. One of the surveyors, 1850, quoted in Trowell, *Mansfield Torrance Survey*, 29.

66. Miller B. Grant, "Okefenokee," 85.

67. Charles Pendleton to *Atlanta Constitution*, October 23, 1875, quoted in Trowell, *Letters from the Expeditions*, 55.

68. Charles Pendleton to *Atlanta Constitution*, September 11, 1875, quoted in Trowell, *Letters from the Expeditions*, 29; Izlar, "Hebard Lumber Company"; Johnson, "Among the Georgia Crackers," 526; one of the surveyors, quoted in Trowell, *Mansfield Torrance Survey*, 29; Laura Singleton Walker, *History of Ware County, Georgia*, 84.

69. Walker and King, *About "Old Okefenok,"* 57–61; Hopkins, "Forty-five Years," 57–58.

70. Hunter, *Report*, 6; Miller B. Grant, "Okefenokee," 53.

71. Dodson, "Old Man and the Swamp," 15.

72. Trowell, *Mansfield Torrance Survey*, 21; one of the surveyors, quoted in Trowell, *Mansfield Torrance Survey*, 28.

73. Miller B. Grant, "Okefenokee," 21, 24, 30; Hunter, *Report*, 8.

74. Miller B. Grant, "Okefenokee," 49; Hunter, *Report*, 4.

75. Miller B. Grant, "Okefenokee," quoted in Trowell, *Richard L. Hunter Survey*, 52, 58.

76. Trowell, *Letters from the Expeditions*, 9.

77. Charles Pendleton, editorial, *Valdosta (Ga.) Times*, February 8, 1890, and May 15, 1875, both quoted in Trowell, *Letters from the Expeditions*, 10, 12–15.

78. Charles Pendleton, editorial, *Valdosta (Ga.) Times*, May 15, 1875, and Charles Pendleton to *Savannah Morning News*, May 25, 1875, both quoted in Trowell, *Letters from the Expeditions*, 16, 21.

79. Charles Pendleton to *Savannah Morning News,* May 25, 1875, quoted in Trowell, *Letters from the Expeditions,* 22.

80. Charles Pendleton to *Atlanta Constitution,* September 11, 1875, and Charles Pendleton to *Atlanta Weekly Constitution,* October 12, 1875, both quoted in Trowell, *Letters from the Expeditions,* 28, 55.

81. *Waycross Reporter,* May 24, 1890, ORL, microfilm.

82. Hopkins, "Forty-five Years," 20–21.

83. Delma E. Presley, "Life and Lore," in Cohen et al., eds., *Okefenokee Swamp,* 36.

84. Thrift, *Coxes of Okefenokee,* 10–11.

85. Ibid., 10–11, 38, 40, 44, 45, 50–51.

86. Ibid., 52, 53; Dickson, "Alligator Poacher Remembers."

87. Dickson, "Okefenokee Yields a Living Grudgingly."

88. Mays, *Settlers of the Okefenokee,* 1–7.

89. Dodson, "Old Man and the Swamp"; Mays, *Settlers of the Okefenokee,* 1–2, 3, 4, 7, 11–14.

90. Trowell, *Billy's Island.*

91. McQueen, *History of Charlton County,* 84.

92. Henry Jackson, "Message to the Board," quoted in Trowell, *Billy's Island,* 10.

93. Pope Barrow to W. M. Oliff, December 15, 1900, quoted in Trowell, *Billy's Island,* 11.

94. Trowell, *Billy's Island,* 15–17.

95. Ibid., 17; Dickson, "Little House"; Walter C. Hill, "Okefenokee," *Inspection News* (Atlanta: Retail Credit, April 1929).

96. *Charlton County Herald,* April 8, 1932, and *Hebard Lumber Company v. Harrison Lee,* April 13, 1932, Charlton County Superior Court, quoted in Trowell, *Billy's Island,* 24.

97. *Charlton County Herald,* May 27, 1932, quoted in Trowell, *Billy's Island,* 24–25.

98. Hopkins, "Forty-five Years," 44.

99. Ibid., 58.

100. Dickson, "Okefenokee Yields a Living Grudgingly"; Dickson, "Okefenokee Gator Poacher Remembers."

101. Mays, *Settlers of the Okefenokee,* 92–94.

*Five. A Refuge for Birds: Okefenokee Preservation*

1. Roland Harper to F. V. Coville, December 12, 1901, and June 29, 1902, quoted in Trowell, *Roland M. Harper,* 3, vi.

2. Nash, *Wilderness and the American Mind,* 96; Marsh, *Man and Nature;* Jacoby, *Crimes against Nature,* 15; Wild, *Pioneer Conservationists,* 15–23.

3. Bouchier and Cruikshank, "'Sportsmen and Pothunters,'" 1; Dunlap, "Sport Hunting and Conservation," 54; Reiger, *American Sportsmen,* 29–34.

4. Reiger, *American Sportsmen*, 39, 139–40; Laurence C. Walker, *Southern Forest*, 137, 192–93, 170; Gonzalez, "Conservation Policy Network," 275.

5. *Waycross Journal-Herald*, January 22, 1919, ORL, microfilm.

6. Farber, *Emergence of Ornithology*, 122.

7. As the ornithological discipline grew and expanded at the turn of the twentieth century in America, ornithology began to embrace the anatomical details and morphology of bird specimens (usually studied from stuffed birds) and what might be called "bird culture"–the habits and habitat of birds in the "wild." Attention to bird culture meant that ornithologists placed importance on field observations. Thus, at the very moment that American ornithology was becoming a distinct scientific discipline, scientific professionals began to embrace the field experiences of amateur collectors and bird-watchers. Orr, *Saving American Birds*, 1, 7, 18, 21–29, 44–52, 73–74, 83, 190; Barrow, *Passion for Birds*.

8. Gonzalez, "Conservation Policy Network," 277, 281, 289.

9. Wright and Harper, "Biological Reconnaissance," 481; Trowell, *Roland M. Harper*, 12, 21.

10. Wright and Harper, "Biological Reconnaissance," 482.

11. Roland Harper, "Journal of a Botanical Exploration of the Okefenokee Swamp" (1902), manuscript, Botany Library, Smithsonian Institution, as quoted in Trowell, *Roland M. Harper*, 6–8, 10–11, 36, 37, 41, 48; Roland Harper, "Okefinokee Swamp," 596–614.

12. Francis Harper, "Report of Expedition," 402, 406; Presley and Harper, *Okefinokee Album*, xi.

13. Francis Harper, "Sojourn in the Primeval Okefinokee," 230; Francis Harper, Chesser Island journal, September 1, 1922, quoted in Presley and Harper, *Okefinokee Album*, 170.

14. Francis Harper, "Report of Expedition," 406.

15. Dr. William Baldwin of St. Marys claimed to have gone on a botanical tour that extended "within about twelve miles of the celebrated Okefanoka Swamp" in February 1814, but the earliest recorded naturalist exploration of the swamp was that of the ornithologist Maurice Thompson in 1885. Like Charles Pendleton and the surveyors who had entered the swamp only ten years before, Thompson felt himself to be a kind of explorer, but for the purposes of science, not development. Francis Harper, "Report of Expedition," 402; Roland Harper, "Okefinokee Swamp," 597; Thompson, "Red-Headed Family," 23.

16. Formal studies of birds had been part of American travel literature from the earliest years of the colonial period. A shift in bird study from an amateur pastime to a profession occurred in the late eighteenth century as European governments began to establish museums to house avian collections. Other countries (including the United States) followed suit, and in the nineteenth century many ornithological and natural history museums became attached to universities. In America, Alexander Wilson's nine-volume *American Ornithology* (1808–14) and John James Audubon's *Birds of America* (1826–38) raised the illustrative art of birds to a new

level and gave Americans their first great national bird collections in print. Amateur birders and collectors became avid consumers of such ornithological research. Alan Feduccia, introduction to *Catesby's Birds of Colonial America,* edited by Feduccia, 3, 5–6, 8, 10; Farber, *Emergence of Ornithology,* xv, xix, 1–2, 8–13, 17–25, 38–43, 49–53, 100–104; McFeely, "Collecting Ourselves," 98–99; Barrow, *Passion for Birds.*

17. Francis Harper, "Report of Expedition," 405. Francis Harper, "Sojourn in the Primeval Okefinokee," 242. For a discussion of the extinction of the passenger pigeon see, Jennifer Price, *Flight Maps.*

18. Francis Harper, "Mammals of the Okefinokee Swamp," 205–6.

19. Francis Harper, "Okefinokee Swamp as a Reservation," 28–41.

20. Barrow, *Passion for Birds.*

21. J. F. Wilson to James G. Needham, February 21, 1919, quoted in Trowell, *Seeking a Sanctuary,* frontispiece.

22. Pearson had grown up in Florida and as a young boy had collected bird eggs and contributed essays to the boys' magazine *Oologist.* The same year he became an Okefinokee Society board member, he published *Birds of North Carolina,* a text based on twenty years of fieldwork and research. Orr, *Saving American Birds,* 236.

23. Francis Harper, "Okefinokee Swamp as a Reservation," 40.

24. Trowell, *Seeking a Sanctuary,* 3; McQueen and Mizell, *History of Okefenokee Swamp,* 188–89.

25. J. F. Wilson to James G. Needham, August 8, 1919, quoted in Trowell, *Seeking a Sanctuary,* 3.

26. Francis Harper, "Okefinokee Swamp as a Reservation," 40.

27. Ibid.; Trowell, *Seeking a Sanctuary,* 3; Trowell, *Roland M. Harper,* 13.

28. Trowell, *Seeking a Sanctuary,* 6.

29. Ibid., 6–7.

30. Hebard, "Winter Birds," 8–10.

31. Trowell, *Seeking a Sanctuary,* 9.

32. Dieffenbach and Reddington, "Report on the Value of the Okefenokee Swamp" (1932), quoted in U.S. Congress, *Senate Special Committee on Conservation,* 1.

33. Bartram, *Travels,* 179.

34. Trowell, *Roland M. Harper,* vi, 6; Roland Harper, journal, August 6, 1902, quoted in Trowell, *Roland M. Harper,* 37, 41.

35. Francis Harper, "Sojourn in the Primeval Okefinokee," 229–30, 231, 235.

36. Ibid., 232; Hebard, "Winter Birds," 8, 22; McQueen and Mizell, *History of Okefenokee Swamp,* 31; Scoville, "Secret Island," 244.

37. Francis Harper did engage in some specimen hunting himself. In 1922 Harper wrote in his journal from Chesser Island that "the specimen of the king rail" had "jumped from the prairie along the 'water-road'; I let my push-pole fly, grabbed the gun, drew more or less of a bead, and pulled the trigger. Down then came his kingship with a big splash in the water-road ahead." Harper, Chesser Is-

land journal, September 4, 1922, quoted in Presley and Harper, *Okefinokee Album,* 170; Francis Harper, "Mammals of the Okefinokee Swamp," 262.

38. Francis Harper, "Mammals of the Okefenokee Swamp," 347, 262; Francis Harper, Chesser Island journal, June 18, 1922, quoted in Presley and Harper, *Okefinokee Album,* 165.

39. Francis Harper, "Report of Expedition," 404.

40. Francis Harper, journal, April 17, 1968, quoted in Presley and Harper, *Okefinokee Album,* 12.

41. Francis Harper, "Dweller in the Piney Woods," 181.

42. Nicole Hahn Rafter, introduction to Rafter, ed., *White Trash,* 1–2.

43. McQueen and Mizell, *History of Okefenokee Swamp,* 22, 23.

44. Ibid., 23.

45. Andrews, "Cracker English," 85–88; B. P., "Cracker's Retort," 644–45; Cocke, "Cracker Jim," 51–70; Graffenried, "Georgia Cracker," 483–98; Johnson, "Among the Georgia Crackers," 522–31; Remington, "Cracker Cowboys of Florida," 339–43; Urmston, "Our Folk," 283–94.

46. McQueen and Mizell, *History of Okefenokee Swamp,* 24–25.

47. Matschat, *Murder in Okefenokee,* 87, 266, 273.

48. Francis Harper, "Sojourn in the Primeval Okefinokee," 231; Presley and Harper, *Okefinokee Album,* 5–6.

49. Francis Harper, Chesser Island journal, August 21, 1922, quoted in Presley and Harper, *Okefinokee Album,* 167–68.

50. Francis Harper, "Report of Expedition," 406; Wright and Harper, "Biological Reconnaissance," 492. The slaughter of egrets was dramatized in the most famous Okefenokee novel of the twentieth century: Vereen Bell's *Swamp Water.* Silas and Bud Dorson, a pair of Swamper brothers and hog stealers (perhaps modeled on the Steedley brothers), hunt egrets almost to extinction in the Okefenokee. Their illegal poaching activities foreshadow their demise in the novel. Vereen Bell, *Swamp Water.*

51. Jacoby, *Crimes against Nature,* 16, 19.

52. Francis Harper, "Tales of the Okefinokee," 407–8.

53. Francis Harper, "Mammals of the Okefinokee Swamp," 210.

54. Francis Harper, "Sojourn in the Primeval Okefinokee," 234.

55. Presley and Harper, *Okefinokee Album,* 27; Francis Harper, "Notes on Two Georgia Species," 159; Francis Harper, "Okefinokee Swamp as a Reservation," 618; Francis Harper, "Voice from the Pines," 280.

56. Trowell, *Seeking a Sanctuary,* 9; Francis Harper, Chesser Island journal, April 10 and 12, 1932, quoted in Presley and Harper, *Okefinokee Album,* 174–75.

57. Trowell, *Seeking a Sanctuary,* 11; "Okefenokee Scenic Highway, 1934–1935," CCPL.

58. Jean Harper to Franklin Delano Roosevelt, November 25, 1933, quoted in Presley and Harper, *Okefinokee Album,* 7–8.

59. Franklin Delano Roosevelt to Jean Harper, December 19, 1933, quoted in Presley and Harper, *Okefinokee Album,* 8.

60. Wong, "FDR and the New Deal," 173–91.

61. *Folkston (Ga.) Progress,* June 14, 1935, CCPL, microfilm.

62. Trowell, *Seeking a Sanctuary,* 13; John R. Eadie, "History of the Okefenokee Wildlife Refuge," in Cohen et al., eds., *Okefenokee Swamp,* n.p.

63. Executive Order No. 7593, as quoted in Eadie, "History of the Okefenokee," n.p.

64. Hebard, "Winter Birds," 26.

65. Harold Martin, "Just a Sketch of the Okefenokee"; Baker, "Okefenokee Swamp," 119.

66. Francis Harper, Chesser Island journal, March 28, 1938, and January 17, 1851, quoted in Presley and Harper, *Okefinokee Album,* 176.

67. *Charlton County Herald,* March 19, 1937, CCPL, microfilm.

68. *Folkston (Ga.) Progress,* April 16, 1937, and *Charlton County (Ga.) Herald,* April 16, 1937, CCPL, microfilm.

69. *Charlton County (Ga.) Herald,* October 22, 1937, CCPL, microfilm.

70. Hopkins, "Forty-five Years," 55; Baker, "Okefenokee Swamp," 119.

71. Jacoby, *Crimes against Nature;* Warren, *Hunter's Game.*

72. Hopkins, "Forty-five Years," 54.

73. Wade Chesser to Robin Harper, August 30, 1941, quoted in Presley and Harper, *Okefinokee Album,* 8–9.

74. Jacoby, *Crimes against Nature;* Warren, *Hunter's Game;* Bouchier and Cruikshank, "'Sportsmen and Pothunters.'"

75. Hopkins, "Forty-five Years," 54, 58.

76. Ibid., 67, 68.

77. Jacoby, *Crimes against Nature,* 146; Manning, "Okefenokee."

78. "First Citizen [of Okefenokee] Ralph Davis Prepares Swamp History"; Dickson, "Alligator Poacher Remembers."

79. Kelly, preface to *Pogo Papers,* n.p.

*Epilogue. Tourist Attraction: The Most Photogenic Spot in America!*

1. Sesonske, "Jean Renoir in Georgia," 29–30.

2. Ibid., 57–60; *New York Times,* November 17, 1941, p. 15; *Waycross (Ga.) Journal-Herald,* October 15, 1941, p. 8, ORL, microfilm.

3. "Okefenokee Swamp Park: Land of Trembling Earth," Hargrett.

4. Barthes, *Camera Lucida,* 80–81, 82.

5. Hopkins, "Forty-five Years," 69; Barthes, *Camera Lucida,* 40.

# BIBLIOGRAPHY

*Manuscript Sources*

Charlton County Public Library, Folkston, Georgia. J. E. Brantley, "A Second Trip into the Okefenokee Swamp, Georgia," 1915. *Charlton County Census,* 1860. Warren Lott et al., *The Okefenokee Swamp,* August 12, 1889. Harold Martin, "Just a Sketch of the Okefenokee," March 15, 1954. "Okefenokee Scenic Highway, 1934–1935," 1935. E. A. Smith, "Sawmill Railroading," 1959. *Ware County Census,* 1830–60.

Georgia Historical Society, Savannah, Georgia. Cornelius Rea Agnew Papers (collection no. 926). Victor Hugo Bassett Papers, 1907–38 (collection no. 55). John Avery Gere Carson Collection, 1881–98 (collection no. 123). Chatham County Commissioners Records, 1889–98 (collection no. 135). Chatham Hunt Club Papers, Minute Book, 1906–9 (collection no. 142). Langdon Cheves Papers (collection no. 144). City and Suburban Railway Company Papers (collection no. 147). Colonial Dames of America (collection no. 965). Marmaduke Hamilton and Dolores Boisfeuillet Floyd Papers (collection no. 1308). Solomon Gleason Diary, 1870–76 (collection no. 1577). Gordon Family Papers (collection no. 318). Keith-Read Collection (collection no. 648). Letter to the Chatham County Superior Court, March 1895 (collection no. 138). John McLaughlin Papers (collection no. 990). Louis Leclerc Milfort, "Memoir or Short Sketch of my Different Voyages and My Stay in the Creek Nation, 1775–1795" (collection no. 989). Edwin Parsons Collection, 1759–1862 (collection no. 608). James Louis Rossignol Papers, 1839 (collection no. 669). Savannah Benevolent Association Minute Book, 1854–1928 (accession no. 99–193). Savannah Historical Research Association Papers (collection no. 994). Willie Swoll Sawyer Papers, 1858–1931 (collection no. 713). Varner Family Papers (collection no. 1256). Antonio J. Waring Papers (collection no. 1287). Joseph Frederick Waring Papers (collection no. 1275). Alfred A. Woodhull Papers (collection no. 879). Naomi Stanton Wylly Papers, 1757–1937 (collection no. 887). Yellow Fever Collection (collection no. 1529).

Hargrett Rare Book and Manuscript Library, University of Georgia, Athens, Georgia. Samuel Edward Butler Diary (February 10, 1748–December 15, 1809), 1784 (transcript). John Clark Family Papers (St. Andrews Bay Company Papers). E. M. Coulter Collection. Creek Indian Collection. James Diamond Family Papers, 1831–91. Barnard Elliott Habersham Family Papers. A. T. Havens Journal, 1842–43. Ebenezer Kellogg Diary, 1817–18. George J. Kollock Family Papers. Julius Caesar LeHardy Papers, 1874–89. Lachlan McIntosh Family Papers, Keith Read Collection. "Okefenokee

Swamp Park: Land of Trembling Earth" (MS2869 no. 119). Ellen Buchanan
Screven Reminiscences (1841–1915). Seminole War Collection, 1836–37.
C. Mildred Thompson Papers.
Okefenokee Regional Library, Waycross, Georgia. Dot Rees Gibson, "Billy's
Island," 1974. Larry Purdom, "Logging Lowdown."
Private Collections. Charles Rinaldo Floyd Diary, 1816–45 (original and
typescript in the possession of Brice McAdoo Clagett, Friendship, Maryland).

## Newspapers and Newspaper Collections on Microfilm

*Atlanta Constitution* (1870–1940).
*Charlton County Herald* (1936–38).
*Early American Newspapers,* 1801–19. Boston: American Antiquarian Society, n.d.
*East Florida Papers.* Washington, D.C.: Library of Congress, 1964–65.
*The Eighteenth Century.* Woodbridge, Conn.: Research Publications, 1982.
*Folkston Progress* (1936–37).
*Georgia Gazette* (1763–70).
*Milledgeville Federal Union* (1834–36).
*Milledgeville Reflector* (1817–18).
*New York Times* (1941).
*Records of Southern Ante-Bellum Plantations: From the Revolution through the Civil
War.* Edited by Kenneth M. Stampp and Randolph Boehm. Frederick, Md.:
University Publications of America, 1985.
*Savannah Daily Morning News* (1850–54).
*Savannah Daily Republican* (1838, 1839, and 1845).
*Savannah Morning News* (1893–1941).
*Waycross Journal-Herald* (1890–1940).
*Waycross Reporter* (1890–95).
*Western Americana.* New Haven, Conn.: Research Publications, 1975.

## Printed Primary Sources

*Abbreviations following an entry denote special collections where the rarer printed
primary sources may be found.*

Anderson, Edward C. *Report of Edward C. Anderson, Mayor of the City of Savannah,
December 1854.* 1854. (GHS)
Arnold, Richard D. *An Essay upon the Relation of Bilious and Yellow Fever.* Augusta,
Ga.: McCafferty's Office, J. Morris, Printer, 1856. (GHS)
Barker, Thomas Herbert. *On Malaria and Miasmata and Their Influence in the
Production of Typhus and Typhoid Fevers, Cholera, and the Exanthemata.* London:
John W. Davies, 1863. (Countway)

Bartram, William. *Travels.* 1790. Reprinted and edited by Francis Harper. Athens: University of Georgia Press, 1998.

Bell, Vereen. *Swamp Water.* Boston: Little, Brown, 1941.

Black, G. V. *The Formation of Poisons by Micro-Organisms; A Biological Study of the Germ Theory of Disease.* Philadelphia: P. Blackiston, Son, 1884. (GHS)

Blandford, R. A. *Reports on the Proposed Drainage of the Watershed of Musgrove Creek.* Savannah: Morning News Print, 1892. (GHS)

Brown, John. *Slave Life in Georgia: A Narrative of the Life, Sufferings, and Escape of John Brown, a Fugitive Slave.* 1855. Reprinted and edited by F. N. Boney. Savannah: Beehive Press, 1991.

Cable, George Washington. *The Grandissimes.* 1880. Reprint, New York: Penguin Group, 1988.

Candler, Allen D., ed. *The Colonial Records of the State of Georgia.* 23 vols. Atlanta: Franklin-Turner Company, 1907.

Carpenter, Wesley M. *Sketches from the History of Yellow Fever; Showing Its Origins, Together with Facts and Circumstances Disproving Its Domestic Origin, and Demonstrating Its Transmissibility.* New Orleans: J. B. Steel, 1844. (Countway)

Chatham County Commissioners of Drainage. *Report to His Excellency, A.H. Colquitt, Governor of Georgia.* 1879. (GHS)

Cohen, M. M. *Notices of Florida and the Campaigns.* Charleston: Burges and Honour, 1836.

*Conclusions of the Board of Experts Authorized by Congress to Investigate the Yellow Fever Epidemic of 1878.* Washington, D.C.: Judd and Detweiler, Printers, 1879. (GHS)

Delany, Martin R. *Blake; or the Huts of America.* 1861–62. Reprint, Boston: Beacon Press, 1970.

Donaldson, J. L. *Sergeant Atkins: A Tale of Adventure; Founded on Fact.* Philadelphia: J. B. Lippincott, 1871.

Doubleday, Abner. *My Life in the Old Army: The Reminiscences of Abner Doubleday from the Collections of the New York Historical Society.* Edited by Joseph E. Chance. Fort Worth: Texas Christian University Press, 1998.

Douglass, Frederick. *The Heroic Slave.* 1853. Reprinted in *Steal Away: Stories of the Runaway Slaves.* Edited by Franklin Chapman. New York: Praeger Publishers, 1971.

"Drainage Needed Near City Limits." *Savannah Morning News.* September 8, 1897. Reprinted in pamphlet form, 1897. (GHS)

Ellicott, Andrew. *The Journal of Andrew Ellicott.* 1803. Reprint, Chicago: Quadrangle Books, 1962.

Elliott, William. *Carolina Sports by Land and Water.* Columbia, S.C.: State Co., 1918. (GHS)

Falligant, Louis A. *A Monograph on the Yellow Fever of 1876 in Savannah, Georgia.* Savannah: Morning News Print, 1888. (GHS)

Giddings, Joshua R. *The Exiles of Florida; or, the Crimes by Our Government against the Maroons.* Columbus, Ohio: Follett, Foster, 1858.

Glascock, Thomas. *Speech of Mr. Glascock, of Georgia, on the Bill Making a Partial Appropriation for the Suppression of Indian Hostilities for the Year 1838.* Washington, D.C.: Globe Office, 1838.

Grant, Hugh Fraser. *Planter Management and Capitalism in Antebellum Georgia: The Journal of Hugh Fraser Grant, Ricegrower.* Edited by Albert Virgil House. New York: Columbia University Press, 1954.

*Health Statistics: Report of the Board of Health of the State of Georgia for 1876 with Appendix and Mortuary Record of the Epidemic in Savannah in 1876.* Savannah: Morning News Office, J. J. Estill, 1877. (GHS)

Henle, Jacob. *On Miasmata and Contagia.* Translated by George Rosen. 1840. Reprint, Baltimore: Johns Hopkins Press, 1938. (Countway)

Hentz, Charles A. *A Southern Practice: The Diary and Autobiography of Charles A. Hentz, M.D.* Edited by Steven M. Stowe. Charlottesville: University of Virginia Press, 2000.

*History of the Discovery and True Nature of Pathogenic Bacteria, the Germ Theory of Disease, in the Epidemic at Savannah.* Report of the Medical Officer to Her Majesty's Government, 1887. (GHS)

Hunter, Richard L. *Report upon the Survey of Okefenokee Swamp.* Milledgeville, Ga.: Federal Union Print, October 21, 1857. (Hargrett)

Jones, Joseph. *Original Investigations on the Natural History, (Symptoms and Pathology) of Yellow Fever.* 1854–94. Chicago: American Medical Association Press, 1894. (GHS)

Kelly, Walt. *The Pogo Papers.* New York: Simon and Schuster, 1953.

Kemble, Frances Anne. *Journal of a Residence on a Georgian Plantation in 1838–1839.* Edited by John A. Scott. Athens: University of Georgia Press, 1984.

Kennedy, John Pendleton. *Swallow Barn; or, A Sojourn in the Old Dominion.* 1832. Reprint, Baton Rouge: Louisiana State University Press, 1986.

King, Spencer B., Jr., ed. *Georgia Voices: A Documentary History to 1872.* Athens: University of Georgia Press, 1966.

LaRoche, Rene. *Yellow Fever, Considered in Its Historical, Pathological, Etiological, Therapeutical Relations . . .* 2 vols. Philadelphia: Blanchard and Lea, 1855. (Countway)

LeHardy, Julius Caesar. *Quarantine: Its Sanitary and Political Aspect in Relation to the Spread of Epidemic Diseases.* Atlanta: James P. Harrison, 1879. (GHS)

———. *The Rational Method of Preventing Yellow Fever on the South Atlantic Coast.* Augusta: J. M. Richards, 1889. (GHS)

———. *Yellow Fever. The Epidemic of 1876 in Savannah.* Atlanta: James P. Harrison, 1878. (GHS)

———. *Yellow Fever: Its Relations to Climate and to Hygienic Measures in the United States. Virginia Medical Monthly,* June 1894. (GHS)

———. *The Yellow Fever Panic.* Savannah: Townshend, October 3, 1888. (GHS)

———. *Yellow Fever the American Plague–through Drainage and Municipal Cleanliness the Only Means of Insuring Its Extinction.* Read before Congress of Immigration, June 1894. (GHS)

Lewis, Henry Clay. *Odd Leaves from the Life of a Louisiana Swamp Doctor.* 1850. Reprint, Baton Rouge: Louisiana State University Press, 1997.

Longfellow, Henry Wadsworth. *The Complete Poetical Works of Henry Wadsworth Longfellow.* Boston: Houghton Mifflin, 1882.

Matschat, Cecile Hulse. *Ladd of the Big Swamp; A Story of the Okefenokee Settlement.* Philadelphia: John C. Winston, 1954.

———. *Murder in Okefenokee.* New York: Farrar and Rinehart, 1941.

———. *Suwannee River: Strange Green Land.* New York: Literary Guild of America, 1938.

McCall, George A. *Letters from the Frontiers.* Philadelphia: J. B. Lippincott, 1868.

Metcalfe, John T. *Report of a Committee of the Associate Members of the Sanitary Commission, on the Subject of the Nature and Treatment of Miasmatic Fevers.* Washington, D.C.: McGill, Witherow, 1862. (Countway)

Miller, Caroline. *Lamb in His Bosom.* 1933. Reprint, Atlanta: Peachtree Publishers, 1993.

Mitchell, Samuel Latham, and Edward Miller, M.D., eds. *The Medical Repository, and Review of American Publications on Medicine, Surgery, and the Auxiliary Branches of Science.* 4 vols. New York: T and J Swords, 1806–7. (GHS)

Motta, Jacob de la. *An Oration, on the Causes of the Mortality among Strangers during the Late Summer and Fall, 1820.* Savannah: Kappel and Bartlet, 1820. (Countway)

Muir, John. *A Thousand-Mile Walk to the Gulf.* 1916. Reprint, Boston: Houghton Mifflin, 1998.

Munn, Vella. *Seminole Song.* New York: Tom Doherty Associates, 1997.

Munroe, Kirk. *Through Swamp and Glade: Tale of the Seminole War.* New York: Charles Scribner's Sons, 1896.

*Names of the Dead, Being a Record of the Mortality in Savannah during the Epidemic of 1854, with a List of the Donations in Aid of the Sick, Also a Brief Account of the September Gale, with Other Matter Compiled from the Daily Morning News.* Savannah: Daily Morning News Press, 1854. (GHS)

*An Official Register of the Deaths Which Occurred among the White Population in the City of Savannah during the Extraordinary Season of Sickness and Mortality Which Prevailed in the Summer and Fall Months of the Year 1820.* Savannah: Henry P. Russell, 1820. (GHS)

Olmsted, Frederick Law. *The Cotton Kingdom.* 1861. Reprint, New York: Modern Library, 1984.

———. *A Journey in the Seaboard Slave States.* New York: Dix and Edwards, 1856.

*The Origin, Cause, and Distinctive Features of Yellow Fever.* 1879. (GHS)

Paine, Lewis W. *Six Years in a Georgia Prison; Narrative of Lewis W. Paine, Who Suffered Imprisonment Six Years in Georgia, for the Crime of Aiding the Escape of a Fellow-Man from That State, after He Had Fled from Slavery.* New York: Printed for the author, 1851. (GHS)

Pearson, Edward A., ed. *Designs against Charleston: The Trial Record of the Denmark Vesey Slave Conspiracy of 1822.* Chapel Hill: University of North Carolina Press, 1999.

Pendleton, Louis. *Bewitched and Other Stories.* New York: Cassell, 1888. (ORL)

———. *In the Okefenokee: A Story of War Time and the Great Georgia Swamp.* Boston: Roberts Brothers, 1895. (ORL)

———. *King Tom and the Runaways; The Story of What Befell Two Boys in a Georgia Swamp.* New York: D. Appleton, 1891.

Pope, Edith. *River in the Wind.* New York: Charles Scribner's Sons, 1954.

Prince, Henry. *Amidst a Storm of Bullets: The Diary of Lt. Henry Prince in Florida, 1836–1842.* Edited by Frank Laumer. Tampa: University of Tampa Press, 1998.

Purse, Benjamin S. *Yellow Fever: Its Treatment and Pathology.* Savannah: Morning News Print, 1898. (GHS)

Rawlings, Marjorie Kinnan. *The Yearling.* 1938. Reprint, New York: Simon and Schuster, 2002.

*Report of John E. Ward, Mayor of the City of Savannah, for the Year Ending 31st October, 1854.* Savannah: Purse's Print, 1854. (GHS)

*Revised Rules of the Board of Health of the City of Savannah, for 1866, Together with the Report of the Poudrette Committee.* Savannah: Charles E. O'Sullivan, Printer, 1866. (GHS)

Simmons, William Hayne. *Notices of East Florida, with an Account of the Seminole Nation of Indians, by a Recent Traveller of the Province.* 1822. Reprint, Gainesville: University Press of Florida, 1973.

Simms, William Gilmore. *Helen Halsey; or, The Swamp State of Conelachita.* 1845. Reprint, Fayetteville: University of Arkansas Press, 1998.

———. *The Scout; or, The Black Riders of Congaree.* 1841. Reprint, Chicago: Donohue, Henneberry, 1890.

Smith, John. *The Generall Historie of Virginia.* 1624. Reprint, Murfreesboro, N.C.: Johnson Publishing, 1970.

Sprague, John T. *The Origin, Progress, and Conclusion of the Florida War.* 1848. Reprint, Gainesville: University Press of Florida, 1964.

Starke, W. W. *W.W. Starke's "Amusing Sketch" Resketched by an Irish Ditcher.* Boston: Tobias Partington, 1851. (GHS)

Stork, William. *Account of East-Florida.* London: Printed for G. Woodfall, 1766.

Stowe, Harriet Beecher. *Dred; A Tale of the Great Dismal Swamp.* 1856. Reprint, London: Edinburgh University Press, 1999.

———. *Palmetto-Leaves.* 1873. Reprint, Gainesville: University Press of Florida, 1999.

Tailfer, Patrick, Hugh Anderson, and David Douglas. *A True and Historical Narrative of the Colony of Georgia in America.* 1741. Reprint, Athens: University of Georgia Press, 1960.

Thomas, J. G. *Address by J.G. Thomas, M.D., Savannah, Georgia, in Defense of the National Board of Health against Attacks in Congress, and on the Importance of Sapelo Quarantine Station as a Place of Refuge for Dangerous and Infected Vessels for the South-Atlantic States.* Savannah: Morning News Steam Printing House, 1883. (GHS)

Thomas, J. G., J. F. Gilmer, John F. Wheaton, C. C. Casey, and John Screven. *Report of the Commissioners of Drainage, Chatham, County, to His Excellency, A.H. Colquitt, Governor of Georgia.* Savannah: George N. Nichols, 1879. (GHS)

Thrift, Luther. *The Coxes of Okefenokee.* J. L. Thrift, 1984. (Hargrett)

Turner, Nat. *The Confessions of Nat Turner.* 1832. Reprint, Boston: Bedford Books of St. Martin's Press, 1996.

Tyndall, John. *Essays on the Floating-Matter of the Air in Relation to Putrefaction and Infection.* London: Longmans, Green, 1881. (GHS)

U.S. Congress. *Senate Special Committee on Conservation of Wildlife Resources: Okefenokee Swamp.* 1932. (Hargrett)

*U.S. Statutes.* Washington, D.C.: U.S. Government Printing Office, 1980.

Wall, John P. *Yellow Fever and the Fallacy of the Germ Theory in Connection with Its Spread and Epidemicity.* Atlanta Medical and Surgical Journal, n.d. (GHS)

Waring, James J. *Supplement to the Mayor's Report, January 1, 1879. The Epidemic at Savannah, 1876. Its Causes—the Measures of Prevention.* Savannah: Morning News Steam Printing House, 1879. (GHS)

Waring, William R. *Report to the City Council of Savannah, on the Epidemic Disease of 1820.* Savannah: Henry P. Russell, 1821. (GHS)

——. *A Summary of the Climate and Epidemics of Savannah during the Series of Years from 1826 to 1829, Part I (April, 1830) and Part II (July 1830).* 1831. (GHS)

White, Octavius A. *Report upon Yellow Fever as It Appeared in Savannah, Georgia, in 1876.* New York: D. Appleton, 1877. (GHS)

Whitman, Albery A. *The Rape of Florida.* St. Louis: Nixon-Jones Printing, 1884.

Woodhull, Alfred A. *Of the Causes of the Epidemic of Yellow Fever at Savannah, Georgia, in 1876 in* The American Journal of the Medical Sciences. 1877. (GHS)

Woodworth, John M. *Annual Report of the Supervising Surgeon-General of the Marine-Hospital Service of the United States, for the Fiscal Year 1875.* Washington, D.C.: Government Printing Office, 1876. (GHS)

*Yellow Fever Record, Year 1876.* Savannah: Ely Otto, 1876. (GHS)

## Secondary Sources

Adelman, Jeremy, and Stephen Aron. "From Borderlands to Borders: Empires, Nation-States, and the Peoples in Between in North American History." *American Historical Review* 104, no. 3 (1999): 814–41.

Andrews, E. F. "Cracker English." *The Chautauquan: A Monthly Magazine* 23–24 (April 1896–September 1896): 85–88.

Anzaldua, Gloria. *Borderlands/La Frontera: The New Mestiza.* 2nd ed. San Francisco: Aunt Lute Books, 1999.

Aptheker, Herbert. *American Negro Slave Revolts: Nat Turner, Denmark Vesey, Gabriel, and Others.* New York: International Publishers, 1943, 1974.

———. "Maroons within the Present Limits of the United States." *Journal of Negro History* 24, no. 2 (April 1939): 167–84.

Arthur, Timothy Shay, and W. H. Carpenter. *The History of Georgia from Its Earliest Settlement to the Present Time.* Philadelphia: Lippincott, Grambo, 1853.

Ayers, Edward L. *The Promise of the New South: Life after Reconstruction.* New York: Oxford University Press, 1992.

Ayers, Edward L., Patricia Nelson Limerick, Stephen Nissenbaum, and Peter S. Onuf. *All over the Map: Rethinking American Regions.* Baltimore: Johns Hopkins University Press, 1996.

Babb, Valerie. *Whiteness Visible: The Meaning of Whiteness in American Literature and Culture.* New York: New York University Press, 1998.

Baird, Nancy D. "The Yellow Fever Plot." *Civil War Times Illustrated* 13, no. 7 (1974): 16–23.

Baker, Woolford B. "The Okefenokee Swamp–Land of Trembling Earth." *The Emory University Quarterly* 5, no. 2 (June 1949): 110–19.

Barnes, Jay. *Florida's Hurricane History.* Chapel Hill: University of North Carolina Press, 1998.

Barron, Hal S. "Rediscovering the Majority: The New Rural History of the Nineteenth-Century North." *Historical Methods* 19, no. 4 (1986): 141–52.

Barrow, Mark V., Jr. *A Passion for Birds: American Ornithology after Audubon.* Princeton, N.J.: Princeton University Press, 1998.

Barthes, Roland. *Camera Lucida: Reflections on Photography.* Translated by Richard Howard. New York: Hill and Wang, 1981.

Bass, Robert D. *Swamp Fox: The Life and Campaigns of General Francis Marion.* New York: Henry Holt, 1959.

Becker, Jane S. *Selling Tradition: Appalachia and the Construction of an American Folk, 1930–1940.* Chapel Hill: University of North Carolina Press, 1998.

Beckett, Ian Frederick William. *Encyclopedia of Guerrilla Warfare.* Santa Barbara: ABC-CLIO, 1999.

Bederman, Gail. *Manliness and Civilization: A Cultural History of Gender and Race in the United States, 1880–1917.* Chicago: University of Chicago Press, 1995.

Bell, Whitfield J. *The College of Physicians of Philadelphia: A Bicentennial History.* Canton, Mass.: Science History Publications, 1987.

Berlin, Ira. *Many Thousands Gone: The First Two Centuries of Slavery in North America.* Cambridge, Mass.: Harvard University Press, 1998.

Berlin, Ira, and Ronald Hoffman, eds. *Slavery and Freedom in the Age of the American Revolution.* Urbana: University of Illinois Press, 1983.

Bittle, George C. "Florida Frontier Incidents during the 1850s." *Florida Historical Quarterly* 49, no. 2 (1970): 153–60.

Blassingame, John. *The Slave Community: Plantation Life in the Antebellum South.* Oxford: Oxford University Press, 1972, 1979.

Bouchier, Nancy B., and Ken Cruikshank. "'Sportsmen and Pothunters':

Environment, Conservation, and Class in the Fishery of Hamilton Harbour, 1858–1914." *Sport History Review* 28 (1997): 1–18.

B. P. "The Cracker's Retort." *Harper's New Monthly Magazine* 67, no. 400 (September 1883): 644–45.

Brown, Canter, Jr. "The 'Sarrazota,' or Runaway Negro Plantations: Tampa Bay's First Black Community, 1812–1821." *Tampa Bay History* 12 (1990): 5–19.

Brown, Leon. "The Logging of the Okefenokee." *TOPS* (September 1983): 12–14.

Buker, George E. "Francis's Metallic Lifeboats and the Third Seminole War." *Florida Historical Quarterly* 63, no. 2 (1984): 139–51.

———. *Swamp Sailors: Riverine Warfare in the Everglades, 1835–1842.* Gainesville: University Press of Florida, 1975.

Cadle, Farris W. *Georgia Land Surveying History and Law.* Athens: University of Georgia Press, 1991.

Carnes, Mark C. *Secret Ritual and Manhood in Victorian America.* New Haven, Conn.: Yale University Press, 1989.

Carney, Judith A. *Black Rice: The African Origins of Rice Cultivation in the Americas.* Cambridge, Mass.: Harvard University Press, 2001.

Chaplin, Joyce. *An Anxious Pursuit: Agricultural Innovation and Modernity in the Lower South, 1730–1815.* Chapel Hill: University of North Carolina Press, 1993.

*Charlton County, Georgia: Historical Notes, 1972.* Folkston, Ga.: Charlton County Historical Commission, 1972.

*Charlton County Gets a Chance to Tell Her Story.* Folkston, Ga.: Charlton County Herald, 1933.

Chew, Sing C. *Logs for Capital: The Timber Industry and Capitalist Enterprise in the Nineteenth Century.* Westport, Conn.: Greenwood Press, 1992.

Clark, Thomas D. *The Greening of the South: The Recovery of Land and Forest.* Lexington: University Press of Kentucky, 1984.

Clary, George E., Jr. "Research Paper Tells of Hebard Lumber Company." *Waycross Journal-Herald,* April 9, 1981.

Cocke, Zitella. "Cracker Jim." *The Overland Monthly* 10, series 2 (July–December 1887): 51–70.

Cogswell, Robert. "Cultural Intervention in Southern Appalachia: Agents and Agendas." *Journal of Southern Folklore* 49, no. 3 (1992): 196–220.

Cohen, A. D., D. J. Casagrande, M. J. Andrejko, and G. R. Best, eds. *The Okefenokee Swamp: Its Natural History, Geology, and Geochemistry.* Los Alamos: Wetland Surveys, 1984.

Colburn, David R., and Jane L. Landers, eds. *The African American Heritage of Florida.* Gainesville: University Press of Florida, 1995.

Coleman, Kenneth. *Colonial Georgia: A History.* New York: Charles Scribner's Sons, 1976.

———. *Georgia History in Outline.* 2nd ed. Athens: University of Georgia Press, 1978.

——, ed. *A History of Georgia*. 2nd ed. Athens: University of Georgia Press, 1991.

Coleman, Kenneth, and Charles Stephen Gurr, eds. *Dictionary of Georgia Biography*. 2 vols. Athens: University of Georgia Press, 1983.

Cothran, Kay L. "Talking Trash in the Okefenokee Swamp Rim, Georgia." *Journal of American Folklore* 87 (1974): 340–56.

Covington, James W. "Billy Bowlegs, Sam Jones, and the Crisis of 1849." *Florida Historical Quarterly* 63, no. 3 (1990): 299–311.

——. "An Episode in the Third Seminole War." *Florida Historical Quarterly* 45, no. 1 (1966): 45–59.

——. *The Seminoles of Florida*. Gainesville: University Press of Florida, 1993.

"Cracker Dialect in South Carolina." *Atlantic Monthly* 53 (March 1884): 435–37.

Crass, David Colin, Steven D. Smith, Martha A. Zierden, and Richard D. Brooks, eds. *The Southern Colonial Backcountry: Interdisciplinary Perspectives on Frontier Communities*. Knoxville: University of Tennessee Press, 1998.

Cronon, William. *Nature's Metropolis: Chicago and the Great West*. New York: W. W. Norton, 1991.

Cronon, William, Jay Gitlin, and George Miles, eds. *Under an Open Sky: Rethinking America's Western Past*. New York: W. W. Norton, 1992.

Cumming, William, ed. *The Southeast in Early Maps*. 3rd ed. Chapel Hill: University of North Carolina Press, 1998.

D'Elia, Donald J. "Dr. Benjamin Rush and the Negro." *Journal of the History of Ideas* 30, no. 3 (1969): 413–22.

Denham, James. "The Florida Cracker before the Civil War as Seen through Travelers' Accounts." *Florida Historical Quarterly* 72, no. 4 (April 1994): 453–68.

Dickson, Terry. "Alligator Poacher Remembers." *Florida Times-Union*, July 11, 1983.

——. "A Little House Deep in 'Ok-fenoke.'" *Florida Times-Union*, June 20, 1983.

——. "Okefenokee Yields a Living Grudgingly." *Florida Times-Union*, June 1983.

Dodson, Jim. "The Old Man and the Swamp." *The Atlanta Journal and Constitution Magazine*, November 18, 1979, p. 15.

"The Drainage of the Everglades." *Harper's New Monthly Magazine* 68 (December 1883–May 1884): 598–605.

Drobney, Jeffrey A. *Lumbermen and Log Sawyers: Life, Labor, and Culture in the North Florida Timber Industry, 1830–1930*. Macon, Ga.: Mercer University Press, 1997.

Dunlap, Thomas R. "Sport Hunting and Conservation, 1880–1920." *Environmental Review* 12, no. 1 (1988): 51–60.

Dusinberre, William. *Them Dark Days: Slavery in the American Rice Swamps*. New York: Oxford University Press, 1996.

Elliott, William. *Carolina Sports by Land and Water including Incidents of Devil-Fishing, Wild-Cat, Deer and Bear Hunting, Etc.* Columbia, S.C.: The State Co., 1918.

Ellis, Richard J. "Legitimating Slavery in the Old South: The Effect of Political

Institutions on Ideology." *Studies in American Political Development* 5, no. 2 (1991): 340–51.

Farber, Paul Lawrence. *The Emergence of Ornithology as a Scientific Discipline.* Dordrecht, Holland: D. Reidel Publishing, 1982.

Faris, John T. *Seeing the Sunny South.* Philadelphia: J. B. Lippincott, 1921.

Farley, M. Foster. "John Elliott Ward, Mayor of Savannah, 1853–1854." *Georgia Historical Quarterly* 53, no. 1 (1969): 68–77.

———. "The Mighty Monarch of the South: Yellow Fever in Charleston and Savannah." *Georgia Review* 27, no. 1 (1973): 56–70.

Farmer, Laurence. "'Moschetoes Were Uncommonly Numerous.'" *American Heritage* 7, no. 3 (1956): 55–57, 99.

Farnham, Thomas J., and Francis P. King. "'The March of the Destroyer': The New Bern Yellow Fever Epidemic of 1864." *North Carolina Historical Review* 73, no. 4 (1996): 435–83.

Feduccia, Alan, ed. *Catesby's Birds of Colonial America.* Chapel Hill: University of North Carolina Press, 1985.

Finlay, Mark. "Panic in Savannah: The Yellow Fever Era." *Coastal Current Insight,* n.d.

"First Citizen of Okefenokee Ralph Davis Prepares Swamp History." *Charlton County Herald,* August 29, 1979.

"Folk-Lore." *Southern Review* 13 (July 1873): 153–78.

Francis, David W. "Antebellum Agricultural Reform in DeBow's Review." *Louisiana History* 14, no. 2 (1973): 165–67.

Franklin, John Hope, and Loren Schweninger, eds. *Runaway Slaves: Rebels on the Plantation.* New York: Oxford University Press, 1999.

Fraser, Walter J., Jr., and Winfred B. Moore Jr., eds. *The Southern Enigma: Essays on Race, Class, and Folk Culture.* Westport, Conn.: Greenwood Press, 1983.

Frazer, John E. "America's 'Turbulent Spirit': Dr. Benjamin Rush." *American History Illustrated* 9, no. 7 (1974): 20–31.

Fredrickson, George M. *The Black Image in the White Mind: The Debate on Afro-American Character and Destiny, 1817–1914.* Middletown, Conn.: Wesleyan University Press, 1987.

Galishoff, Stuart. "Drainage, Disease, Comfort, and Class: A History of Newark's Sewers." *Societas* 6, no. 2 (1976): 121–38.

Gannon, Michael, ed. *The New History of Florida.* Gainesville: University Press of Florida, 1996.

Genovese, Eugene D. *From Rebellion to Revolution: African American Slave Revolts in the Making of the Modern World.* Baton Rouge: Louisiana State University Press, 1979.

———. *Roll, Jordan, Roll: The World the Slaves Made.* New York: Random House, 1972.

Ghachem, Malick. "Sovereignty and Slavery in the Age of Revolution: Haitian Variations on a Metropolitan Theme." PhD diss., Stanford University, 2001.

Ghosh, Amitav. "Mythic Swamps." Public lecture, Harvard University, March 6, 2003.

Gifford, George Edmund. "The Charleston Physician-Naturalists." *Bulletin of the History of Medicine* 49, no. 4 (1975): 556–74.

———. "Edward Frederick Leitner (1812–1838), Physician-Botanist." *Bulletin of the History of Medicine* 46, no. 6 (1972): 568–90.

Gonzalez, George A. "The Conservation Policy Network, 1890–1910: The Development and Implementation of 'Practical' Forestry." *Polity* 31, no. 2 (Winter 1998): 269–99.

Goodyear, James D. "The Sugar Connection: A New Perspective on the History of Yellow Fever." *Bulletin of the History of Medicine* 52, no. 1 (1978): 5–21.

Gorn, Elliott. "'Gouge and Bite, Pull Hair and Scratch': The Social Significance of Fighting in the Southern Backcountry." *American Historical Review* 90, no. 1 (February 1985): 18–43.

Graffenried, Clare de. "The Georgia Cracker in the Cotton Mills." *The Century Magazine* 41, no. 4 (February 1891): 483–98.

Gray, Lewis Cecil. *History of Agriculture in the Southern United States to 1860*. Washington, D.C.: Carnegie Institution of Washington, 1933.

Greeley, William B. *Forests and Men*. Garden City, N.J.: Doubleday, 1951.

Greenberg, Kenneth. *Honor and Slavery: Lies, Duels, Noses, Masks, Dressing as a Woman, Gifts, Strangers, Humanitarianism, the Proslavery Argument, Baseball, Hunting, and Gambling in the Old South*. Princeton, N.J.: Princeton University Press, 1996.

Greenblatt, Stephen. *Marvelous Possessions: The Wonder of the New World*. Chicago: University of Chicago Press, 1991.

Hahn, Steven. *The Roots of Southern Populism: Yeoman Farmers and the Transformation of the Georgia Upcountry, 1850–1890*. New York: Oxford University Press, 1983.

Hahn, Steven, and Jonathan Prude, eds. *The Countryside in the Age of Capitalist Transformation*. Chapel Hill: University of North Carolina Press, 1985.

Hale, Grace Elizabeth. *Making Whiteness: The Culture of Segregation in the South, 1890–1940*. New York: Pantheon Books, 1998.

Haller, John S. "The Negro and the Southern Physician: A Study of Medical and Racial Attitudes, 1800–1860." *Medical History* 16, no. 3 (1972): 238–53.

Harper, Francis. "Alligators of the Okefinokee." *The Scientific Monthly* 31, no. 1 (1930): 51–67.

———. "The Chuck-Will's Widow in the Okefinokee Region." *The Oriole* 3, no. 2 (June 1938): 9–14.

———. "Distribution, Taxonomy, Nomenclature, and Habits of the Little Tree-Frog." *The American Midland Naturalist* 22, no. 1 (1938): 134–49.

———. "A Dweller in the Piney Woods." *The Scientific Monthly* 32, no. 2 (1931): 176–81.

——. "The Mammals of the Okefinokee Swamp Region of Georgia." *Proceedings of the Boston Society of Natural History* 38, no. 7 (March 1927): 191–396.

——. "Notes on Two Georgia Species of Pseudacris." *Copeia* 4 (December 28, 1931): 159–61.

——. "Okefinokee Swamp as a Reservation." *Natural History* 20, no. 1 (1920): 28–41.

——. "The Okefinokee Wilderness: Exploring the Mystery Land of the Suwannee River Reveals Natural Wonders and Fascinating Folklore." *National Geographic Magazine* 65, no. 5 (1934): 597–624.

——. "Records of Amphibians in the Southeastern States." *The American Midland Naturalist* 16, no. 3 (1935): 275–310.

——. "Report of Expedition into Okefenoke Swamp, Georgia." *Bird-Lore* 14, no. 6 (1912): 402–7.

——. "A Season with Holbrook's Chorus Frog." *The American Midland Naturalist* 18, no. 2 (1937): 260–72.

——. "A Sojourn in the Primeval Okefinokee." *The Brooklyn Museum Quarterly* 2, no. 1 (April 1915): 226–44.

——. "A Southern Subspecies of the Spring Peeper." *Notulae Naturae of the Academy of Natural Sciences of Philadelphia* 27 (September 14, 1939): 1–4.

——. "Tales of the Okefinokee." *American Speech* 1, no. 8 (May 1926): 407–20.

——. "A Voice from the Pines." *Natural History* 32, no. 3 (May–June 1932): 280–88.

Harper, Roland. "The Okefinokee Swamp." *Popular Science Monthly* 74, no. 6 (June 1909): 596–614.

Hebard, Frederick V. "Winter Birds of the Okefinokee and Coleraine: A Preliminary Check-List of the Winter Birds of the Interior of Southeastern Georgia." *Georgia Society of Naturalists Bulletin No. 3.* Atlanta: Georgia Society of Naturalists, December 1941.

Hedges, William L. "Benjamin Rush, Charles Brockden Brown, and the American Plague Year." *Early American Literature* 7, no. 3 (1973): 295–311.

Heidler, David S., and Jeanne T. Heidler. *Old Hickory's War: Andrew Jackson and the Quest for Empire.* Mechanicsburg, Pa.: Stackpole Books, 1996.

Herndon, G. Melvin. "Forest Products of Colonial Georgia." *Journal of Forest History* 23, no. 3 (1979): 130–35.

Heuman, Gad, ed. *Out of the House of Bondage: Runaways, Resistance, and Marronage in Africa and the New World.* London: Frank Cass, 1986.

Hill, Mike, ed. *Whiteness: A Critical Reader.* New York: New York University Press, 1997.

Holmes, Chris. "Benjamin Rush and the Yellow Fever." *Bulletin of the History of Medicine* 40, no. 3 (1966): 246–63.

Hopkins, John M. "Forty-five Years with the Okefenokee Swamp, 1900–1945." *Georgia Society of Naturalists Bulletin No. 4.* Atlanta: Georgia Society of Naturalists, December 1945.

Howarth, William. "Imagined Territory: The Writing of Wetlands." *New Literary History* 30 (1999): 509–39.

Humphreys, Margaret. *Yellow Fever and the South.* Baltimore: Johns Hopkins University Press, 1992.

Hurd, Barbara. *Stirring the Mud: On Swamps, Bogs, and the Human Imagination.* Boston: Beacon Press, 2001.

Hurst, Robert Latimer. *This Magic Wilderness: Historical Features from the Wiregrass.* N.p., 1974.

Hyde, Samuel C., Jr., ed. *Plain Folk of the South Revisited.* Baton Rouge: Louisiana State University Press, 1997.

Izlar, Robert L. "The Hebard Lumber Company in the Okefenokee Swamp: Thirty-six Years of Southern Logging History." Master's thesis, University of Georgia, 1971.

Jabour, Anya. "Male Friendship and Masculinity in the Early National South: William Wirt and His Friends." *Journal of the Early Republic* 20, no. 1 (Spring 2000): 83–111.

Jacoby, Karl. *Crimes against Nature: Squatters, Poachers, Thieves, and the Hidden History of American Conservation.* Berkeley: University of California Press, 2001.

Johnson, Clifton. "Among the Georgia Crackers." *Outing: The Gentleman's Magazine of Sport, Travel, and Outdoor Life* 43 (1903–4): 522–31.

Jones, Anne Goodwyn, and Susan Donaldson, eds. *Haunted Bodies: Gender and Southern Texts.* Charlottesville: University of Virginia Press, 1997.

Joyner, Charles. *Down by the Riverside: A South Carolina Slave Community.* Urbana: University of Illinois Press, 1984.

Kantrowitz, Stephen. "Ben Tillman and Hendrix McLane, Agrarian Rebels: White Manhood, 'The Farmers,' and the Limits of Southern Populism." *Journal of Southern History* 66, no. 3 (August 2000): 497–524.

Killian, Lewis M. *White Southerners.* New York: Random House, 1970.

Killion, Ronald G., and Charles T. Waller. *Georgia and the Revolution.* Atlanta: Cherokee Publishing Company, 1975.

Kimmel, Michael. *Manhood in America: A Cultural History.* New York: Free Pres, 1996.

King, Lester S. *Transformations in American Medicine: From Benjamin Rush to William Oster.* Baltimore: Johns Hopkins University Press, 1991.

Kiple, Kenneth F., and Virginia H. Kiple. "Black Yellow Fever Immunities, Innate and Acquired, as Revealed in the American South." *Social Science History* 1, no. 4 (Summer 1997): 419–36.

Kirby, Jack Temple. *Poquosin: A Study of Rural Landscape and Society.* Chapel Hill: University of North Carolina Press, 1995.

Knight, Lucian Lamar. *A Standard History of Georgia and Georgians.* Vol. 1. Chicago: Lewis Publishing, 1917.

Koeniger, A. Cash. "Climate and Southern Distinctiveness." *The Journal of Southern History* 54 (February 1988): 21–44.

Kriegel, Leonard. *On Men and Manhood.* New York: Hawthorn Books, 1979.

Kulikoff, Allan. "Households and Markets." *William and Mary Quarterly* 50, no. 2 (1993): 342–55.

———. *Tobacco and Slaves: The Development of Southern Cultures in the Chesapeake, 1680–1800.* Chapel Hill: University of North Carolina Press, 1986.

Kuritz, Hyman. "Benjamin Rush: His Theory of Republican Education." *History of Education Quarterly* 7, no. 4 (1967): 432–51.

Landers, Jane L. *Black Society in Spanish Florida.* Urbana: University of Illinois Press, 1999.

———. "A Separate Nation: Free Blacks and Indians on the Florida Frontier." Paper presented at the Society for Historians of the Early American Republic Meeting, Lexington, Kentucky, July 1999.

———, ed. *Against the Odds: Free Blacks in the Slave Societies of the Americas.* London: Frank Cass, 1996.

Larson, Ron. *Swamp Song: A Natural History of Florida's Swamps.* Gainesville: University Press of Florida, 1995.

Leavitt, Judith Walzer, and Ronald L. Numbers, eds. *Sickness and Health in America: Readings in the History of Medicine and Public Health.* 2nd ed. Madison: University of Wisconsin Press, 1985.

Lewis, James A. "Cracker – Spanish Florida Style." *Florida Historical Quarterly* 43, no. 2 (October 1984): 184–204.

Limerick, Patricia Nelson. *The Legacy of Conquest: The Unbroken Past of the American West.* New York: W. W. Norton, 1987.

Limerick, Patricia Nelson, Clyde Milner II, and Charles Rankin, eds. *Trails: Toward a New Western History.* Lawrence, Kans.: University Press of Kansas, 1991.

Littlefield, Daniel. *Rice and Slaves: Ethnicity and the Slave Trade in Colonial South Carolina.* Baton Rouge: Louisiana State University Press, 1981.

MacManus, Elizabeth R., and Susan A. MacManus. *Citrus, Sawmills, Critters, and Crackers: Life in Early Lutz and Central Pasco County, Florida.* Tampa: University of Tampa Press, 1998.

Malone, Patrick M. *The Skulking Way of War: Technology and Tactics among the New England Indians.* Baltimore: Johns Hopkins University Press, 1991.

Manning, James. "The Okefenokee: Backyard for Florida Swamp Folk." *St. Petersburg Times,* n.d.

Marsh, George Perkins. *Man and Nature; or Physical Geography as Modified by Human Action.* 1864. Reprint, Cambridge, Mass.: Belknap Press of the Harvard University Press, 1965.

Martin, Joel W. *Sacred Revolt: The Muskogees' Struggle for a New World.* Boston: Beacon Press, 1991.

Martin, Scott C. "Don Quixote and Leatherstocking: Hunting, Class, and Masculinity in the American South, 1800–1840." *The International Journal of the History of Sport* 12, no. 3 (Dec. 1995): 61–79.

Mayfield, John. "'The Soul of a Man!' William Gilmore Simms and the Myths of Southern Manhood." *Journal of the Early Republic* 15, no. 3 (1995): 477–500.

Mays, Lois Barefoot. *Settlers of the Okefenokee: Seven Biographical Sketches.* Jacksonville, Fla.: Rascoe Photo/Type, 1975, 1999.

McFeely, Eliza. "Collecting Ourselves: A Field Guide to the Culture of American Ornithology." *Reviews in American History* 27, no. 1 (1999): 98–104.

McNeill, J. R. "Ecology, Epidemics, and Empires: Environmental Change and the Geopolitics of Tropical America, 1600–1825." *Environmental History* 5, no. 2 (1999): 175–84.

McQueen, Alexander S. *History of Charlton County.* Atlanta: Stein Printing, 1932.

McQueen, Alexander S., and Hamp Mizell. *History of Okefenokee Swamp.* 1926. Reprint, Folkston, Ga.: Charlton County Historical Society, 1992.

Melish, John. *Travels in the United States of America, in the Years 1806 and 1807, and 1809, 1810, and 1811; Including an Account of Passages betwixt America and Britain, Ireland, and Upper Canada.* Illustrated with eight maps. 2 vols. Philadelphia: T and G Palmer, Publishers, 1812.

Merchant, Carolyn. *Ecological Revolutions: Nature, Gender, and Science in New England.* Chapel Hill: University of North Carolina Press, 1989.

Meyer, William B. "When Dismal Swamps Became Priceless Wetlands." *American Heritage* 45, no. 3 (1994): 108–16.

Miller, David C. *Dark Eden: The Swamp in Nineteenth-Century American Culture.* Cambridge: Cambridge University Press, 1989.

Miller, Henry. *On the Fringe: The Dispossessed in America.* Lexington, Mass.: D. C. Heath, 1991.

Miller, James J. *An Environmental History of Northeast Florida.* Gainesville: University Press of Florida, 1998.

Mormino, Gary R. "'The Firing of Guns and Crackers Continued till Light': A Diary of the Billy Bowlegs War." *Tequesta* 45 (1985): 48–72.

Morrison, Toni. *Playing in the Dark: Whiteness and the Literary Imagination.* Cambridge, Mass.: Harvard University Press, 1992.

Mullin, Michael. *Africa in America: Slave Acculturation and Resistance in the American South and the British Caribbean, 1736–1831.* Urbana: University of Illinois Press, 1992.

Mulroy, Kevin. *Freedom on the Border: The Seminole Maroons in Florida, the Indian Territory, Coahuila, and Texas.* Lubbock: Texas Tech University Press, 1993.

Nash, Roderick Frazier. *Wilderness and the American Mind.* 4th ed. New Haven, Conn.: Yale University Press, 2001.

Neill, Wilfred T. "Surveyors' Field Notes as a Source of Historical Information." *Florida Historical Quarterly* 34, no. 4 (1956): 329–33.

Nelson, Megan Kate. "The Landscape of Disease: Swamps and Medical Discourse in the American Southeast, 1800–1880." *Mississippi Quarterly: The Journal of Southern Cultures* 55, no. 4 (Fall 2002): 535–67.

Newitz, Annalee, and Matt Wray, eds. *White Trash: Race and Class in America.* New York: Routledge, 1997.

"A Night with a Mosquito." *Harper's New Monthly Magazine* 16 (December 1857–May 1858): 89–92.

Nothen, William J., ed. *Men of Mark in Georgia.* 1907. Reprint, Spartanburg, S.C.: The Reprint Co., 1974.

Oates, Stephen B. *The Fires of Jubilee: Nat Turner's Fierce Rebellion.* New York: Harper and Row, 1975.

Odum, Howard. *Folk, Region, and Society: Selected Papers of Howard W. Odum.* Edited by Katharine Jocher et al. Chapel Hill: University of North Carolina Press, 1964.

Ogle, Maureen. "Water Supply, Waste Disposal, and the Culture of Privatism in the Mid-Nineteenth-Century American City." *Journal of Urban History* 25, no. 3 (March 1999): 321–47.

Okihiro, Gary, ed. *In Resistance: Studies in African, Caribbean, and Afro-American History.* Amherst: University of Massachusetts Press, 1986.

Orr, Oliver H., Jr. *Saving American Birds: T. Gilbert Pearson and the Founding of the Audubon Movement.* Gainesville: University Press of Florida, 1992.

Otto, John Solomon. "Oral Traditional History in the Southern Highlands." *Appalachian Journal* 9, no. 1 (Fall 1981): 20–31.

———. "Plain Folk, Lost Frontiersmen, and Hillbillies: The Southern Mountain Folk in History and Popular Culture." *Southern Studies: An Interdisciplinary Journal of the South* 26, no. 1 (Spring 1987): 5–17.

Ownby, Ted. *Subduing Satan: Religion, Recreation, and Manhood in the Rural South, 1875–1920.* Chapel Hill: University of North Carolina Press, 1990.

Owsley, Frank L. *Plain Folk of the Old South.* Chicago: Quadrangle Books, 1949.

Porter, Kenneth W. *The Black Seminoles: History of a Freedom-Seeking People.* Revised and edited by Alcione M. Amos and Thomas P. Senter. Gainesville: University Press of Florida, 1996.

Prassel, Frank Richard. *The Great American Outlaw: A Legacy of Fact and Fiction.* Norman: University of Oklahoma Press, 1993.

Pratt, Mary Louise. *Imperial Eyes: Travel Writing and Transculturation.* London: Routledge, 1992.

Presley, Delma E. "The Crackers of Georgia." *Georgia Historical Quarterly* 60, no. 2 (1976): 102–16.

Presley, Delma E., and Francis Harper. *Okefinokee Album.* Athens: University of Georgia Press, 1981.

Price, Jennifer. *Flight Maps: Adventures with Nature in Modern America.* New York: Basic Books, 1999.

Price, Richard, ed. *Maroon Societies: Rebel Slave Communities in the Americas.* New York: Doubleday/Anchor Press, 1973.

Prince, Hugh. "A Marshland Chronicle, 1830–1960: From Artificial Drainage to

Outdoor Recreation in Central Wisconsin." *Journal of Historical Geography* 21, no. 1 (1995): 3–22.

———. *Wetlands of the American Midwest: A Historical Geography of Changing Attitudes.* Chicago: University of Chicago Press, 1997.

Rafter, Nicole Hahn, ed. *White Trash: The Eugenic Family Studies, 1877–1919.* Boston: Northeastern University Press, 1988.

Reed, John Shelton. *Southern Folk, Plain and Fancy: Native White Social Types.* Athens: University of Georgia Press, 1986.

Rees, Ronald. "Under the Weather: Climate and Disease, 1700–1900." *History Today* 46, no. 1 (1996): 35–41.

Reiger, John F. *American Sportsmen and the Origins of Conservation.* 3rd ed. Corvallis: Oregon State University Press, 2001.

Reiss, Oscar. *Blacks in Colonial America.* Jefferson, N.C.: McFarland, 1997.

Remington, Frederic. "Cracker Cowboys of Florida." *Harper's New Monthly Magazine* 91 (1895): 339–43.

Risse, Guenter B. "Epidemics and Medicine: The Influence of Disease on Medical Thought and Practice." *Bulletin of the History of Medicine* 53, no. 4 (1979): 505–19.

Robins, Joseph. *The Miasma: Epidemic and Panic in Nineteenth-Century Ireland.* Dublin: Institute of Public Administration, 1995.

Roediger, David R. *The Wages of Whiteness: Race and the Making of the American Working Class.* London: Verso Press, 1991.

Rosenberg, Charles E., and Janet Golden, eds. *Framing Disease: Studies in Cultural History.* New Brunswick, N.J.: Rutgers University Press, 1992.

Rummel, Virginia C. "Crackers and Cattle Kings." *Americas* 22, no. 9 (September 1970): 36–41.

Scoville, Samuel. "Secret Island." *The Forum* (April 1929): 243–47.

———. *Wild Honey.* Boston: Little, Brown, 1929.

Sesonske, Alexander. "Jean Renoir in Georgia: Swamp Water." *Georgia Review* 26, no. 1 (1982): 24–66.

Sidbury, James. *Ploughshares into Swords: Race, Rebellion, and Identity in Gabriel's Virginia, 1730–1810.* Cambridge: Cambridge University Press, 1997.

Sikes, Lewright. "Medical Care for Slaves: A Preview of the Welfare State." *Georgia Historical Quarterly* 52, no. 4 (1968): 405–13.

Simms, William Gilmore. *The Life of Francis Marion.* New York: J. and H. G. Langley, 1846.

Skaggs, Merrill Maguire. *The Folk of Southern Fiction.* Athens: University of Georgia Press, 1972.

Smith, Billy G., and Richard Wotjowicz. *Blacks Who Stole Themselves: Advertisements for Runaway Slaves in the Pennsylvania Gazette, 1728–1790.* Philadelphia: University of Pennsylvania Press, 1989.

Smith, Julia Floyd. *Slavery and Plantation Growth in Antebellum Florida, 1821–1860.* Gainesville: University Press of Florida, 1973.

———. *Slavery and Rice Culture in Low Country Georgia, 1750–1860.* Knoxville: University of Tennessee Press, 1985.

Starr, Paul. *The Social Transformation of American Medicine.* New York: Basic Books, 1982.

Stavins, Robert N., and Adam B. Jaffe. "Unintended Impacts of Public Investments on Private Decisions: The Depletion of Forested Wetlands." *American Economic Review* 80, no. 3 (1990): 337–52.

Steiner, Roland. "Superstitions and Beliefs from Central Georgia." *The Journal of American Folk-Lore* 12 (1899): 261–71.

Stevens, William B. *A History of Georgia.* 2 vols. 1859. Reprint, Savannah: Beehive Press, 1972.

Stewart, Mart A. *"What Nature Suffers to Groe": Life, Labor, and Landscape on the Georgia Coast, 1680–1920.* Athens: University of Georgia Press, 1996.

Stilgoe, John R. "Jack-o'-lanterns to Surveyors: The Secularization of Landscape Boundaries." *Environmental Review* 1 (1976): 14–31.

Stovall, Mary E. "'To Be, to Do, and to Suffer': Responses to Illness and Death in the Nineteenth-Century Central South." *Journal of Mississippi History* 52, no. 2 (1990): 95–109.

Strozier, Charles B. "Benjamin Rush, Revolutionary Doctor." *The American Scholar* 64, no. 3 (1995): 415–21.

Swierenga, Robert P. "The New Rural History: Defining the Parameters." *Great Plains Quarterly* 1, no. 4 (1981): 211–23.

———. "Theoretical Perspectives on the New Rural History: From Environmentalism to Modernization." *Agricultural History* 56, no. 3 (1982): 495–502.

Taylor, Joseph E. "Negotiating Nature through Science, Sentiment, and Economics." *Diplomatic History* 25, no. 2 (2001): 335–39.

Taylor, Robert A. "Unforgotten Threat: Florida Seminoles in the Civil War." *Florida Historical Quarterly* 69, no. 3 (1991): 300–314.

Thompson, Maurice. "A Red-Headed Family (Ivory-Billed Woodpeckers)." *By-Ways and Bird Notes* (New York, 1885): 23–39.

Tiger, Peggy, and Molly Babcock. *The Life and Art of Jerome Tiger: War to Peace, Death to Life.* Norman: University of Oklahoma Press, 1980.

Tomes, Nancy. *The Gospel of Germs: Men, Women, and the Microbe in American Life.* Cambridge, Mass.: Harvard University Press, 1998.

Trowell, Chris T. "Another Description of the Okefenokee Swamp in 1850." *OWL News* 1 (March 2000): 1–2.

———. *Billy's Island: An Historical Sketch.* Okefenokee Wildlife League Special Publication no. 7, 2000.

———. *Exploring the Okefenokee: Letters from the Expeditions in 1875.* Nicholls, Ga.: Smith Printing Service, 1989.

———. *Exploring the Okefenokee: Roland M. Harper in the Okefenokee Swamp, 1902 and 1919.* Nicholls, Ga.: Smith Printing Service, 1988.

———. *Exploring the Okefenokee: The Mansfield Torrance Survey of 1850.* Nicholls, Ga.: Smith Printing Service, 1989.

———. *Exploring the Okefenokee: The Richard L. Hunter Survey of the Okefenokee Swamp, 1856–7.* Nicholls, Ga.: Smith Printing Service, 1988.

———. *The Hebard Lumber Company.* Okefenokee Wildlife League Special Publication no. 5, 1998.

———. *Life on the Okefenokee Frontier.* Okefenokee Wildlife League Special Publication no. 3, 1998.

———. "Preserving a Wilderness–Timetable." Typed sheet found at the Charlton County Historical Society, Folkston, Ga. November 15, 1999.

———. *Roland M. Harper in the Okefenokee Swamp, 1902 and 1909.* Nicholls, Ga.: Smith Printing Service, 1988.

———. *Seeking a Sanctuary: A Chronicle of Efforts to Preserve the Okefenokee.* Okefenokee Wildlife League Special Publication no. 6, 1998.

———. *The Suwanee Canal Company in the Okefenokee Swamp.* Douglas, Ga.: South Georgia College, 1984.

Trowell, Chris T., and Lorraine Fussell. *Exploring the Okefenokee: Railroads of the Okefenokee Realm.* N.p., 1998.

Trowell, Chris T., and Robert L. Izlar. *Jackson's Folly: The Suwanee Canal Company in the Okefenokee Swamp.* Okefenokee Wildlife League Special Publication no. 4, 1998.

Urmston, Emmeline. "Our Folk." In *Southern Bivouac: A Literary and Historical Magazine,* 283–94. Louisville, Ky.: B. F. Avery and Sons, June 1885.

Vaught, David. "State of the Art: Rural History or, Why Is There No Rural History of California?" *Agricultural History* 74, no. 4 (2000): 759–74.

Vileisis, Ann. *Discovering the Unknown Landscape: A History of America's Wetlands.* Washington, D.C.: Island Press, 1997.

Vlach, John Michael. *Back of the Big House: The Architecture of Plantation Slavery.* Chapel Hill: University of North Carolina Press, 1993.

Vocelle, James T. *History of Camden County, Georgia.* 1914. Reprint, Kingsland, Ga: Southeast Georgian, 1967.

Walker, Laura Singleton. *History of Ware County, Georgia.* Macon: J. W. Burke, 1934.

Walker, Laura Singleton, and Sara Singleton King. *About "Old Okefenok."* 1947.

Walker, Laurence C. *The Southern Forest: A Chronicle.* Austin: University of Texas Press, 1991.

Waring, George E., Jr. "The Sanitary Drainage of Houses and Towns I–III." *Atlantic Monthly* 36 (1875): 339–55, 427–42, 535–53.

Waring, Joseph Ioor. "Asiatic Cholera in South Carolina." *Bulletin of the History of Medicine* 40, no. 5 (1966): 459–66.

———. "John McKenzie: A Carolina Herb Doctor of the Early Nineteenth Century." *South Carolina Historical Magazine* 69, no. 2 (1968): 97–100.

——. "The Yellow Fever Epidemic of Savannah in 1820, with a Sketch of Dr. William Coffee Daniell." *Georgia Historical Quarterly* 52, no. 4 (1968): 398–409.

Warner, Margaret. "Local Control versus National Interest: The Debate over Southern Public Health, 1878–1884." *Journal of Southern History* 50, no. 3 (1984): 407–28.

Warren, Louis S. *The Hunter's Game: Poachers and Conservationists in Twentieth-Century America.* New Haven, Conn.: Yale University Press, 1997.

Weisman, Brent R. *Like Beads on a String: A Culture History of the Seminole Indians in North Peninsular Florida.* Tuscaloosa: University of Alabama Press, 1989.

Whisnant, David E. *All That Is Native and Fine: The Politics of Culture in an American Region.* Chapel Hill: University of North Carolina Press, 1983.

White, George. *Historical Collections of Georgia.* New York: Pudney and Rassell, Publishers, 1855.

White, Richard. *"It's Your Misfortune and None of my Own": A History of the American West.* Norman: University of Oklahoma Press, 1991.

——. *The Middle Ground: Indians, Empire, and Republics in the Great Lakes Region, 1650–1815.* New York: Cambridge University Press, 1991.

Wickman, Patricia. "'A Trifling Affair': Loomis Lyman Langdon and the Third Seminole War." *Florida Historical Quarterly* 63, no. 3 (1985): 303–17.

Wild, Peter. *Pioneer Conservationists of Eastern America.* Missoula, Mont.: Mountain Press Publishing, 1986.

Wilson, Charles Reagan, ed. *The New Regionalism.* Jackson: University Press of Mississippi, 1998.

Wilson, James Grant, and John Fiske, eds. *Appleton's Cyclopaedia of American Biography.* 2 vols. New York: D. Appleton, 1888.

Wong, John. "FDR and the New Deal on Sport and Recreation." *Sport History Review* 29 (1998): 173–91.

Wood, Betty. *Slavery in Colonial Georgia, 1730–1775.* Athens: University of Georgia Press, 1984.

Wood, Peter H. *Black Majority: Negroes in Colonial South Carolina from 1670 through the Stono Rebellion.* New York: W. W. Norton, 1974.

Woodward, C. Vann. *The Burden of Southern History.* 3rd ed. Baton Rouge: Louisiana State University Press, 1993.

Worster, Donald. *Dust Bowl: The Southern Plains in the 1930s.* 2nd ed. New York: Oxford University Press, 1982.

——. *A River Running West: The Life of John Wesley Powell.* New York: Oxford University Press, 1992.

——. *Rivers of Empire: Water, Aridity, and the Growth of the American West.* New York: Oxford University Press, 1992.

Wright, Albert Hazen. *Our Georgia-Florida Frontier: The Okefinokee, Its History and Cartography.* Ithaca, N.Y.: A. H. Wright, 1945.

Wright, Albert Hazen, and Francis Harper. "A Biological Reconnaissance of the

Okefinokee Swamp: The Birds." *The Auk: A Quarterly Journal of Ornithology* 30, no. 4 (October 1913): 477–505.

Wright, J. Leitch, Jr. *Creeks and Seminoles: The Destruction and Regeneration of the Muscogulge People.* Lincoln: University of Nebraska Press, 1986.

Writer, James V. "Did the Mosquito Do It?" *American History* 31, no. 6 (1997): 44–51.

Wyatt-Brown, Bertram. "The Antimission Movement in the Jacksonian South: A Study in Regional Folk Culture." *Journal of Southern History* 36, no. 4 (1970): 501–29.

——. *The Shaping of Southern Culture: Honor, Grace, and War, 1760s–1880s.* Chapel Hill: University of North Carolina Press, 2001.

——. *Southern Honor: Ethics and Behavior in the Old South.* New York: Oxford University Press, 1982.

Young, Jeffrey R. *Domesticating Slavery: The Master Class in Georgia and South Carolina, 1670–1837.* Chapel Hill: University of North Carolina Press, 1999.

——. "Ideology and Death on a Savannah River Rice Plantation, 1833–1867: Paternalism Amongst 'a Good Supply of Disease and Pain.'" *Journal of Southern History* 59, no. 4 (November 1993): 673–706.

# INDEX

Upper Creek tribe, 42, 52. *See also* Creek
    tribe
Upper Guinea Coast (West Africa), 21
Upton, Benjamin, 89
U.S. Army, 4, 56–57, 59, 60, 67, 68, 69, 72
U.S. Biological Survey, 168, 170, 189, 190
U.S. Department of Agriculture, 157, 159,
    189
U.S. Department of Treasury, 213 (n. 6)
U.S. Navy, 63, 68
U.S. Senate Special Committee on
    Conservation of Wildlife Resources, 170
U.S. Tenth Census Report (1880), 95

*Valdosta Times* (Ga.), 82–83, 134
value of land in the Okefenokee, 74, 89
Vanderbilt, George Washington, 159
Vileisis, Ann, 6–7
Violet (slave in custody of Gulford
    Dudley), 131
Vlach, John Michael, 23

Wahoo Swamp (Fla.), 54, 55, 58, 59
Waite, Captain, 63
Walcott, Frederick C., 170
Walker, S. T., 97
Walker, W. H. T., 159
Walton, George, 47
Ware County (Ga.), 62, 74, 75, 124, 125,
    130, 131, 199; and Confederate
    deserters, 129; and Crackers, 128
Ware County Militia, 61, 129
Waresboro (Ga.), 75
War of 1812, 52, 101
War of Jenkins Ear, 27
Warren, John, 54
Warren, Louis, 193–94
Washington, Madison (in *The Heroic Slave*),
    37
Washington County (Ga.), 47
Waycross (Ga.), 80, 125, 170, 192, 194,
    199; and lumber industry, 104, 106, 113
Waycross and Jacksonville Railroad, 89
Waycross and Southern Railroad, 109,
    110
Waycross Chamber of Commerce, 167
*Waycross Journal-Herald* (Ga.), 159

weather, and the Okefenokee, 20
West as "frontier," the, 6, 205 (n. 5)
Whan (fugitive slave), 25
whiskey, 105, 143–44
White (Spanish colonial Governor of
    Florida), 31
"White Trash." *See* Crackers
Wild Cat (Coacoochee; Creek leader), 61,
    62
Wild family, 63
wildfires, 187
wildlife, 173, 174, 175, 185, 189–90, 193;
    rare specimens, 173, 175, 224 (n. 37). *See
    also* alligators; bears; birds; hunting,
    trapping, and fishing
Wildlife Refuge Center, 2
Williams family, 140
Wilson, J. F., 167, 169
Windsor Springs (Ga.), 159
Withlacoochee River, 54, 56, 57; Cove of
    the Withlacoochee, 56, 57, 59, 60
Witten, Glasgow, 30
Witten, Judy, 30
Witten, Polly, 30
Witten, Prince, 30, 40, 52
women: Cracker, 121, 123; and fugitive
    slavery, 32
Wood, Peter, 207 (n. 52)
woodpecker, 2, 165, 189. *See also* birds
Worsham, E. L., 161
Worth, Colonel, 69
Wright, Albert Hazen, 161, 162, 167
Wright, James, 119, 120
Wright, J. Leitch, Jr., 42

Yamacraw Bluff (Ga.), 12, 14
Yamassee tribe, 42, 45
Yarborough, "Uncle" Ben, 85, 146–48, 172
*Yearling, The* (Rawlings), 127, 134
yellow fever, 14–16. *See also* diseases
Yellowstone National Park, 159
Yosemite Valley, 159
Young, P. M. B., 90, 91
Yuchi tribe, 42

Zanuck, Darryl, 199–200
Zespedes, Don Vicente, 119, 120, 123

CPSIA information can be obtained
at www.ICGtesting.com
Printed in the USA
LVHW041952031120
670609LV00005B/525